G000272711

Pigeons for Everyone

By Douglas McClary

Acknowledgements

The author wishes to acknowledge the assistance provided by many friends and advisers who have greatly helped in the writing of these chapters. From the first ideas to the final product, many have been involved and without such help this book would not have been possible.

Published by Winckley Press
5 Winckley Street
Preston PR1 2AA

© Copyright D McClary and Winckley Press.
No part of this publication may be reproduced,
stored in a retrieval system, or transmitted in any form
or by any means, electronic, mechanical, photocopying,
recording or otherwise, without prior permission
in writing of the publisher

ISBN 0-907769-28-4

1999

Set in 10 on 11 Arial
Designed and typeset by Winckley Press
Printed and bound in Great Britain

About the Author

Doug McClary has been a pigeon fancier for most of his life. His main interest has always been the promotion of the show racer. He has maintained a family of show racers since the early 1960's, concentrating on and enjoying most his original powder blues. However most colours are kept, and latterly, with an interest in the rarer colours. As well as showing, he races pigeons at club, federation and national level and has kept a number of breeds of fancy and flying variety pigeons.

Doug is pictured holding a magnificent blue cock 'Louisville Slugger' bred by Jim Isselhardt of Illinois. He judged the blue as a young bird at the National Young Bird Show in Louisville awarding it best in show and four years later when judging in North Carolina again awarded it best in show. He is pictured holding the bird several years later as a form of reunion when staying in Wisconsin with the cock's final owner, Dick Lipski. It reinforces a philosophy that a good pigeon is a good pigeon whenever and wherever.

He is married to Ann and they have three children and a growing number of grandchildren.

His interest in pigeons has taken him to many parts of the world, especially to the United States where he has judged at several of the classic shows.

He is the author of two previous books on pigeons, 'The Show Racer' and 'Pigeon Showing' and for many years has written for pigeon magazines on a weekly and monthly basis.

He is a founder member and President of the British Show Racer Federation, a founder member and long-serving secretary of the Devon and Cornwall Show Racer Society, and has held numerous offices within the sport of pigeon racing and organised numerous shows at both local and National level.

Now retired, he was a career police officer and following retirement from the police service worked in his own business enterprises. Pigeons however, continue to influence life and commitment.

KEY TO FRONT COVER ILLUSTRATION

First published in 'Boy's Own Paper. Drawn by A F Lydon

1. Black mottled Short Faced Tumbler. 2 Red Long Faced Tumbler. 3. Beard Tumbler.
4. Almond Tumbler. 5. Suabian Pigeon. 6. Fantail. 7. Priest. 8. Magpie.
9. Jacobin. 10. Baldhead. 11. Turbit. 12. Barb. 13. Domi. 14. English Owl.
15. Blondinette. 16. Turbiteen. 17. Trumpeter. 18. Swallow. 19. White-spot Pigeon.
20. Dragoon. 21. Antwerp. 22. Runt. 23. Carrier. 24. Pouter. 25. Norwich Cropper. 26.
Nun. 27. Yellow Spot. 28. Shield. 29. Frillback. 30. Homer. 31. Archangel.
32. Swift. 33. Triganica or Modena. 34. Hyacinth.

Pigeons for Everyone

INTRODUCTION

THE keeping of pigeons must be one of the most fascinating hobbies in the world. It is of universal interest and man has kept and enjoyed the pigeon from time immemorial. Indeed the pigeon or dove has always been regarded as a symbol of peace.

For many, it is more than a hobby - it is a way of life - an obsession, an all-absorbing love of the pigeon as a companion. It dominates the life and interests of so many who consider their birds at all times, where living is more arranged to accommodate the pigeons than the pigeons having to fit in with domestic arrangements.

Of course, not many fanciers will admit to this state of affairs, but it is with such observation in mind that I present this book to the fancy. As an enthusiast of many years I considered that a general book on pigeons, especially one with a base of advice on pigeon showing, would be a useful addition to pigeon literature. I have been involved with pigeon showing throughout my life in pigeons and have decided to present some of my experiences by way of advice and commendation to the readership. Showing continues to flourish despite all the odds of additional attractions presented by modern life and technology.

The section on pigeon racing has been aimed at the fancier who needs to accommodate his sport in accordance with other constraints on time and family commitments. In other words, it is a suggested manner of racing pigeons for the busy man (or woman).

I sought to widen the appeal of the book by the inclusion of subjects of wider interest such as the general management of pigeons, and information on show racers, fancy pigeons and the flying breeds. Research has revealed a huge subject concerning the use of pigeons in the service of their country and a chapter deals mainly with the British use during two world wars. It illustrates the great debt owed by country to the humble pigeon. Pigeon books have always been of great interest to me and the chapter on books old and new is the result of this. The books chosen are mainly those which have provided me with interest, guidance and information over the years and I trust that many readers will whet their appetites for more reading on pigeon matters - whether for new information or for more historical content.

My idea in planning this book was to provide a wide range of pigeon related subjects so that it is of interest to most pigeon fanciers and hopefully to people who are considering pigeons as their hobby. The intent therefore was to present information in an interesting and readable manner and to provide guidance to the novice, as well as thought or ideas to the more experienced fancier.

Mankind owes a great deal to the pigeon. Throughout history the pigeon has been kept and nurtured as a companion, as a source of food and as a means of competition through showing and racing. The attraction of companionship must never be underestimated as numerous people with no desire to compete in any way with their birds, enjoy the company of pigeons and the thrill of seeing them out on the wing. The spectacle of a kit of pigeons, whether they are fancy breeds, racers or the little flying machines of the flying breeds, out in the morning sunshine, is one which is almost breathtaking. Little wonder therefore that the pigeon continues to be so popular.

Every breed of pigeon has its admirers, for every derivation from the original rock pigeon carries with it a personality, character and appeal. It is truly a case of beauty being in the eye of the beholder. It is with this thought in mind that I have included as many aspects as possible in this book and trust that if interest is provided that it is accompanied by the pleasure and passion which pigeons provide to countless people throughout the world.

Contents

Part   4   A PIGEON MISCELLANY

**Part 5   THE PIGEON YEAR – A MONTH BY
                MONTH GUIDE**

PART 1

Chapter 1

Pigeons, making a start and basic care

MOST people who read this book will already be pigeon fanciers. But, hopefully there will be some who are hoping to become fanciers; to make a start into this fascinating hobby or sport. This chapter is really addressed to the potential fancier, to the novice, or to anyone who is contemplating changing direction within the fancy such as taking up a new or additional breed.

What comes first, the pigeon or the pigeon fanciership? In other words do people normally commence to keep pigeons before deciding on their direction, or do they decide first on how they want to exercise their pigeon keeping before taking on a particular breed or type? My own experience was that as a boy I was introduced to pigeons one day and was immediately smitten. I decided to keep some of the homer type and to have them flying out. It was some time before I had the introduction to pigeon showing and from that time onwards, all effort was directed to producing pigeons for showing purposes. Yet I have always maintained my desire to have pigeons flying freely from their loft.

My view is that the majority of pigeon fanciers start with racing pigeons. Pigeon racing appears to be in decline for various reasons yet it remains as a most popular sport demanding much hard work and attention to detail. The racer is a hardy breed, quite easy to look after and extremely rewarding in flying ability and appearance. However there are several ways of enjoying the hobby or sport and even more if the aim is simply to keep pigeons for their decorative company. Let us examine in brief detail some of the ways of introduction to the joys of keeping pigeons:

■ **Racing pigeons.** Racers are probably the easiest birds to make a start with. They are hardy, they breed and feed well and of course are full of flying ability and young racers are easy to 'break' to their new abode and to fly out freely. They are reasonably easy to acquire and can cost from little or nothing right up to the highest of prices for birds with proven ability or if from proven and valuable stock. There are racing pigeon clubs in most localities so there is plenty of opportunity to learn about

1

the sport and to compete at the novice stage. Performances of speed and long distance are the base of legend, and I can tell anyone that there are few sights to match that of a returning racer dropping from the skies on to the loft.

Even when competition is not envisaged this is an excellent pigeon to keep for ease of management and because of the many colours available. In my own case the attraction was with the bright coloured pied pigeons and no bird carried too much white for my liking. Even today I still carry a high regard for the pieds.

■ **Show Racers.** These beautiful birds are kin to the pure racer, being the show variety. They are slightly larger in size and are bred for their conformity to show requirements rather than flying ability. However, they have the ability to fly out and home to their loft. They are equally hardy to keep and breed and of course seem to have an even greater range of attractive colours. Please see Chapter 23 for further details.

■ **Fancy Pigeons.** There are numerous breeds of fancy pigeon of all sizes, colours and types. The expression that 'beauty is in the eye of the beholder' is especially applicable to keepers of fancy pigeons, for what is attractive to one person is not so to another. However, each breed of whatever type is a pigeon with all the attributes of attractiveness. Each is a pigeon in its own right with all the ability to respond to good and proper management. Each breed will repay care and kindness with endless hours of pleasure.

It would be impossible to deal with all the breeds in such a short treatise as this but in very basic terms, the easiest to keep and breed are the long-faced varieties, while those with short faces are the most demanding and requiring of experience. Divisions within breeds can be listed in many ways but this is one way:

■ **Faces** - long faced, short faced, medium faced and down faced.

■ **Legs and feet** - clear of feather, muffed - with a profusion of foot feathering, slippered with medium length feather cover, and groused meaning a small covering of closely adhering small feathers.

■ **Face markings,** badge or pied marked, bearded, baldheaded, spot, bibbed or helmeted.

■ **Crested** including shell crested, peak crested, double crested, hooded, breast frilled or rose marked.

Fancy pigeons are kept most for showing purposes but many fanciers keep them simply for their decoration or for their pleasant companionship. See chapter 21.

- **Performing Pigeons.** These are the beautiful little pigeons which are kept for their flying ability, both in competition and in sheer flying ability as a wonderful spectacle when flying high or in tumbling or rolling performances. These include flying tumblers, Birmingham rollers and flying tipplers in their most numerous, with other high-flying breeds from various parts of the world. They are full of vigour, carry a full range of colours, are easy to 'break' to fly from a new loft and are excellent breeders and feeders. They present a challenge for new fanciers, yet are easy enough to satisfy even the novice to pigeon keeping. They will provide great pleasure to all fanciers and further information can be found in Chapter 22.

So with decisions made as to intentions within the selected breed, whether to race, show, fly competitively or merely to keep and admire them, the next consideration is where to keep them and on what scale.

Size of the Operation

There are mainly three main considerations or restrictions on the size of the loft or coop into which the acquired birds will be kept:

- The space available to site the structure

- The size of loft for the size of the intended operation

- The amount of finance available.

These are the decisions which have to be made at the beginning. I am sorry to say that most of these decisions will be the subject of modification later on when experience causes a re-think of the aims and intentions based upon the practicalities involved. The biggest mistake always is in the size of the loft or coop and the best advice to be offered is to make it as large as possible. Base it on today's thinking and the chances are that in the climate of the future, more space will be needed.

However, to enjoy pigeons it is not necessary to have a large purpose-built structure in which to house them. My first start was by keeping them in a large box attached to a wall and I found great enjoyment with them. The first time I was able to physically go in with my birds was when I partitioned our chicken house so that my little team could be housed with more space and with more ventilation.

Nowadays though I know of fanciers who actually race their birds to hutch-like structure in their gardens. For those who suffer from an aversion to pigeon protein this is the only way they can keep pigeons, ensuring that they are in the open air when they tend to their birds. The hutch-like structure is not too far removed from the pigeon cotes found in many gardens for decorative purposes.[1]

The Commitment

Pigeon fancying is not a hobby that is either part-time, or one which can be put aside from time to time. When any form of livestock is acquired it requires constant and daily attention with the same being applicable to pigeons as to dogs, cats, poultry, goats, indeed anything living and kept by man. The pigeon fancier will therefore have to be able to find the time necessary on a daily basis, and at other times when he wishes to be away such as on holiday, there will be a need for someone to step in to do the chores. Whilst most is included in the other chapters of this book, a reference at this early stage may prove to be of assistance:

- **Cleaning.** The loft or coop will require cleaning almost on a daily basis. It will depend to some extent on the sort of loft management to be practised but some attention will always be necessary. Some scrape the floors while other maintain a covering of deep litter of some sort to save on the scraping, by using sand, straw, sawdust, shavings or some other product. Over the years I have tried them all but have now reverted to the use of the scraper as the best means of maintaining the birds in top condition and by removing dust and other problems at source. It is purely a matter of preference within the management plan but even where litter is used on the floors, or even where floor grills are fitted, the perches will still want cleaning and also the nest boxes and other loft areas.

- **Food and Feeding.** The system of management will to a large extent decide the commitment on the feeding. Whether to feed once or twice a day for instance or perhaps to use a hopper system to ensure that food is always available. It must be regular whatever system is used so that the birds know roughly when the food is due to be delivered and thus avoid the stress of fretting for food while in a state of hunger.

- **Water.** The same remarks about feeding pertain to the supply of water. Fresh water should be provided in 'drinkers' which

---

[1] Please see photograph on page 60

are covered and which cannot be fouled in any way. Ideally they should be off the ground - on a shelf or raised position. A very good solution is to have the ability to replace the water from outside the section of compartment. Water fountains can be used to keep water present at all times and are especially suitable for times when the fancier is forced to spend some while away.

■ **Baths and Bathing.** The birds will enjoy bathing and baths must be provided quite frequently. The ideal situation is to have a bath mounted outside the loft for birds which are able to fly freely, or in an aviary. However when the baths have to be provided inside the loft, high sides baths are best to prevent too much spillage of water

■ **Pests.** Pests come in all forms and have to be guarded against. Rats, mice, mink, cats, squirrels, crows, magpies and hawks all predate on pigeons and will have to be kept out. The use of wire mesh will ensure this. Inside the loft and on the pigeons are the insect life or external parasites, while worms, as internal parasites will need treatment from time to time.

■ **Care of Health.** So there we have it, the basics required in order to keep and enjoy pigeons. The list is not a long one and neither is it one which should give anxiety for most of the so-called chores are pleasant ones as the bond between pigeon and pigeon fancier becomes more established. However, there is one further matter which must be addresses and that is the health of the pigeon fancier. Just as certain complaints or illnesses have become more common because of modern life and its pace, such as asthma, so the number of fanciers suffering an allergy to pigeon protein through the dust has also increased.

It is sound policy to be careful about this by using a mask when cleaning the birds and by wearing a loft coat and hat when in the lofts. This is simple common sense, for the allergy does not depend entirely upon the length of time spent with the birds but more on how susceptible the individual is to the problem. A spare pair of 'slip-on' shoes will prove to be a useful aide to ensure that nothing from the loft floor is inadvertently taken indoors.

■ **Enjoyment** is the key to pigeon fancying. Whether the fancier enters into competition by racing, showing or flying the birds, the main aim is to enjoy the pigeons as a hobby. It is an extremely rewarding one and enthusiasts like myself would never be able to imagine life without them.

Chapter 2

Pigeon Lofts, Coops and Cabins

Housing for Pigeons

WHAT is a pigeon loft? Ask that question of a member of the public and there will be a picture of a shed for racing pigeons, fitted with trapping arrangements and often painted in bright colours. Ask a pigeon fancier and the answers will be quite different for there is no general guide, no model, anything which is typical for the rest to follow. In this chapter I hope to explore the needs of the pigeons and the fancier and to discuss some considerations.

The term 'loft' derives from the days when pigeons were kept in the loft areas above stables and other substantial outbuildings. Most pigeon lofts, which are constructed and sold, are intended for racing pigeons. As a result, there will generally be fittings to allow the birds out and to encourage them to enter at the fastest possible manner on race days. The needs of the show fancier, the flying breed enthusiast, the keeper of fancy pigeons and the hobby fancier, are quite different and subject to other considerations. I am therefore aiming my remarks at the novice, to the newcomer within the sport. However, I would also be thinking of fanciers who are either returning to the keeping of pigeons or to racing fanciers who are now thinking of changing course and keeping birds for showing purposes. Perhaps a good way to start would be to state some principals which might help in the selection of the structure:

- Look at as many lofts as possible especially those maintained by successful fanciers
- Think ahead and plan for the future
- Always purchase the best possible
- The most expensive solution is often, in the long run, the cheapest

These are general rules but there are further considerations which need to be addressed at the earliest stage and I would list these as follows:

6

- The space available - a small garden or yard will allow only a small loft which even then should not dominate all else. Likewise a sloping piece of ground will restrict the available space and the options for its siting.
- The size of the loft required. This will depend on the types of birds to be kept, numbers and style of management.
- How it will look - its general appearance to avoid problems with neighbours
- The environment for the birds - their comfort
- The comfort and convenience of the fancier and his style of management.

Portable Buildings

My discussion on pigeon lofts is mainly concerned with portable structures, for few are able to afford the luxury of brick or block built lofts which are usually purpose designed and constructed for the discerning and generally well-off fanciers. Most fanciers are back yard or garden fanciers who have to operate within the constraints of what can be achieved by the building of a wooden pigeon loft.

The average fancier can only gaze in awe at some of the wonderful lofts which are permanently situated and built of brick or block. Some of the finest lofts to be seen anywhere are those in European countries such as Belgium, many of which are part of or built above the fancier's own residence. I have visited several such lofts and they are absolutely superb, being dry and warm yet ventilated to perfection. Most of those I have seen have been environmentally perfect with a special sort of calmness to be seen in the birds. Having said that, I have also seen lofts which I have found repulsive and running in vermin - and that over the fancier's own house! So my remarks are intended for those using or planning to use a portable structure to house the pigeons.

Experiences

I guess that I can speak on this subject with some experience because over many years I have owned several lofts in several locations and in most of those years, the structures have been mainly for the use of show pigeons. As a boy my first birds were kept in rabbit hutch style houses to start off with, and then I went on to take over a poultry house which was constructed of corrugated metal sheeting. Those were magical days when I first gained my love of the pigeon, of its ability to fly free and to return to its home. What joys were experienced in those simple buildings, with those simple pigeons, but the impressions left me with a lasting love for pigeons and I thank God for that!

I endured a short break away from pigeons when I left home to work at my chosen profession and when I lived in lodgings as a single man. However, when I married and moved into my first house which was set in a wonderful flat garden, pigeons soon followed. The biggest consideration in those days was portability because my profession was one which forced me to move from town to town on a fairly regular basis so I needed to know that I could easily dismantle and re-erect without too much upset to the birds. My first loft was hopelessly small, as a garden shed seven foot by five foot (210 cm by 150 cm). I tried enlarging it by using bays and then an aviary but it was always going to be inadequate as by this time I was well into showing and building a comprehensive little team.

My next loft was larger but still allowed only two compartments, though each had a large bay at the front. That particular garden had a block-built summerhouse with slate floor. A wooden floor and partitions made two more compartments and for the first time I had the luxury of space. Another change of town and house followed, and without my summerhouse I was lost for space so invested in a large garden shed for conversion into a pigeon house. That was a mistake. My carpentry skills are just above zero so I relied heavily on friends. The result was a good working structure but it lacked rigidity. When I had to move to yet another house the removal was most difficult because my converted shed was taken apart into many pieces - almost like a giant jig-saw when it had to be re-assembled.

A purpose-built pigeon loft was ordained and duly followed. It was eighteen feet by six feet (550 cm by 180 cm) in three compartments or sections, proving to be a great success with the production of some super show racers. I even managed to race to it, using my show racers as race candidates. I well recall the garden when the loft was erected in it - almost like a waste tip, but when we moved on it was surrounded by lawns and flowers.

That loft endured two more moves. One, into a temporary location in a flat garden, and the second to the address at which I now reside. Its final resting-place teaches another lesson for my garden here is quite sloping. I wanted it to face the house so it had to be built up on columns at one end. However, to have it facing the house, it had to face east and this proved to be its undoing. I will talk about facing direction later but that east facing loft which had been so successful in one location which faced south, was suddenly not at all ideal because I could not condition my winning pigeons in it.

This brings me into the final chapter of my lofting experiences. Having decided that my loft would have to be dismantled yet again and re-erected in a south-facing mode, I decided to sell it and to have a new one built. This would enable me to have it exactly as I wanted it, and so it all came about. Constraints of space and the sloping garden made some of my decisions especially as by this time I had erected a new garage and a racing loft. The new loft could only be eighteen feet in length but with a corridor at the front, there was a great deal more space. I will describe this more fully later in the chapter. Most fanciers do not have the considerations of portability faced by 'nomads' such as myself. How I dreaded those moves, yet having something which is purpose-built and easily bolted together does have attractions still.

Considerations for planning and construction

In my loft - which has now stood the test of time for nearly two decades there were some priorities which I included in my planning. As stated, eighteen feet (550cm) was the space available to me so it followed that three six by six feet (180 x 180cm) compartments would provide the best use of the space. I wanted the tallest part to be at the south-facing front of the loft so that the rain would fall away at the rear out of harm's way. I wanted a corridor to run along the entire front. It had to be waterproof; it had to have a smooth floor for ease of scraping and cleaning, and it had to have ample light and excellent ventilation. I also wanted it to be as vermin-free as possible.

The ventilation and light I managed by using sets of adjustable glass louvres through the entire front of the loft providing excellent light, waterproofing and draught proofing all in one. Extra ventilation was provided at the rear of each compartment using high level adjustable louvres. As the rear wall is north facing, it is a bonus and indeed a necessity to be able to keep those cold north winds out. The partitions between the compartments were made of solid boarding which provided privacy in each compartment and gave rigidity to the whole structure. The doors to each compartment, and the entire front facing divisions were constructed of doweled sections which provide maximum light, air and vision in for me and vision out for the birds. Each compartment door corresponded to an outer door, so ensuring that in good weather the outside doors could be left open providing sunshine to the inmates I have never raced pigeons to this loft but would be confident that it would make an ideal racing loft.

The corridor has proved to be excellent. My advice would be to have it as wide as possible. Mine has been widened slightly by pushing the doweled sections back into the compartments a few inches, adding six inches (15cm) to the original 2feet 6inches. (45cm) I would urge a corridor to be at least three feet (90cm) in width. Moving about is made so much easier especially when basketing the birds for shows. I also wanted my corridor to provide feeding trays and drinkers so that these could be serviced from the corridor without having to enter the compartments with the birds. This has also proved to be a great success.

I have mentioned my thoughts in the matter because they may provide pointers for readers who are thinking of designing a loft at any time. My earlier advice applies in this, to visit as many lofts as possible and to speak to their owners about advantages and drawbacks to their design. It is all so straightforward and sensible to do this to avoid making costly mistakes.

Further considerations and ideals.

My twenty-year-old loft is not the same as when I first took possession of it. I am constantly looking for fresh ideas and ways to improve it. Bays have been added so that the show birds can get out into the light, air and sunshine, but a way had to be found of getting them across the corridor, so high level walk-ways were constructed. Normally I would have added an aviary but this was out of the question because constructed in front of the loft is a large fishpond!

Given my time over again, I would have made the loft taller by a foot (30cms) all round. Extra height is invaluable for many purposes. I once saw a loft in the United States which was extra high, and the perches consisted of a row around the four walls at their highest point. His birds had constant exercise in rising to those top perches. The extra height provides extra possibilities for ventilation and of course the more modern pent roofed lofts clad in tiles takes care of this. Of course the higher the loft, the more chance there is of it being damaged by gales. Secure anchorages should be used as a means of keeping the loft in place even in the highest winds. Stakes should be concreted into the ground and the loft secured to then using screws, bolts or hawser. Such work well implemented will provide great peace of mind.

It is important to arrange for the structure to be off the ground enough to prevent vermin from getting underneath and staying there. Ideally 12inches(30cms) should be clear underneath so that a good terrier can regularly check the area out for unwanted guests! It is always useful to give thought to keep mice out of the loft and some elementary steps can achieve this. Small mesh wire netting should be used to cover openings especially those which are low down but it must be remembered that rats, mice, stoats etc are very clever and can get to and into most openings, so small mesh is invaluable to keep such pests at bay.

I must say that it is a great attraction to have a pigeon loft within view of the house, both for the aesthetic point of view and for security. Therefore when siting a loft one will have this in mind, but must also consider the existing services such as paths, walkways, electricity and a water supply. All these considerations will ensure more comfort and easier work in the future. The easier the work, the better the management is likely to be.

Aspect

I earlier mentioned that a successful loft when moved to a new address and erected so as to face east, proved to be less than successful. It caught the early morning sunshine, but after that was facing away from where the health-giving sunshine could be seen. My advice would be to have the loft facing the direction which attracts most sunshine, and here in Britain, this is in a southerly facing direction. Obviously there will be gardens or yards which do not allow this, and if this is so, then other steps can be taken to ensure reception of sunshine, such as by the use of glass in the roof or by added windows to attract the sunshine. Pigeons do need the sun to prosper so when siting the loft. always be aware of this fact.

To paint or not to paint

The appearance of the housing for pigeons is very important, not only for the pride of the fancier but also for him to present a good impression to neighbours. Many lofts are painted in bright colours and stripes. They can be very pleasing to the eye. I do not paint my lofts, preferring the use of wood protection and preservative finishes. They are easily applied and easily renewed - with a couple of hours seeing a reasonably sized loft treated. I tend to use creosote on the sides and rear, with a more expensive, longer lasting and better-looking finish to the front facing area. However, it is very much a matter of personal taste. However, I am adamant that I will not use paint on the outside.

But what of the inside? Here again I do not decorate the inside of my lofts, preferring to see plain wood which can be scrubbed and scrubbed again. It is very nice seeing the inside of a loft painted out in white paint but when this needs to be done again, the work involved is very great and the upset to the birds likewise traumatic. Here again, it is a matter of taste and I doubt that there is a right way for all.

Size and numbers

I would like to discuss how to arrive at the size of structure required. Which way around the decision should be made is a little unsure. Some fanciers will buy a loft - possibly second hand - and then decide how to stock it. Others - and the best way I imagine, is to plan what sort of team is required depending on the type of competition envisaged. This will also depend on the time available, so that someone who is at work, labouring long hours will be more limited in his ability to manage numbers than someone who is retired or someone who is professional and who can afford to pay for some help.

Each pigeon will require a certain amount of space. In his famous book 'Pigeon Racing', Dr W.E. Barker stated that each pigeon should have 27/28 cubic feet (2.8m^3) of space. I believe that this is rather luxurious because if applied to my present loft, each compartment measuring six feet by six feet would allow only eight or nine pigeons, making a maximum of 27 for the loft. Thinking of my loft again, I think that in ideal circumstances, if we add the length by the breadth (12 feet) twelve pigeons could be kept in each compartment. In practice I have six nest boxes in each to allow for the twelve pigeons but this state of affairs only exists when the breeding season commences. The young bird compartment often holds more than twelve pigeons - in fact more than double that number. With a virtually uncluttered space, this seems quite reasonable and I never feel that the overcrowding is very noticeable.

Some of the decisions will include the numbers of compartments required. This will depend on the type of racing, the type of showing or whatever other purposes are in mind. Looking at showing, my three compartments I would like to increase to five. I doubt that this would entail the keeping of more pigeons but the management would be much easier. Two compartments would contain nest boxes for the adults; there would be one each for the young cocks and young hens, and one to house any spare and unmated birds. Hopefully, at times of the year one or two of the compartments would be empty and then could be used as a penning room or the opportunity taken to thoroughly scrub and disinfect that particular living space. Five compartments would be a luxurious amount of space but wonderful in the interests of good management. For instance, some of the finest racing lofts in Europe have a 'hospital' section for sick, injured and stray pigeons, an invaluable asset to better management.

Now to the corridor space. I would always recommend a corridor on any loft for what it amounts to, other than extra air space, is an area for the fancier to work in. It allows the fancier to work without disturbing the birds and allows observations at all times. If this space can be coupled with arrangements which can allow the feeding and watering from the corridor area then so much the better. It allows the birds to be serviced without too much interference with them and their lifestyle. Obviously there will be times when entry is necessary, for cleaning, for handling and other work but proper use of the corridor helps greatly in creating a settled environment.

I would urge that the corridor be made as wide as possible. There is little worse than having a corridor which is too narrow for ease of movement. Remember that baskets, show containers and the like have to be taken into lofts and used, so how much better to have the room available to handle them in comfort. It is also so much easier to entertain visitors to the loft, to allow them to view the birds. When building a loft it is always tempting to economise on timber or other requirements but as stated earlier, the dearest can often be the cheapest in the long run.

Sunshine

I briefly referred to the desirability of allowing access to sunshine. My own loft is well suited to this because the three outside doors can be opened so that the sun can shine right into the compartments through the doweling. In the summer they are able to enjoy many hours of sunshine in this way but I also encourage them to get out into the open air by the use of bays or viewing areas. The benefits of this are enormous for the birds really enjoy being out and in being able to view what is outside the loft.

I once had a stock loft which had a full-length aviary with all birds having access to it. This arrangement was excellent for the prisoners. They spent most of their days out in the weather and of course they bathed there also. I would have preferred to have this type of arrangement for my show loft but have to rely on small bays instead. However these are very good for adding space to the loft and in addition allow birds to fly out and having trapping arrangements also.

Allowing the sun's rays in is an important matter and I would suggest that consideration should always be given to this facility. In tiled roofs clear or plastic tiles can be used and clear sheets can be inserted into any roof to allow light and sun in. I do not recommend that the entire roof be made of a see-through material as this makes the loft too light and too hot.

Health of the fancier

Nowadays there is a greater consideration for the health of the fancier with the realisation that too much contact with pigeons can lead to complications with health owing to a complaint known loosely as 'pigeon fanciers' lung'. It goes without saying that a mask should be worn especially when performing heavy work in the loft including cleaning the loft, but in the design and construction planning of a loft, though should be given to this aspect. Dust accompanied by feather protein is the problem and the better the ability to get this out of the loft the better. Grilled flooring areas are the obvious answer to this, for all dust falls through to be collected in the area under the grills. All such dust removed is dust which will never be breathed by fancier or his birds.

Some lofts are constructed with a grilled area so that dust and feather particles can fall through out into the open where they are dealt with by the elements. Indeed, instead of being open to the ground, they can be boxed so that debris falls into the box where it can be periodically removed. Other ideas are the use of extractor fans to be used while the fancier is at work in the loft - or in some cases operating all the time, low level louvered areas, indeed anything which allows the dust created by pigeons to be taken away rather than being recirculated and breathed in by fancier or birds. I would urge anyone to think about this when designing, building or altering a loft.

Future Developments

I feel sure that fanciers returning to the sport after an absence of a decade or more would hardly recognise pigeon housing and its fitments. How things have developed in the last decade or so - just as they have in other fields such as in professional breeding studs and the like. We are influenced by the continental flair from where new ideas seem to be flowing almost constantly. A few years ago tiled roofs were hardly ever seen, whereas today they are quite common place. Grills for the floor, louvres, new style feeding trays, drinkers and a multitude of other improvements can be seen. Doubtless the process will continue so that the new ideas will always be a part of the sport leading to better conditions for both birds and fancier.

Pigeon perfection – Loft by Petron Lofts

Within this fad for ideas, trends come and pass. There was a time when lofts were not considered healthy for the birds unless the wind blew freely through. There was a desire to have maximum access to the elements but with the acceptance of widowhood racing, the lofts were designed to be kept warm, they were insulated and where ventilation was by a more planned method of foul air escaping through the tiles in the roof or through some other high area of the loft.

Show lofts always required a degree of protection from the elements for a cold wind will strip condition off show candidates and cause a quick loss of form. Show fanciers therefore always sought a quiet environment where the need to get birds out for a fly was one of the least important considerations. Indeed many top show lofts never allow their birds to fly freely.

Even with a settled and successful loft the fancier must always be looking for improvements, new ideas and ways to improve pigeon fancying. The past is important for not all ideas are good ones and many of the tried and tested methods are still those which produce consistent results, but an open mind is a necessary ingredient of success in the sport.

Let me finish with a simple but true statement mentioned earlier in the chapter, that when planning a pigeon loft, always afford more than what seems affordable, for the dearest is often the cheapest in the long run.

Chapter 3

Breeding

General Management to produce good results

MOST fanciers I imagine would rate the breeding season as their favourite time within the loft in any period of twelve months. The thought of producing young pigeons to race well, to be good show specimens or merely to keep and enjoy or to fly out, makes us all a little excited. After all, it is all about our birds, our efforts and our skills which when arranged together produce the pigeons which represent the future of our lofts.

The decisions are all ours, when to start, when to finish, which birds to pair, the nest boxes and their fittings - all these are matters which determine the success or otherwise of the breeding programme. Yet, the quality of the progeny is decided by the quality of the parentage, directed to some extent by the intervention of 'Lady Luck' in causing some pairings to 'click' to produce the outstanding youngsters we all seek.

Nest boxes

Unless you are happy to have your birds nesting in corners, on perches or other places, there needs to be some order and this generally starts with the design and layout of the breeding boxes. Plenty of thought needs to be applied to this matter, with some fanciers preferring ordered banks of boxes - pleasing to the eye of the fancier, or in creating conditions which the birds like i.e. shelves, boxes placed at differing levels and in places which they find attractive to use. Birds determined to breed will find a way and some of the very best birds are bred in those corners, perhaps protected by a piece of board or a brick, or in some other inaccessible place so it does not pay to have set, inflexible ideas on the subject.

My own management dictates that I prefer the boxes in a set order but I would never criticise a fancier who allowed his birds some freedom to determine their own destinies! I like boxes to be as large as space allows for I believe that birds like plenty of room, and of course, the larger the box, the more flexibility there is to allow them to have more than one nest at a time. A large box with a shelf therein is ideal and I am always impressed with the amount of thought fanciers apply to the subject, judging by the vast array of nest boxes which are now to be seen on the market. For ease of management also, I prefer smaller numbers within each compartment of section of the loft, say six boxes for six pairs or at the most eight boxes for eight pairs. Lucky is the fancier who has single-pen breeding arrangements.

If breeding is the best time in the loft, I would also guess that the actual pairing process is one of the most hated. Birds which are mild in manner can suddenly become awkward, obstructive and downright aggressive both to their intended mate and to other birds. Some decide that they want boxes other than the one offered and others decide suddenly to dominate the floor area. This is where having smaller numbers of boxes per section pays off, for management becomes far easier.

I would always like to have nest boxes with a floor area of at least 576 square inches (3600cm^2) and if these can be tall enough to allow for a shelf to be fitted, large enough to take a nest bowl, then so much the better. A shelf adds to the area available to the birds and is especially valuable when they have large young birds in the nest and are looking to lay again. A fresh bowl placed on the shelf provides them with a new area and allows the new eggs to remain unsoiled and undamaged by the young birds in the nest. Of course some pairs prefer to continue to use the same bowl but this is their interpretation of nature at work!

In the early stages of breeding, the pairs seem to like a measure of privacy and react well to having an area of darkness to themselves. Boxes which have half the front blocked off fulfil this purpose well but I have seen small cardboard boxes inserted in the nest box with one end open to allow the birds in and out, taken readily by the nesting birds. In other words, the inner box provides the privacy and in the worst of the cold weather, a retreat from the lowest of the temperatures. This 'inner sanctum' idea can be especially useful where loft fronts are fairly open to the elements.

I have always tried to keep my nest boxes clean and use newspaper on the floor area, several layers thick. This enables the floor area to be kept clean by regular changing of the paper but also provides good insulation - as well as nesting material for many birds like to rip the paper up and to use it in their nests. I also use nest pan surrounds - either of plastic construction, or of cardboard to keep the droppings from the nest away from the nest box sides. Cardboard boxes cut down are very good, so that the corner of the box can provide privacy, insulation and cleanliness all in one and can easily be disposed of after use. A suitable cardboard box can provide up to four such corner protectors.

The pairing

The methods of introducing the pairs are many. Showmen often use show pens for this purpose, where the two birds selected can get on nodding terms by being placed in adjacent show pens. This is an excellent way and one I would recommend immediately after a show season when the show birds may be carrying weight which is too much for the breeding operation. The birds in the pens can be fed and watered to order with an exact intake of food measured. Racing enthusiasts would also find this method most useful. It does not cost time, for immediately the birds are placed in the pens so that they can see only themselves, they are engaged in the pairing process.

However, if penning is not available, then the birds can be placed in their chosen boxes either together, or one of the pair to start off with and with the opposite sex introduced later. I would recommend at this stage that a chart be prepared of the layout of the boxes on to which the ring numbers of the chosen inmates are recorded. Leaving this to memory can cause confusion both to fancier and birds.

Once the birds are in their boxes, there are useful little precautions which can be used to prevent damage to either. Place a small block or a brick in each box so that the more timid of the two - usually the hen - can retreat from the full attentions of the keen mate. All too often birds can be scalped at this stage - even cocks by strong-willed hens - so the placing of a block can help to avoid the situation.

Next follows the time-consuming stage. One pair should be allowed out at a time. This allows them to feed and to drink, but more importantly the way back to their own box. During the first day or so, this should be done hourly with a new pair being liberated and the previously freed pair shut back into their correct box. If the birds can be allowed out of the loft together at such times they are certain to find bonding opportunities and greatly enjoy the company of each other out on the wing. For fanciers who are away at work, assistance will be required for the regular changing, but is a matter well worth doing to get the birds to settle more quickly. When the birds are becoming settled and then two pairs can be allowed out at a time and then three and so on. Generally a couple of days is enough for this hard work stage and only the most awkward pairs need to be shut in after this sort of attention. There will often be a difficult bird or two which fail to recognise the need for a settled life and can take a week - almost to the laying stage before they accept the situation of one pair to one box!

Nesting time

Once the birds are settled, it is time to take the matter one stage further by providing them with a suitable receptacle for their egg laying attentions. Nest bowls can be put in to the boxes after about four days, though an upturned nest bowl can be used instead of a block to prevent damage or injury to a bird from an ardent mate. However, once the nest bowl is installed ready for the egg laying thoughts can be directed to nesting material. I like to use dry sand or wood shavings in the bottom of each bowl with some coarse straw on top. A point worth making is to stagger the position of the nest bowl in each box, especially where the boxes are in banks. In one box place the bowl in a left-hand corner, and in the next to the right. This will help in preventing mistakes when birds inadvertently enter the wrong nest box, as with the bowl in a position not familiar to them, they seem to know immediately that they have gone wrong.

The best nesting material however is whatever the birds find for themselves. Birds which have their liberty from the loft obey nature by finding and carrying their own nesting material. They greatly enjoy the work and this is part of nature's way of getting them fit for the laying and breeding. Suitable twigs can be left close at hand, including coarse straw, tobacco stalks etc but whatever they use, there is little more satisfying than in seeing a pair busily at work flying to and from the loft building their own nests.

For birds which are not allowed liberty from the loft; stock birds, show racers and fancy pigeons, nature can be imitated by a suitable supply of twigs, straw or stalks which hopefully the birds will enjoy carrying to their own boxes. However, some pairs will not carry for themselves so some assistance in nest building may have to be given by the fancier.

I would urge fanciers to treat his pigeons carefully at this stage, but whatever the breed is involved, to treat them as close as possible to what nature intended. The racing pigeon is a good guide, for a good fit racer seems to want to have its liberty, to build its own nest and to fly itself fit. With captive pigeons it is not so simple, but a basic regard to the characteristics of the racer will generally pay off. Some of the racers in their back to nature routine will build huge nests, the product of hours of flying and foraging work. I have even had to remove some of the nest to provide better balance for it and those precious eggs.

Another point which is worthy of mention is that when pairing during the worst of the winter weather, sometimes as early as December or early January, the birds can be manipulated to some degree by the use of electrical lighting controlled by the use of a time switch. This will lengthen the days and bring the birds into a 'Spring season mode' and thus induce them to pair and breed more readily. For really early breeding the use of artificial lighting is all-important. If possible, any lighting system should be coupled to a dimmer to allow the light to fade gently to allow the birds back to their nests. A sudden cut-off is not suitable for any pigeon loft.

The Laying Process

No pigeon fancier would admit to failing to be moved by the sight of that first egg appearing in the nest. In ideal conditions these start appearing after about day eight after pairing. I say ideal for in the real world it does not work exactly as some writers would have us believe. According to them all their pigeons lay on day eight and so on, but there are bound to be variations just as there are many variations in the age, demeanour and temperament of the pairings. However, if the birds are fit, in the right sort of condition, then the eggs should appear within the space of 8-10 days. The first egg is laid at the end of the afternoon with the second appearing some 45 hours or so later.

All eggs should be checked. Ideal are those which are clean, even shaped and smooth for they are likely to contain healthy embryos. Beware of eggs which are rough in texture, mis-shaped or which carry blood traces. These indicate that something is amiss and it is often better to discard them immediately. I often replace such eggs with one or both from another suitable nest as it allows the hen laying the doubtful eggs to rest up, hatch healthy young birds and then after rearing them to find the better health to enable her to produce better eggs. This is an excellent ploy for the older hen.

Eggs can become dented, perhaps owing to another pigeon getting into the box and being repulsed, but unless the inner skin is broken when the egg is useless, a small cover can be placed over the dent. Masking tape or clear tape can be used and this will generally enable the egg in question to hatch. Typewriter fluid can also be used for this but I have always preferred tape, as there is less likelihood of chemicals being present. Eggs often become soiled in the nest and here I recommend that they be cleaned using a cloth moistened with warm soapy water.

The general rule with the eggs is that the better the egg, the better the youngster that is likely to emerge from it. The best eggs produce the best young birds so the advice always is to discard bad eggs to avoid future troubles. It also follows that if a hen is laying poor eggs, or failing to produce two on time, that there is something wrong and that this can be taken as a warning sign. To produce good eggs of course, the hens require large amounts of good grit and my advice always is to have two or three types of grit available including clay block. The use of oyster shell grit equates to calcium so necessary for the production of the eggs and shells and this should always be available.

I think that it would be fair to say that the later in the season that breeding commences, the better are the chances of success. Very early breeding is a little contrary to nature but fanciers have to choose a commencement date in line with their future requirements. Hence, those who use widowhood systems for racing will need to pair early, whereas fancier who use the natural system can start much later, and the same considerations apply to show enthusiasts according to whether they need earlier bred youngsters or not. The later the better for more assured results and unless early-bred birds are required, why feed youngsters for a couple of months longer than actually required?

Whatever the time of year however, the birds need to be prepared for breeding especially the hens. Fat pigeons do not produce well and neither do birds which are not entirely fit and well. Fat pigeons can be brought down to a more suitable weight by adjusting their intake and type of food - more barley and less protein - while birds under weight may be brought up to better fitness by supplying them with good quality food including a vitamin based supplement.

The Sitting Process

As soon as the second egg is safely laid, the incubation period begins. Calculations can be made by adding nineteen days to the time of the first egg or seventeen days to the laying of the second. Generally speaking the cocks sit by day and the hens take over late afternoon until the following morning. There are variations to this of course and some really keen pairs seem to want to sit together.

After they have been sitting for some four to five days it is worth checking whether the eggs are fertile. Often the colour change in the egg clearly shows this, when the pristine white has changed to a more opaque colour and where the eggs are somewhat denser to the feel. However the easiest way is to hold each egg to a light, a torch or something similar and to note whether the embryo inside is visible with the appearance of vein-like strands. Great care must be taken when removing or replacing eggs. It is better to use both hands, one to shield the bird and the other to remove the egg. Where one hand only is free, the back of the hand should be turned towards the bird so that a beating wing or a beak can only be directed at it, allowing removal of the egg in safety. We have all done it! We have all dropped eggs or even young birds in this way when surprised by an attack from the sitting bird.

If the eggs are clear or infertile, then they should be either discarded or replaced by others which have been taken from other pairs. Two days difference is about the maximum difference in dates to make this changing over successful, though eggs which have been sat for a couple of days can be stored for a couple of days without harm in warm conditions. I have been told that eggs travel much better when they have been so incubated for a couple of days before being taken away.

It is probably a good time to mention about the storage of eggs. There are many reasons to do this, such as wishing to concentrate on a pairing to produce more young birds; one of the breeding pair being lost or where good eggs are required to be placed under feeders. Keep the eggs in a safe place, in a suitable receptacle and packed in cotton wool, sawdust, polystyrene chips or some other suitable material. The eggs should be turned every day to help them be kept as fertile prospects.   Treated in this way the eggs should last for a week or more and I have known them to keep for much longer periods than this.

Particularly with older birds and more especially with older show birds or fancy pigeons, it is quite likely that they will not produce good eggs in the first nest or in the early part of the season. To help the situation it is a good strategy to give the pair in question another pair of good eggs, so that they can sit, enjoy parenthood and bring themselves into good breeding condition to be able to produce good eggs. As stated, the supplied eggs should be in the same time scale of two days or less. This is a useful ploy for older pairs or for older birds within pairings. Other aids to fertility in older birds can include:

■   to pair old birds to younger mates.

■   by trimming the mass of feathers near the vent.

- reducing fatness by suitable diet.
- use of 'heat' seeds such as hemp.

All these are matters of good management within a loft. It is also a good time to treat sitting birds for canker as birds carrying the disease can easily pass it on to squabs.

The eggs when being incubated should be left without disturbance as much as possible. Apart for the check for fertility, the 'sitters' are best left alone though they are better if the eggs can be kept clean. A soft cloth dampened with warm water is ideal for this and as eggs benefit from moisture, the sitting birds should be given ample bathing opportunities. However, being careful to allow peace and quiet for the birds while incubating, does not mean ceasing to be observant, for often some intelligent observations can avoid eggs being lost to a pair which look like as though they are going to leave the nest. If this looks like happening, try to place the eggs elsewhere if they are from a valued pairing.

One of the most common reasons for sitting birds to leave the nest is the presence of red mite. Often invisible, these mites trouble pigeons and force them off the nest. Although red mite occur mostly in warm weather, they can wreak havoc at almost any time of the year and I sincerely urge fanciers who's experience tells them that a sitting pair are uneasy, to examine nests very carefully for signs of the red mite infestation. Routine treatments of the nest boxes and loft walls, as well as bowls can overcome this problem but it must be taken most seriously. Straw can be a hiding place for them so if there is a problem, tobacco stalks may be a more suitable nesting material especially if they have been soaked in a solution of Ivomec then dried prior to use.

To round off the sitting process period, let me say a few words about eggs which appear to have gone cold. My advice is always to give the benefit of the doubt to the egg by warming it up gently in heat or under another sitting pair, at which stage the sitters may have been induce to start sitting again and the egg(s) can be replaced. Over the years I have been amazed by eggs which have seemed icy cold but which have recovered to hatch out perfectly healthy young birds. There are many reasons why eggs go cold, a bird being shut out of the loft, kept out of the nest box by another bird or some other reason.

Young Birds in the Nest

If all goes well, the young birds should break free from their shells on the 19th day after the lying of the first. Normally this happens without any help from outside forces such as intervention by the fancier. Over many years I have done the following when I detect that the eggs are 'pipping'. I use my thumb nail to indent the line of perforations made by the youngster in the egg and before returning the egg(s) to the nest I moisten the palm of my hand and rub the egg in it so that some of the moisture is transferred to the egg. Moisture, when it dries, makes the shell even more brittle and thereby renders assistance to the potential squab. Extreme care must be taken in removing or replacing eggs, as at this stage the sitting birds will become quite possessive and aggressive towards disturbance.

Under the previous heading I gave advice about cold eggs and the same applies to young birds which appear cold or even dead. Always give them the benefit of the doubt and provide warmth because often revival is the result. I recall a fancier telling me how he found a young bird out of the nest apparently dead, in sub-zero temperatures. He carried the bird to discard it in the rubbish bin and as he placed it in, he thought he detected a slight movement. Warmth revived the bird which went on to be a show champion with several classic wins and a long life. The cock filled its eggs when in its fourteenth year. It taught me to give the benefit of the doubt. Since hearing that particular story I have revived many youngsters with no apparent ill to them in the long term.

Particularly in northern climes but wherever in extreme cold temperatures, early breeding is assisted by using some form of heating. At the very least steps should be taken to reduce draughts by shielding open areas of the loft using plastic, hardboard and some other suitable material. Icy winds allowed to blow in will affect young birds in the nest where the adults leave the nest to feed or to drink. As for heating, it does not need to be expensive and low wattage tubular heaters can be used safely especially when used in conjunction with a thermostat. I would also once again mention the benefits of lighting when coupled to a dimmer as providing a longer day and hence a longer feeding time for the youngsters in the nest.

It hardly needs saying that the very best of food must be provided during the rearing time and in bountiful quantities. The better the start a youngster gets through diet, the better chance it will have of being a champion. Good food, good water and suitable nutritional supplements are vital, as are plenty of grits, picking stones, minerals and other additions. In the latter category I would mention greenstuffs such as lettuce, indeed anything which adds value to the food intake. There are plenty of good supplements on the market, some in food form, others to be added to the drinking water.

The fancier decides for himself and his birds just what and how to administer these but over many years I have used a supplementary feed consisting of pinhead oatmeal, cod liver oil, calcium and vitamins and the birds love it and seem to derive great benefit from it. Feed this and you will avoid having birds which look as though they are feeding, i.e. with greasy wattles etc. Garlic in clove or soluble powder form can be used in the water or in powder form on the food as it is a good natural product which helps to guard against coccidiosis and canker. Canker is a scourge which needs to be in management thought at any time of the year but especially when the youngsters are being fed. I believe that most young bird fatalities can be put down to canker inherited in the nest. The sad thing is that if it can be identified, it is generally too late to treat as by this time the resistance is severely reduced.

The other aspect which is decided by management and individual preferences is that of how to feed at this time of the year. Food can be provided in the hopper, on trays, in the nest boxes or whatever. I will not advise on this for over the years I have tried it all and have found that I revert back to what suits me best. I use hoppers with the birds having to feed at them and to carry their food back to the youngsters. I always feel that the secret of pigeon fancying is not only working hard but also not making a great chore out of doing things. If the enjoyment is lost or if it all becomes more like hard work than relaxation, then pigeon fancying might become a drag and I have never felt that I wanted to get to that stage. Hence, management has to be easy as well as effective

As in this chapter earlier, I must again mention red mite and the need to be watchful for it. They cannot easily be spotted in the nest but can more easily be seen on the youngsters before and during the feathering process and at night times. Examine frequently for they hide easily and just because there is a negative search one day, it does not imply that no red mite are present. To see one is enough to be certain that there are numerous ones lurking, feeding off the youngsters and troubling the adults also. If you notice adults leaving the nest for periods of time always think of the possible presence of red mite. Should you find any, then treat immediately by spraying, using a proprietary treatment but being careful to keep it well away from the actual youngsters. Some treatments are so strong that they can kill. I would like to couple these remarks by again mentioning the use of straw on the floor and in the boxes. Straw can harbour mite but can also be a haven to vermin and rodents, so be watchful and exercise care

Development and Identification

If all goes well, a pair of young birds will quickly grow and develop growing daily and feathering up. Ideally they should be matched for size but if there is an obvious weakling it is better suppressed at an early stage. Spiky feathers, constantly squeaking are warning signals that something is wrong with the young bird(s). There may be problems of internal health, the presence of red mite or other factors. Unless the cause can be remedied, dispose of the suspect bird as soon as possible.

When the birds are six to eight days of age, they need to be rung or banded. Breeds and families within breeds will vary as to when the ringing is necessary and it can vary considerably. Some birds carry larger limbs than others do and good substance also comes with good feeding and breeding. The fancier will choose which leg will carry the ring. Rings should be applied over the three front toes of the young bird, with the bottom of the ring going on first as this ensures that the ring can be read when the bird is held normally throughout its life. The three toes and main foot should go through the ring easily, and then the back claw can be eased through the ring. When performing this fairly routine task, it is better to place the youngster on a piece of cloth such as towelling so that it doesn't slip about. They can be held in the hand of course but often cause a mess when put under such stress. Should the leg be fairly large, then use can be made of a suitable lubricant such as liquid soap. Ideally, when the ring is on and properly applied, it should not slip off but in any case it is wise to check for a couple of days to ensure that the ring will not be slipped off by the youngster moving about in the nest.

A note must be made at the time of the ring numbers applied. Indeed notes should be made of just about everything that goes on in the loft and especially during the breeding operation. Nowadays I make an outline plan of my nest box positions and insert in each box for each nest box, dates, ring numbers and any other relevant information. It is amazing just how fickle the memory can be so my advice is always to make a note of things as they occur. Contemporaneous notes are the very best and certainly outrank the value of my memory!

Such a plan is invaluable in another matter and that is the planning of numbers to be bred. Thought must be directed throughout the breeding season to what is required from which pairs. Plan this very carefully, making notes of what is actually wanted for the race, show or flying team and from which pigeons. Much thought must be applied to this for without such planning a team can easily be made up from birds which breed freely, and which may not be the birds thought to be valuable as breeding candidates. This is very necessary where the fancier manages more than one loft. I often find myself taking the outline plans indoors to make notes and charts of requirements and also as a progress check.

Weaning

Another important decision becomes necessary when the good management has produced youngsters large and mature enough to leave the nest and to be able to fend for themselves. The age varies with the breed and of the family within the breed of pigeon. The youngster must be capable of fending for itself. There are several useful guides for this and these include the following:

- when it is noticed that the young birds are taking food them-selves - a definite benefit of feeding in the nest box

- when the young birds begin to wander and to look to leave the nest for short periods

- when the tail is two inches or more in length

- when the feathering under the wing is complete and acts as a covering.

These factors are also more noticeable when the parents have other interests such as sitting the next round of eggs and when it looks that they wish their young charges to become more independent. Observation and presence within the loft will often decide the day on which the weaning should be done. I prefer to wean birds in groups so that they find comfort together. There are many methods of weaning them away, show fanciers might like to use show pens, while racing enthusiasts may prefer to wean them into race crates so that they learn at an early stage how to feed and drink in a pannier. Show racers weaned into show pens gain that early advantage of being made familiar with being in a wire pen and where to find food and water. If these facilities are not available they can be placed into a spare compartment or section which has been prepared with a layer of sawdust or wood shavings. For a day or so it may be necessary to dip the beaks of the youngsters into the water so that they learn quickly how to drink and they will always learn from others which have been weaned for a few days.

Considerable stress is caused when the birds are removed from their parents so good management of the situation is very important.

Kindness shown will always be remembered and every minute spent with the young birds is well used for the bond which is formed or encouraged at that stage will always be an important relationship between fancier and the birds. Pigeons made tame and friendly at this age will generally always be so.

In retrospect

The breeding season is one of the most labour intensive but is a most enjoyable experience and many fanciers claim to enjoy the breeding season more than any other. The early cold days turn into warm long days of enjoyment with the birds. It just doesn't happen, it has to be worked at and planned and managed at every stage. The great satisfaction is in producing a team for the future of the loft as a result of sound planning and management. After all, the future of the loft depends upon the quality of the birds produced in those vital weeks.

Chapter 4

The Moult and its Management.

THE pigeon is a most beautiful creature when seen in its finished coat of feathers. Pigeons when in the very peak of condition with a lovely lustre and intensity of colour in their feathering present one of the loveliest sights in nature, and unlike the majority of avian species, the colouration of the sexes is identical. Nature, in its provision of feathers for birds, has bestowed one of the most wonderful products for their protection and beauty. This chapter explores the growth and development of feathers and their annual replacement known as the moult. The subject is a fascinating one for those who seek knowledge beyond the fact that feathers are necessary for flight and for very existence, and some additional information will enable explanation of some of the factors which occur in every loft in every year as the moult starts and proceeds to completion.

To the majority, the moult is the phenomenon which occurs every year and is a period which has to be endured rather than enjoyed. Some even regard the moult as a disease or ailment and in the past I have seen writers referring to the moult in these terms. I firmly believe that the contrary is the case and that the moult should be welcomed as the start of another year in the loft. Indeed the enlightened fancier will look upon the moult at its peak as the challenge to start the new year of pigeon fancying. The fancier who keeps away from the birds during the moult will be most likely to allow matters to develop which could result in a poor moult. Good fanciership is so very important during this most exacting time within a loft.

A good moult is a sure indication of good health and clearly suggests a state of good management. The reverse situation most certainly applies. It also follows that a considerable strain is placed upon the pigeon when it is growing the new plumage, and at such times of stress or strain other diseases can manifest themselves, taking the opportunity to attack while the immune system of the bird is weak.

It is erroneously believed that feathers grow on every part of the body of the pigeon but an examination will reveal that there are no feathers on the flesh on either side of the keel. The feather is a most complicated and beautiful structure possessing great strength and resilience. Its appearance is a sure indication of the health of the bird carrying it. Feathering full of lustre, clarity, and covered in bloom assures one that the health of the bird is good, whereas dull, listless feathering lacking a covering of bloom is a positive indication that something is wrong with the bird.

It follows therefore that when the pigeon enters into the moult it needs to be in perfect health to allow it to go through the trauma of casting its entire plumage and re-growing a new set for the year ahead. It is all a natural and necessary process. However, having said that, as many pigeon fanciers confine their birds to the loft, the situation is not an entirely natural one. Therefore thought must be applied to the provision of environmental factors which will assist the bird to go though a good moult with minimum discomfort, and with maximum success in the production of good healthy feathering.

Good management is absolutely essential and the provision of the following will assist:

■ Good food which is varied and which contains some oil seeds such as rape, linseed, safflower etc as well as a good basic

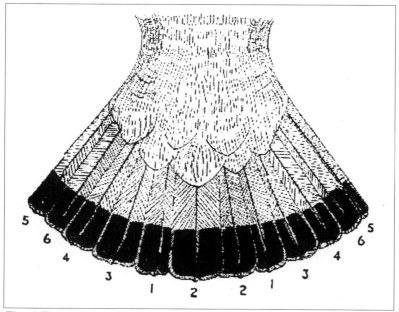

Fig. 1 The tail moult

mixture. The food must be supplied regularly so that there is no anxiety on the part of the birds.

- A good and sustained supply of water This can be supplemented with a tonic or other health-assisting products.

- Grit containing different types such as limestone, oyster shell

- A supply of minerals and clay blocks or picking stones

- Baths are very important at all stages of the year but especially during the moult

- Green foods, lettuce, chickweed, indeed anything which they will take. Carrot in diced form is excellent

- Herbals tonics such as pigeon tea, garlic and other natural products.

Some observations on the progress of the moult

YOUNG BIRDS

Young birds grow their covering feathers at least twice in the year of their birth and in unusual circumstances I have seen a third replacement when birds have been bred at a very early time of the season. The first flight is cast anything from 42 to 75 days and then progresses consecutively until the tenth flight is cast anything from 170-227 days, normally in the range of six or seven months. When the first flight is cast, the body moult will also progress.

Later bred young birds, i.e. those bred from mid-June onwards will moult their cover feathers but will not often drop all ten primary flights in the year or season of their birth. They often have a dual moulting of their primary flights in their yearling year.

The tail feathers, twelve in number in most cases, also drop in pairs. There seems to be a correlation between the casting of the last primary flight and the last pair of tail feathers. *(See illustration Fig. 1.)* As to the moulting of the secondary flights, there is less regularity in this and the author knows of no study which has proved a set progress of this aspect of the moult. Indeed, not all the secondary flights are replaced in any year.

It is quite common for young pigeons in the nest to carry minor fretting and in some cases the marks will be noticed in the majority of feathers. Most writers for racing purposes suggest that this is a weakness, which will prevail into adulthood so that the best course is to cull such birds. I do not necessarily subscribe to this as often the causes are minor in nature and I have witnessed some remarkable examples of birds which have been checked in some way, growing into wonderful adults with great vigour and value.

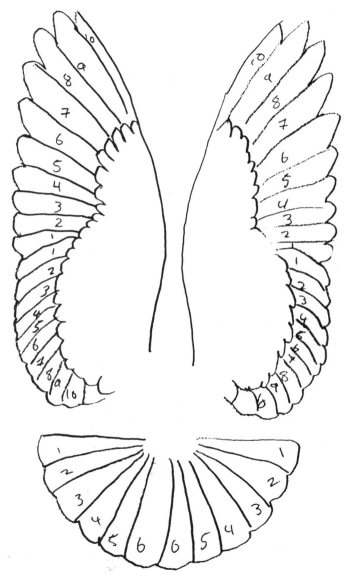

Fig. 2. Feathers of a Homer

ADULTS

The moult of the adult pigeon normally begins in April when the first primary flight is shed and this is normally connected with the breeding cycle, occurring when the first round of youngsters have been reared and the second round of eggs are being incubated. Birds which are unpaired start their moult several weeks later and will maintain condition much longer into the spring and summer.

The moult of the primary flights then takes an orderly programme of casting and growing with the next being cast when the preceding flight is half-grown. By the time the fifth primary is dropped the moult proceeds more rapidly with a more general body moult becoming obvious. The order over the body varies from pigeon to pigeon.

The moulting of the tail is an interesting process with a fairly set order of casting. The tail is generally made up of twelve large feathers or retrices; six on each side of a central and imaginary dividing line. The numbers of retrices can vary with as few as ten and as many as fifteen tail feathers and even more than that in fancy varieties such as the fantails. However, a normal tail when spread takes on the appearance of a fan, without an obvious break. For the purposes of numbering however we will assume that there are two sets of six feathers in the normal tail, numbered from the outside inwards so that the outside pair are numbered as one, and the two central retrices as six.

The first two to drop are the number fives, i.e. the two either side of the central two, and when these are just over half grown, the central two (number six) will be cast, then in order of four, three and one, the remainder will be cast and re-grown. The last to be replaced are the pair numbered as two, those second in from the outside. This apparent order pertains to birds in the very best of health, being another pointer towards the presence of condition, but in some birds under stress, particularly young bird racers, an almost complete tail will be cast and grown at once - with a corresponding strain on the bird.

There seems to be a correlation between the moulting of the tail feathers (retrices) and the primary flights of the wing, in that the tail moult seems to begin when the sixth primary is cast. Also, the last tail feathers to fall (numbered two) seem to coincide with the growing of the tenth primary. *(See illustration Fig. 2.)* The moulting of the ten secondary flights is less orderly and no set order has yet been discovered to my knowledge. Not all secondaries are replaced in a year.

33

Some observations on the moult

- It is known that some feathers change colour in the young bird's first moult. For instance a white nest flight can be re-grown as a normal coloured flight.

- In older birds there is a more common colour change which seems to progress with age, in that birds carrying black splashes will intensify this colour change as the years change. This normally occurs with the reds and mealies and indicates that the bird is heterozygous for colour.

- The moult can be delayed or affected by illness. The delay can be considerable with the progress of the moult being placed 'on hold' during an illness. Birds which experience injury - especially racing pigeons suffering wounds of broken limbs when flying - can have the moult delayed for several weeks. It seems to be nature's way of compensating one problem by providing rest or the correct environment for recovery.

- White feathers or those of the dilute colours seem to be more liable to becoming frayed or damaged especially in younger pigeons.

- It is better to avoid the administration of worming agents during the moult and also of anti-biotics. Their use can cause upset and result in stress marks or frets appearing.

- Birds which seem to lack feather condition should be examined to ensure that the oil gland is not clogged. This is situated on top of the rump near the base of the tail. Gentle pressure will normally allow a small amount of oil to be released. If it becomes blocked in some way, the natural oils will not be available for the bird to maintain its condition by normal preening.

- Young birds troubled in the nest e.g. with red mite attack, or injury of some sort, will suffer in the moult by becoming fret marked and lacking in bar/chequer colouring.

- The famous 'Violette' in his book, The General Management of Pigeons, recommends the use of new grains during the moult. In other words he suggested that newly harvested grains were more beneficial because of their increased vitamin contents. He even suggested that birds should be allowed to 'field' in the late summer and autumn period to enjoy the benefits of field-grown cereals and other seeds.

- A damaged or fretted primary flight or tail feather should not be 'drawn' or 'pulled' while the moult is in progress. If there is an intention to remove such a flight or retrice, it would be far better to cut it to a length of about an inch or so, allowing a natural wasting of the damaged feather, and to remove it in total only when the main moult has been completed. As for a 'blood quill', one full of blood and failing to properly develop, removal of these is never right and may lead to permanent damage of the feather base. It is better to treat this by the application of warm water, gentle steaming or of supplying warm baths.

Loft Hygiene during the moult

It goes without saying that extra work should be applied during the moulting process to keep the lofts clean. The removal of feathers is not only an aesthetic cause but also one which can prevent the outside of the loft looking a mess. A simple method of collecting feathers is to place a board such as a piece of hardboard in each corner resting against the wall. This little enclosed triangle acts as a trap for feathers and keeps them together for ease of removal.

As each feather develops, there is a constant shedding of debris or waste. This will be most clearly seen in the nest pan as young birds change and develop their plumage and in corners of the loft when the adult birds are moulting. It takes the form of a blueish powder and flaking and is best removed on a regular basis. Arrangements which allow the 'dust' to escape - such as floor grills, tobacco stalks or coarse straw in nest pans, and even straw on the loft floors helps in allowing separation of the dust from the normal environment. In my view the dangers of this dust both to fanciers and their birds cannot be overstated. In the wild, birds overcome this problem by building nests of coarse materials such as twigs, which allow the debris from feather changes to fall through and be lost to the winds. Fanciers should wear masks in the lofts during the moult especially but at all other times so as to reduce the likelihood of hazards to health.

It all amounts to good management and as I stated earlier, it is just as important during the moult as during other times of the year. The cleaner the loft the better are the chances of allowing the birds to enjoy a good, sound moult. Nor is it just a matter of cleaning, for time spent in the lofts will enable observation of the birds to prevent the development of illness or individual cases of stress.

Methods of speeding or delaying the moult

The best advice that can be given is to allow the moult to be as natural a function as possible. A good settled environment, which promotes good health, is the surest way of producing a good all-round moult. However, in recent years there have been developments or changes which have been discovered by fanciers with advanced thought which have produced advantages which can be useful to the average show enthusiast. Most of the changes have been produced by top racing fanciers but with some subtle changes can benefit the show or flying lofts.

The most obvious change has been brought about by the need to have young pigeons being at their best when the maximum performances are required i.e. during the longer distance young bird races. Ideally they should be holding a full or nearly full wing of primary flights and have a good cover of body feathers. Birds bred early in the year enjoy a normal moult, which results in the shedding of feathers being at its height when performance is wanted. I have sadly seen young birds sent to races in a state of 'undress' which detracts from their ability to home let alone race effectively. Fanciers enter young birds in such a state that they would not envisage for older birds. I am saddened by what I see and for some of the main classic, end-of-season races, it is often difficult to find youngsters to enter because most are deficient of good feathering around the face and breast and are carrying too few tail feathers. Use of the 'darkness system' overcomes this problem.

Using Darkness

To overcome this, the 'Darkness System' as it has been termed, was discovered to accelerate the body moult but to delay the moulting of primary flights and tail feathers (retrices). The young pigeons are provided with fewer hours of daylight by darkening their section or compartment over a sixteen-hour period, say between the hours of 1700 hrs and 0900 hrs the following morning. Apart from this extended period of darkness or semi-darkness, the loft management is exactly the same with the birds being allowed to feed, bathe and exercise as the normal management dictates. The result is that the youngsters will very quickly change their appearance by moulting their bodies completely but at the same time retaining their flights and tail feather. In racing terms it means that these birds wings and body cover are at their peak when the performance races are held.

The Darkness System has to be ended by about mid-June so that the birds can function more normally but the obvious advantages to the show fancier can be seen, in having fully body-moulted birds ready for the early season shows. The date of removing the darkness system is quite important because if it is kept operating after mid-June, the primary flight moult may not be completed in that year. However, disadvantages follow in that the wing moult is delayed and may hinder the bird's showing availability for the main winter shows and there is the likelihood of a secondary body moult also.

I have one word of warning on the use of the darkness system. If the compartment in question is darkened using dense materials, the free circulation of air may be affected and the birds will probably suffer from the restricted ventilation. The ideal way of darkening the section is to use a dark curtain through which air can pass, or if a dense material is used, a ventilation fan of some sort might be necessary to keep the air moving. Once the autumn approaches, extended periods of light from late September to the end of November will ensure that the birds progress through the wing moult to its completion.

Using Extended light

The exact reverse is in the 'Light System' which encourages the use of artificial lighting to extend the hours of light in the lofts to 16 or 17 hours to promote an early and sustained moult both in primary flights, tail feathers and in the body. The idea of this system is to breed and rear the youngsters in a light period of sixteen hours, then to wean the youngsters into a section which has a light span of sixteen or 17 hours every day. The idea is to use good lighting, preferably fluorescent lighting of the full spectrum specification - the type of lighting used in reptile houses.

It is not good to extend the light beyond the 16-17 hours, as longer periods of light will lead to stress and to a slowing of the moult as a result. I am also advised that it is not good to extend the lighting period both in the morning and evening. In other words, the birds should see either the natural daybreak or the natural dusk. This is more important for those who race or fly birds because for example, if the light is extended until midnight, the birds will think that this is dusk. Therefore if they are allowed out to fly in late afternoon they may get lost, flying into the night as what they believe is their evening. This is a safeguard for the racing enthusiast bur will not affect the show fancier.

The artificial lighting is cut off in May, early in the month for very early bred youngsters and later in the month for birds bred a little later. If the period of natural light is much less than the extended period of lighting, it is possible that the birds will fall into a heavy body moult. Nature tells them that winter is approaching and therefore they need to get on with the moult. This system facilitates the conditions where early-bred young birds will be completely through their moult, both body and primary moult by the end of summer.

Other Theories and ideas

To delay the body moult to enable adult birds to be shown during the summer months, there is a simple method which can be accommodated without great effort. It is to keep the breeding pairs together after they have completed their breeding duties. Their eggs are replaced with pot eggs and they are allowed to sit happily throughout the summer period. The system has two advantages. Firstly they rest thoroughly after their rearing details and this enables them to produce super condition. Secondly, the breeding cycle is not interrupted so that the moult is not induced.

The birds will therefore be in a general show condition for any summer event planned. However, it is very likely that once the show is over, the moult will suddenly take over and the birds will enter into a very heavy fall of body feathers. However, they are in a really good condition and can cope with the situation quite well. Good care and the provision of tonic will also help at this time.

I have seen several ideas on how to speed the progress of the moult. For birds which have been on the darkness system, it will be necessary to provide suitable conditions for them to complete the moult of their primary flights. To enable this to happen it may be necessary to provide extra light. Just as the autumn results in reduced sunshine and natural lighting, it will be necessary to lengthen the lighted periods by the provision of artificial lighting to at least sixteen hours a day. To the birds, summer is thus extended and they will speed through their moult better.

Another old system was to take a crate, a box or a show basket and to line it with dampened hay. The container is then taken into a warm room or place, so that the result is a humid environment within the container brought about by the warmth drying the dampened hay. The resulting humidity is excellent for allowing the moult to progress. Warmth in any case will assist the moult and I have known fanciers to basket their birds and to keep them in a warm place. This is usually practised when the tenth primary is growing, to enable it to grow to its full length, thus completing the moult, in time for a chosen show.

Plenty of baths assist the moult especially when warm water is used. Individual birds can be given individual baths by immersing their bodies in warm water and allowing them to dry themselves in a warm environment.

Managing the Moult

To allow a good, full and complete moult the fancier will have to adhere to the following:

■ Provide extra management and care

■ Provide a wide and varied diet with a constant supply of water

■ Exercise a system of hygiene which allows the birds to enjoy a clean, happy and settled environment

■ To take steps to ensure that the birds enjoy full health.

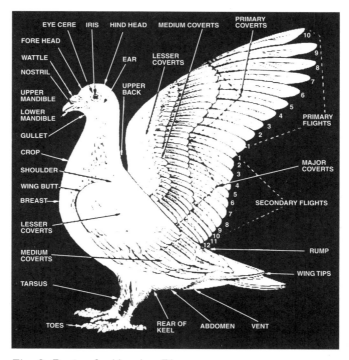

Fig. 3. Parts of a Homing Pigeon

Chapter 5

Good Health, Injuries and Common Ailments

SCIENCE is continually moving on in line with modern living re quirements and this most certainly applies to pigeon diseases and their treatment. One has only to read older books on pigeon fancying to clearly see this, for the terms used there are rather prosaic and bear little resemblance to the current situation and usages.

One is bound to wonder whether the diseases encountered now were experienced in past years or are they new to the pigeon fancy? Previously did fanciers deal with sickness by culling birds involved, thus dispensing with problems at the same time. Has the current situation developed because of a vast increase in the importation of pigeons and the situation where pedigree seems to take precedence over proven ability? In yesteryear, were the present diseases in existence but hidden by a more resolute determination to stamp them out at every source? For instance was there paramyxovirus in pigeons, parvovirus in dogs and virus problems in humans in years gone past or are these the result of the pace of modern life and of man's interference with nature?

As a non-medical person I do not know the answers to such questions and will therefore not even try to pontificate on them. I am always prepared to bow to superior and learned beings who are expert in their fields on such matters and to seek knowledge and guidance as and when required. After all, when ill we consult a doctor, yet pigeon fanciers try to deal with illnesses within their lofts by trying to treat such matters themselves - often with dire consequences.

I therefore approach this subject with some trepidation and to try to deal with it as a practical pigeon fancier with a reasonable experience of the sport. I have met with problems over the years and have made some of the mistakes I am about to warn about, but in general, have sought veterinarian advice or the advice of fanciers who seem to have a sound knowledge of their subject. In no way would I ever attempt to present myself as an expert on pigeon ailments and what I state here in this chapter is basic material, the sort of situation that most fanciers will encounter at some time in their pigeon fancying careers. Most of my advice is 'DON'T' rather than to 'DO'. I could almost sum up my advice as follows:

■ Do not administer anti-biotics unless they are prescribed for you. Far too many gain possession of these drugs and use them improperly, thus building up problems and troubles for themselves. The unmerited use of anti-biotics builds up a resistance to their effectiveness.

■ Do not administer a load of concoctions to the pigeons. Indeed I know of fanciers who rarely have clean water in front of their birds. The wrongful use of treatments for canker, coccidiosis and other diseases can be extremely damaging in the long term.

■ In the event of illness within the lofts, seek professional advice. It is a good idea to try to establish and cultivate a good relationship with a veterinarian with knowledge of pigeons or one who is prepared to learn.

Be determined to be a good pigeon fancier and to provide a good, clean and dry loft with adequate ventilation, a settled environment and to feed the birds with good food, clean water and grit.

The pigeon in its many forms is generally a healthy as well as a beautiful creature. Treated with good and considerate management it maintains form and health quite easily. This should always be the aim, to treat our pigeons as the robust creatures that they are and even in my management of some of the more 'delicate' breeds, my declared intention has always been to 'treat pigeons as pigeons'.

The old adage of suppressing the weak and the sickly birds still has relevance and much ongoing problem would be avoided with such an attitude. Better and more effective treatments however do allow us to deal with illnesses which occur owing to contact from outside sources and it is for each fancier to decide on the needs for such effective treatment within his own team. For instance, the treatments on offer for canker are a great asset to us as even the best birds can succumb to this ailment.

GOOD HEALTH

As my title of the chapter suggests three parts, perhaps a look at good, normal health is worth spending some time in discussing. The normal state of a successful loft, whether it be a backyard shack or a palatial racing establishment depends for success on good health. It is always a joy to witness good health in a loft, where the birds carry a sheen and seem to be content and full of vigour. In normal terms and based upon the premise that the pigeon is a healthy creature, the following are the basic requirements to induce a state of good health:

■ Clean Lofts

■ Clean air with ample and efficient ventilation

■ Clean water which is changed regularly and always available

■ Clean food, in other words good food free from soiling from themselves and from vermin and other pests

■ A supply of grit, minerals, green foods.

Given these factors, the average loft of pigeons will be fit and healthy. However, there may be factors present which are not altogether apparent and which if allowed to remain unchecked will lead to problems. So, to improve the chances of maintaining the good health, one possible routine is to have samples from the birds examined on a routine basis to check that nothing untoward is attacking from within.

Apart from this, there are some basic supplies, which any fancier might do well to keep on hand. I know that fanciers often have a cupboard full of treatments for almost any malady likely to be encountered but in basic terms the following would assist in the maintenance of good health:

■ A verucidal disinfectant. There are some wonderful products available to us now and they can be used routinely not only in the lofts but around them. I keep a pressure sprayer charged with some verucidal disinfectant, which I use, on floors and perches. I also use it in dry, hot periods to spray on the floors to loosen droppings prior to scraping the floors.

■ Jeyes fluid. This is another all-purpose disinfectant, which is hated by moths and other insect-life.

■ Sterilising fluid such as the type used to sterilise baby-feeding equipment. Used in accordance with the instructions on the bottle, this is a wonderful aid to a modern loft and will prevent cross-infection through the drinkers.

■ Iodine or iodine based products, long recognised as bactericides, as antiseptic for minor wounds, sterilisation of instruments and the purification of water.

- Bleach. (Household bleach (5%) available from most super-markets). One of the best products for sterilisation and for the removal of smells.

- A blowtorch as an aide for sterilising floor areas and for the destruction of worm eggs. *Needless to say, extreme care in the use of flame in the loft will be required.*

These are some of the best products available to us and prove that the best are not necessarily the most expensive.

INJURIES

Most injuries occur outside the loft. For those who keep their birds confined to the loft or to an aviary, they are unlikely to have problems associated with injured pigeons. However, those who keep the flying breeds and actually have them out on the wing, then from time to time it is an unpleasant situation that has to be faced. Those who race pigeons will have the most problems as their birds have to navigate wires, trees and numerous other obstacles, included of course, the dreaded hawks and falcons.

A practical look at the most common type of injuries may be useful but the advice is very much the same as already given, if in doubt about the situation of an injured bird, consult a veterinarian or at the very least, someone who is an expert at treating injuries. In nearly every case shock will be present and will need to be treated using care.

Chest Wounds. These are probably the most common injuries to be experienced and are normally the result of a collision with a wire, branch or some other sharp object. They often look worse than they are in actuality and can be treated fairly easily. The wound should be sterilised using a standard cleansing solution, and of course iodine will do the job. If the gash or cut is a long or wide one, a stitch or two may be necessary to bring the two edges together. In the event of the crop being split open, then a sewing of the wound is a must and must be accompanied by the sterilising process. Many fanciers undertake this work themselves but if in doubt, get professional assistance. Damage to the crop area always look terrible especially if food and water are able to escape through the opening, but the pigeon is amazingly resilient and will normally soon recover.

Breastbone injuries. Birds which hit wires, particularly high-tension electricity cables, often experience these. They seem to spot the danger just too late and attempt to rise above them, only to strike them with the lowest part of their body. Broken legs often accompany such injuries. A damaged keel normally heals on its own though it will show signs of the damage forever more. If there is an open wound present it must be sterilised and treated as above. Keels, which are fractured or split, will heal themselves also, but it is always debatable whether the injured bird will ever be able to race again. Each case will have to be treated on its merits and only observation and experience will tell the fancier whether to race or even fly the bird again.

Broken wings. To have a bird with a broken wing is quite rare as for the very obvious reasons; they are rarely able to reach home after such a devastating injury. However, I have known of birds walking home even across difficult terrain and of course such an injury may occur in the precincts of the yard or garden area. Such an injury is most difficult to treat and veterinary help should be sought. In many cases, as splints are not really a feasible option, the wing can be taped to the body in its normal position to allow the body to act as the splint. Such injuries are rarely successful and it is likely that even if the bird is ever able to fly, it will be a restricted sort of flight. Generally, any racing career is well and truly over.

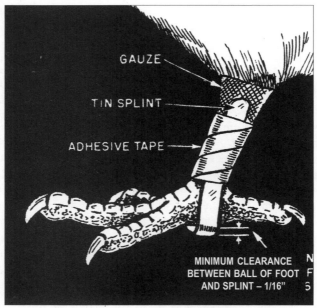

Splint for a broken leg

Broken legs. Those of us who race our pigeons have to face up to this problem just about every year. The main problem seems to come when the young birds are allowed out in their early days and especially when the winds are high. A bird with a broken leg is a dreadful sight, yet despite the injury they seem able to get home and to manage to get back into their lofts.

The most difficult injury is to the thigh as the fleshy thigh makes splinting difficult. Injuries to the lower part of the leg are a little easier but are often complicated owing to the presence of the ring or band. If there is serious swelling the ring/band may have to be removed to prevent further suffering. Broken legs can be splinted using small pieces of wood such as lolly sticks, even matchsticks and it is possible to buy purpose made plastic leg splints into which the entire leg can be placed. The wise fancier will have these in reserve for such eventualities.

There are other ways of mending broken legs, including strapping using bandages or pieces of sticking plaster. For many years my wife and I have mended broken legs using Plaster of Paris. This is a cheap product and if kept dry will keep for years. Small strips of bandage are cut and prepared for use, then dipped into a fairly runny mixture of the plaster, and are then applied to the broken limb. The first layer of bandage should be applied dry as eventual removal is made easier.

The Plaster of Paris dries very quickly and forms an excellent repair. Breaks to both legs require a high degree of skill and I would always advise the assistance of a veterinary surgeon. The bird will have to be suspended in some way using a sling of some sort to remove all its weight from its legs. This is not an easy matter, as the bird will have to have access to food and water and to be able to rid itself of waste products during convalescence.

Hawk and Falcon wounds.

Unfortunately these injuries are becoming all too common. Birds which are lucky enough to survive an attack, arrive home with wounds to the back or wing area. The worst sort of problem would be damage to the oil gland situated on top of the rump at the base of the tail. Falcon attacks are sometimes found on the underside, as often this is the way the attack is made. The wounds can be extremely serious and will require urgent treatment. They will have to be sterilised and the wound may need stitching. It must be remembered also that after such an attack the bird may be severely traumatised and will require very careful handling.

AILMENTS or ILLNESSES

I intend to be brief in my discussion on ailments for the reasons given, that I am not qualified to talk about them but will nevertheless mention them as a practical pigeon fancier. My advice is as before, that if in doubt to go to a veterinarian expert or to other respected source.

Paramyxovirus. This is a terrible disease which is dreadful to witness. It is worse in young birds, killing them in a matter of days or even hours. The disease attacks the nervous system causing neck twisting, an inability to feed, falling over and many more awful consequences. The droppings become watery and smell badly. The disease can be prevented by vaccination and I recommend all to vaccinate their birds immediately they are taken from the nest. I state that without hesitation, as I firmly believe in its necessity. Should there be an outbreak in the vicinity, then full use must be made of disinfectants in and around the lofts.

Canker. Most avian life is affected by the minute organism known as Trichomoniasis but a balance is normally struck in adult birds allowing them to live quite happily with a normal gut. There are three forms, the pharyngeal with yellow cheesy deposits being seen in the throat, the internal form and the navel canker normally seen in young squeakers. The disease is easily treated using either flock treatment in the water or in pillular form. Young birds are worse affected and I make a point of treating each young bird in the day or so after weaning. I strongly recommend this. Remember however that in youngsters, if the birds show the symptoms of canker, it is generally too late to treat, so prevention in this case is a must.

Coccidiosis. This used to be regarded as a killer disease but there are now good treatments available and good management will normally keep the problem in check. Routine treatment is not recommended but a routine testing of droppings will advise on any need to treat. The symptoms are loss of weight, dull condition overall, listlessness, a dull eye and droppings may be watery and discoloured. Where coccidiosis is present in a loft there must be good hygiene with no damp patches, especially around the drinkers. The use of a good virucidal or iodophor disinfectant will kill the Oocysts as will the use of the blowtorch.

Worms - Internal Parasites. It is suggested that worms are present at most times in our pigeons but when in good health they cope and respond to good management. Garlic seems to assist in keeping worms in check as a natural preventative part of general management, but treatment on a twice-yearly basis will keep the problem well under control. Some fanciers rarely if ever treat for worms but again, routine testing will establish any need for treatment. Individual treatments in pillular form are available as well as flock treatment preparations. In outbreaks, the use of bleach or the blowtorch on the floors and perching areas will kill worm eggs effectively.

External parasites. These are one of the modern day curses and the fancier will have to be continually on guard against these pests. Owing to changing regulation treatments seem not as effective as in the past and I tend to keep a variety of treatments to combat the problem which is usually seen as mites and as lice. The newer idea is where a drop of 'Ivomec' is placed on the flesh of the neck. This 'immunises' the bird against parasites for a month or so, and is favoured.

One of the worst problems is that of the dreaded red mite. These creatures live in cracks in lofts and being nocturnal mainly cause their problems as night by sucking blood. This can cause adults to leave their eggs of youngsters and when this happens, the first suspicion always must be that there is an outbreak of red mite. In bad outbreaks the red mite can be seen scurrying about on partially feathered youngsters but are otherwise difficult to spot. Treatment is recommended even if the pest is not visible. They are not easy to shift but a concentrated attack using insecticides, Jeyes Fluid mixture, heat via the blowtorch and other remedies will eventually allow the birds to be able to resume their breeding. This can be a very serious matter and deserves sustained and urgent treatment. The application of the 'Ivomec' type drops on the birds will kill the mite on the birds but the problem will have to be eradicated from the loft structure. Remember, that red mites are extremely dangerous and in most cases they cannot be seen. If birds leave their nests while sitting, always suspect the presence of red mite.

Hypocalcaemia, Eclampsia, hens in trouble after laying.
Unfortunately this is a troublesome and all-too common a problem. Immediately after laying a hen is seen to be off her legs and in some distress. In basic terms she is suffering from a deficiency of calcium caused through the use of all her natural calcium reserves to produce the egg. The situation can be easily treated and even more easily prevented. Treatment is in the provision of a calcium supplement given to her directly in tablet, powder or liquid form, including milk.

Recovery is generally instantaneous. Prevention is by providing ample grit before the birds at all times and by feeding a good calcium based supplement during the breeding season. Old-time pigeon fanciers kept all the eggshells from the kitchen and which were baked and crushed before being fed to the birds as grit.

Feather rot, bare patches on chest.
The bald patches frequently seen on the drop area of pigeons is almost invariably due to one of two main causes and not as many believe by rubbing when in contact with the feeders.

Where the area is completely clear of feather stub, the problem is of a fungal nature. Treatment is by washing the area with a solution of carbolic soap or by the use of modern anti-fungus ointments such as those used for the treatment of 'Athletes Foot'.

Where minute stubs of feathers can be seen, there is a feather mite at work living off the bird and getting transferred from one bird to another. Treatment is by various anti-mite products though the most modern and effective will be the Ivomec type, where a large drop is applied to the neck monthly providing 'immunisation' for the bird, making its blood poisonous to all known varieties of mites and lice. Natural moulting will replace the feathers with good healthy ones.

*   *   *   *

There are many other matters which could be mentioned but I have dealt with only those which may be encountered in day to day pigeon fancying. Be an expert only to yourself within your own loft but be prepared to seek proper and professional advice. The main advice is also a simple one, do not treat unless there is a problem. Over treatment is a curse of our time with 'amateur experts' not understanding what they are doing; yet building up problems for themselves by interfering with the proper balance of nature.

PART 2

Chapter 6

Enjoyable showing

HAVE now been involved in pigeon showing for many years. I enjoy showing my birds and I also enjoy the social pleasures which accompany the exhibition side of the hobby. In my early days I would have asserted that the pleasure was in the exhibiting of the best birds possible with the aim of winning. I still enjoy winning, that hardly needs to be stated, but my emphasis has changed to satisfy myself and to enjoy the company of other fanciers.

Perhaps my enjoyment of showing goes back to schooldays and when I first became smitten by the pigeon. The aim then was a simple one, to have some pigeons of the brightest colours possible - mainly gay pieds, to have them flying out freely, then for them to return to my shed. These birds were acquired from a local farm where they lived as ferals in a large old barn. Night sorties saw myself and friends risking life and limb to catch a few of them.

Then one day something happened which changed my life forever more. I was taken to an agricultural show where there was a pigeon show in progress. From the moment I entered that marquee and gazed upon the wonderful pigeons there I was completely and inextricably hooked on the concept of showing pigeons. My aim changed to the need to be able to show my pigeons.

I soon learned of the existence of a local small livestock fanciers' club and joined it. Evening 'table' shows were held so my first ever experience of placing a pigeon in a show pen was at one of these little events. Many is the time that I had to walk home three miles with my box and birds late into the evening but it did not dampen my spirits towards the pleasures of showing. I was fortunate enough to make friends with some of the local fanciers, most of whom were willing to help out and to put me on the right path to success. Thus my little team was changing and improving so that shows further away could be entered using the railway system for sending the birds and having them returned.

Just as I was producing a useful team, almost good enough to compete with the best local fanciers I had to leave home to start my career. I kept the birds for sometime thanks to the hard work of my mother, but eventually they had to be disposed of and for some years

I had no pigeons while I lived in quarters as a single man. Throughout this period however I never lost enthusiasm for pigeons and despite most of my contacts being in the racing side of the sport, my thoughts and aims remained true to showing.

When I married in the early sixties I was once again able to keep a very small team of pigeons for showing and enjoyed all the emotions of the sheer enjoyment of having birds again and in the building of my own family. I was ecstatic with pleasure and much of what I write about in the following chapters is based upon those early times, for they still seem like only yesterday.

Why Showing?

Obviously I often ask myself why I found myself so keen on the showing rather than on the more common and popular racing side of the sport. I find it difficult to answer even to myself but suppose that it had something to do with my upbringing in the Cornish countryside. I had encountered farmers who took great pride in the showing of their Shire horses for instance, and had met and assisted rabbit fanciers who bred for the show pen, seeking the excellence demanded by it. In other words I was being schooled to look for the quality in livestock which the show pen requires. A further friendship with a pigeon fancier who bred and exhibited Nuns probably gave me the final incentive as I admired his patience in breeding to a standard.

Nowadays I still concentrate on my showing but also enjoy keep and racing a team of racing pigeons. The entry into racing has provided me with good information and knowledge which assists the production of show condition and apart from the obvious strictures in time, I find that one side is quite conducive to the other. If racing had to be given up - and the current hawk and falcon situation is a real threat to it- I would probably throw myself into a new breed for showing and thus test my advice to others on starting up and on how to create a family!

I believe that the real answer to why people enjoy their showing is that which people in all walks of pigeon exhibition find. It is in the joy of producing something approaching excellence and then pitting against the excellence of others in their particular sphere. You need look no further than a top agricultural show to witness this working in all aspects of livestock exhibition, from the horses, cows, sheep, goats, and pigs of the farmyard, to the more domestic nature of dogs, cats, rabbits, cage birds, cavies and pigeons. Each breed will have its devotees who eat, sleep and drink their interests and travel long distances to exhibit and judge them, also to enjoy the social company of others with like interest. The occasion provides a buzz of excitement, a boost of adrenaline and a complete change from the usual stresses of life - though I sometimes think that more stress is endured at shows than anywhere else! Perhaps we all need that sort of stress to keep body and mind functioning.

Showing as an art

I consider showing to be an art in any form of exhibition. Enthusiasts ensure this by producing excellence in any sphere of operation. This most certainly applies to the showing of pigeons in their many exhibition guises. The successful fanciers are those with an extra degree of flair and animal/bird sense who are able to produce birds of the right type and in the best of condition as and when required.

The conditioning of pigeons for the show pen can be hard work but when it is based upon hard-won experience and sound knowledge, then it can become less of a chore and more of a pleasure. The final touches have to be applied to provide that extra chance of success.

Over the years I have never found the need to be apologetic for being a showman. I have always been proud of my birds and in being able to produce them in good order for the attention of the judges. Of course, it isn't only for the views of the judges for the observations and opinions of fellow exhibitors are often much more appreciated. An acknowledgement of a good team from a fellow competitor is always greatly valued. Appreciation is something which should always be expressed, for the good fancier is never afraid to praise the efforts of his fellow exhibitors and of the quality of the birds. Likewise an acknowledgement of the efforts and work of those who produce and organise the shows is well worth passing on.

A pigeon show is the product of the hard work and commitment of someone and provides a forum, a social function where fanciers meet, talk, argue, agree, disagree, boast and enjoy a multitude of emotions. The social aspect presented by a pigeon show is to be encouraged just as is sportsmanship with each being supportive of the other. If there is good sportsmanship present then it is likely that the social aspect will thrive and prosper. The good exhibitor is one who enjoys the competition, who is prepared to acknowledge the success of others and to offer congratulation, who helps out with the arrangements or chores and who encourages others.

Conversely someone in a club or society or at a show, who is out to win at all costs, who can see no virtue in anything not owned by himself, who resents others winning and who generally takes all but gives nothing in return, is likely to blight the whole event. We can all point to examples of both types and our aims should be to be an example of the first type mentioned, the sport, and to be less like the unsporting type who seeks selfish self-glorification.

Social input

Shows are what the exhibitors are prepared to put into them. If only we could produce a recipe for the successful types of show it would be an easy matter where the enjoyment would be even greater. Sometimes a show is just perfect, one where the competition and the judging has been good, the good birds have won and the successful fanciers have enjoyed their success but have been congratulated by fellow fanciers. Yet sometimes shows are the antipathy of this where morose types moan and groan about just about everything, contribute nothing and want to get away with their birds as quickly as possible, leaving the few workers to clear up afterwards.

Possibly the answer is to strive to get the social input right in show organisation. If fanciers can be involved in the show in some way or by attending an arrangement at the show, such as a meal, a drink, a discussion, a lecture/talk, or a specific function, a little something is added to the overall enjoyment. Breed clubs are very good at this and pigeon conventions in the United States and other places are excellent at promoting social enjoyment not only for the fanciers but for spouses and friends.

The success of shows depends on many factors. Shows will be held at most times of the year and will attract a small band of supporters whatever the problems. For instance, shows held immediately following the breeding season - or while some still have pairs together, restrict the entry because of lack of show condition. Yet such shows deserve support for if lost, will be lost forever. Shows held before the moult has fully cleared up will likewise fail to attract as many as desirable because of the need of exhibitors to avoid possible feather damage by exhibiting moulting birds. It is only in the prime time of each show season when the moult has been completed and when most of the birds are in top condition, that the entries will exceed expectations.

Out of Season support

Sadly, there are fanciers who fail to support shows 'out of season'. They act only in their interests and not in the wider implications for the show fancy as a whole. The early season shows are a necessary avenue for newcomers to have a go at and to gain the experience so necessary for success. As stated above, once lost such shows rarely appear in the calendar again and I really would like to see more show enthusiasts entering for the good of showing than for their own selfish expectations. I think back to that agricultural show I first attended for had it not been held I might never have gained my interest. That particular show no longer exists and is yet another example of a 'shop window' for the sport being lost forever.

The more pigeon shows there are where the public can take a look at our hobby, interest or sport, the better for our future in showing. It is mainly through such exhibitions that new members can be attracted. The agricultural events play a most important part in providing that 'shop window' for our pigeons to be viewed. I have always been amazed at the reaction of the public when they see blowers, croppers, the tiny breeds and of course the more ornate spectacle of a jacobin, for they are amazed and surely this is where our hobby should be presenting itself. The sportsmen will support such out of season shows with their entries and efforts, while the selfish will stay away and perhaps one day find themselves with no shows at any time of the year.

Large team, small team

It probably goes without need of saying that the larger the team a fancier is able to exhibit, the better are his chances of success. The same applies in races where the man with a large flying team should in theory multiply his chances over the flier with an entry of one or two birds. I must say that I enjoy showing small teams better than when I take along a larger number. Indeed one of the new ventures has been shows with a restriction on numbers to provide an equal chance to the majority of fanciers. A one exhibit per class per exhibitor is a big attraction to me. Not only are the chances of success evened out but the work involved in preparing the team is reduced greatly. The final benefit comes after the show when it is so easy to return a small team to the loft.

Over the years I have seen examples of small-team fanciers operating in a small loft with a small number of pigeons, yet who have been able to more than hold their own in the most challenging competition. I have great admiration for such people for while I have never operated with large numbers, neither have I been able to reduce down to six to eight pairs. If I ever did this I would be fearful of losing my family pattern.

In any breed the numbers kept will to a large extent depend on the number of shows available and to the number of classes open for competition. The real pleasure is in winning breed or club classes against the best in that breed, rather than in the 'any other variety' type classes where the judging becomes more of a lottery. Fanciers who persevere with the numerically weaker breeds are to be admired for keeping on and in trying to promote their chosen breed against the odds. It is easier for the show racer fancier or one specialising in the popular flying varieties or the more popular fancy breeds to keep an interest than it is for the fancier who competes only in small classes against a small number of exhibitors. I daresay that in many such cases more than one breed will be kept to be able to spread the competing interest in the shows.

As a show organiser of course I have mixed emotions on numbers for it is often the exhibitor with the large team who keeps the show going economically with the larger entries. Each show requires cash to enable it to meet its expenses and so often the balance is a most delicate one. Any losses have to either be absorbed or met from other sources and no show can continue to lose money for long. However, whether the exhibitor possesses a large team or operates from a more restricted base, there must be a welcome for all fanciers are welcome to enable showing to continue in the future.

Classic shows, small-event shows . . .

I have been fortunate to attend shows in all shapes and sizes and in several countries. I have attended some of the largest pigeon shows in the world and some of the smallest and most inconspicuous. The former speak for themselves, being held in huge arenas or complexes and attended by thousands of paying spectators who produce considerable profit to the show organisers - often for charitable aims. I have also attended shows on the other scale, shows held in gardens, in barns, in marquees and in spare rooms.

Whatever the size of the show, there has been enjoyment in them all with some of the more intimate smaller events providing extra friendship and camaraderie. Every pigeon show will have its attractions and these are what should be worked at, the making of a social gathering as well as a serious competition. We all like to win, we all enjoy seeing a first prize on our entries, and we all like winning specials but above all, it is so much better to leave a show with pleasant and enjoyable memories. These are more likely to be gained by a sporting intention to genuinely contribute to the show and the work entailed.

Novices and newcomers

Any time spent with newcomers to the sport or to the breed at shows is time well spent. Experienced fanciers should always be prepared to give advice and to give of their time willingly to help those who are seeking knowledge. Some would-be fanciers are so willing to learn that they will gladly listen to and heed good, genuine advice.

Too often I have seen novices taken in by those who should know better. They spend time with the newcomer but only to be able to sell some birds, sometimes at wildly inflated prices. Of course there are novices and novices, some think that they will be able to purchase their success and are therefore more easily taken in by the fancier seeking to unload some pigeons. I just feel that those who genuinely seek knowledge should be treated with respect and provided with some time from the more experienced person.

Future showing

All pigeon fanciers who enjoy showing will need to give thought to the future. With so many other attractions in this modern world, pigeon showing will have to compete and present itself to remain attractive. The need to be seen by members of the public cannot be overstated because this is where we may attract new fanciers to our ranks. Running shows amongst ourselves may be fine for those who merely want to compete, but there is a wide world out there from where we need to attract new recruits to pigeon keeping.

Yet, even as I write this, I must avoid sounding despondent for in my time in the sport, shows and showing have flourished and will do so hopefully in the future. While some shows disappear, others take their place and while some seem to reduce in attraction, there are events worldwide attracting huge numbers of entries. There will always be room for excellence in livestock keeping and our aim as pigeon show enthusiasts must be to spread the word, our word about the social benefits of enjoying a relaxing yet demanding interest.

We owe it to the sport to be of the sporting types who value what is done for us, to help others and to encourage others especially novices and newcomers. We owe it to the sport to try to enter for the 'out of season' shows even when it would be easier to stay at home and to do something else. Only by competing in this way will we be able to ensure a future for pigeon showing for ourselves and for all those out there who don't even know yet that they are one day going to be pigeon enthusiasts.

Chapter 7

Fittings for the Show Loft

AGREEING that pigeon lofts come in all shapes, sizes and types and the next discussion concerns the question whether a loft intended for show pigeons needs to be different than one for racing purposes. In my view it does.

I base this assertion on the fact that I compete at both sides of the sport and while my present show loft would make a superb racing loft because of its aspect, ventilation, light and access, it would still require adaptation to enable racers to race effectively to it. Likewise as a confirmed showman, I would need to make considerable alteration to my racing loft in order to house the show birds in the manner I like. I would therefore like to examine how a typical loft for show pigeons needs to be for sustained showing success.

First however, let me say that what I am talking about is an ideal and not one which is absolutely necessary. Therefore someone turning to showing from racing or flying the birds, would probably find that the loft would be suitable for most purposes to adequately house a team of show racers or other show pigeons. Pigeons need to be treated as pigeons and the over-riding consideration is that the structure provides an environment which the birds enjoy and therefore become settled to their loft.

And so to those ideals:

Compartments or sections

In my view, the ideal show loft would have at least four sections with five being even better. Good management depends upon space and air and the ability to arrange the birds according to their needs. Sections for old cocks, old hens, young cocks and young hens enables good management and a fifth one would enable a further division in the event of a further division of sexes to be necessary.

The size of each compartment is one for individual preferences but the aim must always be to avoid overcrowding. Good-sized perches are important with numbers being adjusted to allow plenty of air space for the numbers kept - probably in the autumn period when numbers are at their greatest.

For many years I advocated solid partitions between the sections of compartments but I now favour having a free flow of air and light from one end of the loft to another. So long as birds of the opposite sex are unable to have contact leading to a loss of condition, I would prefer to see a gap in the walling with the use of doweling or something similar. Any gap should be inserted so that there is at least fifteen inches or 38cm above the floor so that birds can't linger and pair together. A good sunny aspect from one or more compartments or sections can be enjoyed by birds in other sections by the free circulation of air, light and warmth.

Corridor

A corridor would come very high on my list of priorities for the show enthusiast. The wider it is the better and I would urge anyone starting the design of a show loft from scratch to arrange a good wide corridor from which the servicing of all the sections is arranged. Even in my present loft, the corridor was slightly too narrow and I made adjustments to make more space. A good guide would be to carry a large basket or show container in and to judge the ease or degree of difficulty involved.

A corridor not only allows ease of access to the birds, but also allows the facility to observe them at length without upsetting them by being in with them. The birds get used to the presence of the fancier but without that worrying proximity. This can be done in a dry environment, as one with all the pigeons in the loft off the corridor. I prefer a corridor to run along the front of the loft especially when south facing, but I have seen equally successful lofts where the corridor runs at the rear. It is all a matter of preference and of necessity of design for available space and aspect.

One immediate advantage of a corridor would be the ability to install some pens for pen training. I have used a set of four pens in my show loft for many years and regard them as an essential part of show training and in getting young birds used to being in the pens from an early age. It is very easy to pop birds into the pens on a daily basis if required especially where fanciers are due to call as they can then judge the birds providing them with some additional and beneficial training.

Aviary or bays

In days of growing problems of raptors, it is frequently imprudent to allow the show pigeons their freedom from the loft. Indeed I would assert that one of the greatest changes to be found in showing habit is that show fanciers hardly ever allow their birds out because the average show pigeon is almost a sitting target for a hungry hawk or falcon. Show loft design therefore should take this into account by making provision for the birds to get access to the open air and sunshine.

An aviary is an ideal arrangement so long as thought is given also to control of the birds. It is no use having unlimited access to an aviary if the birds become unmanageable as a result. A smaller area if therefore the ideal, in an area large enough for the birds to be able to fly or flutter about and to enjoy bathing, but with thought given to the fancier's control over his birds.

In the event of an aviary not being possible, then good-sized bays are desirable. These should be constructed so that sunshine can get to the birds yet no rain is able to beat in. Bays come in many sizes and types but the birds gain tremendous benefit from being able to enjoy sight of the outside world. Over the years I have tried various structures and have made mistakes in design and construction but the use of clear glass or clear glass substitute very necessary. The bay can be designed so that it allows the inmates to get out and in from the loft to fly if this is possible and desirable. Something based upon the needs of the racing pigeon will generally act as a guide.

Penning room or facility

The next extension to having some pens installed in the loft is having a separate penning room or at least a facility where pens can be erected. Some fanciers use a compartment within the loft for this purpose combining the space with basket storage, corn bins and for other uses - even as an office. Again I have been fortunate to have a little under-balcony penning room and would find it difficult to operate without it.

Apart from the obvious advantages of pen training, the penning area can be used as an isolation area in the event of new birds being received, in the event of illness or disease and all sorts of other reasons. As a racing enthusiast I use my pens for widowhood hens at certain times of the year and also for pairing birds. It is surprising how quickly birds pair when situated in adjacent pens for a few days prior to being placed in their boxes.

Of course not everybody is fortunate enough to have the facility for separate penning but we are talking about ideals for successful showing and I know full well that some of my greatest successes have come in times when no such luxuries were available to me. It is all a matter of making the best out of what we have.

Perches, type and sizes

Over my many years within the sport I have experimented with all sorts of perches. Even now I have a selection of sizes and types although the trusty box perch still seems the most suitable overall. In my show loft I tended to fit the maximum number of perches into available space, so that in each 72" (180 cm) wide section, seven boxes wide in blocks were selected rather than the six wide would have allowed them to be nearer 12" (30cm) wide each. I cannot claim that this is a wrong choice as the birds seem to cope very well with the narrower box perches but somehow I suspect that the wider size may have been better overall.

I have also used much narrower but deeper perches which resulted in birds being able to face forward only and to have the ability to keep all other birds from invading their space. These were 5" (12cm) wide and fifteen inches (38cm) deep. I used them for several years before disposing of them and replacing with normal box perches. 'V' perches have been used for many years often in smaller areas to provide some additional perching room for the birds and possibly a more interesting site for them. Birds tend to like having their own perch in an isolated position and thereby 'V' or saddle perches come into their own.

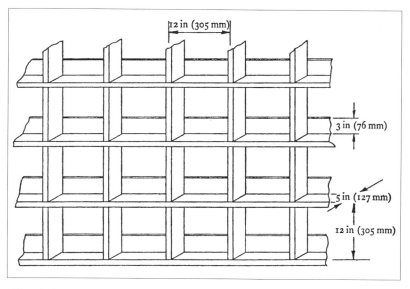

Fig. 4. Box perches, showing 'backing batten'

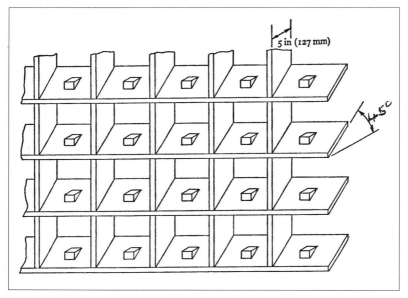

Fig. 5. Box perches with sloping face and block.

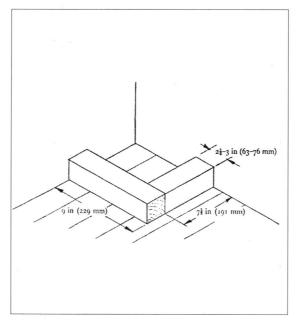

Fig. 6. A simple wood surround to form a corner nest.

I guess that over the years I have tried to make my perching arrangements tidy or symmetrical, generally with a block of perches on one wall only. Nowadays I tend to vary this slightly. However, one interesting use of perching as a conditioning tool I saw in the United States and as mentioned in Chapter 2. A show fancier there had a large cabin for his birds, with higher than normal walls. Around each wall at ceiling height he had a row of box perches and it seemed to take some effort for the birds to reach this height, thus adding to their fitness and thereby condition. In fact, if I had to design another loft I would make it considerably taller than normal so as to provide greater flexibility, better ventilation opportunities and added space and light. The danger is in loss of control but one need not lead to the other.

The conventional box perch has been superseded in some respects by forms of perching which

Are more often than not based upon the box perch idea. I never cease to be amazed at the ingenuity shown by fanciers in trying to establish perfection for them and for their pigeons. These generally involve the birds standing on a slim front perch within the box structure, while behind them there is either a slope or a flat area guarded by wires to prevent the birds standing elsewhere than on the intended perching strip. Another form of perch I am now using is to have the birds standing on pieces of wood four and a half inches square (11 cm by 11 cm), with dividing boards about twelve inches (30cm) apart. The theory is that the birds will face into the perch when defecating so that the droppings fall in front of the perches and never on to the bird on the perch below. Please see illustration Fig. 5. The width between the boards can be varied to suit the breed concerned so while the 12 inches or 30 cm is adequate for show racers, a smaller breed may require less width.

One tip I always use is to have a tray under all sets of perches. This catches the worst of the droppings rather than have them falling on to and building up on the floor area. In some cases I have a conventional tray while in others I use grills so that the dropping fall through allowing a clean area for the birds to walk on. This is especially important for the show racers during the showing season enabling feet and legs to be kept clean.

Lighting, dimmers and heaters

For show lofts I would always recommend that lighting be fitted. Nowadays this is made possible by the fact that the majority of lofts are situated in garden areas of residential property. This provides additional flexibility for basketing birds prior to showing them or on their return from shows.

A dimmer switch fitted in conjunction with the lighting is an added bonus. There are various types on the market, some with timers for use only with conventional bulbs (non-fluorescent) and permit the lighting to come on up to two occasions in a day. This is especially useful for early breeding, where the extra lighting hours can convince the birds that spring has arrived. One of the most useful I have used provides an automatic dimming time of about 15-20 minutes. In other words, when the birds return home from a show and are taken out of their baskets and returned to the loft, they can be fed and watered in the light, and then when the switch is activated, darkness falls in a natural fashion in that space of time.

Baths and bathing

A system for bathing the birds on a frequent basis is an absolute must. Again over many years I have tried all sorts of receptacles for pigeon baths. Again, a corridor is most useful in allowing space for the bathing process. I tend to lay down cloths to catch most of the water, something very necessary when shallow receptacles are used. In the last few years I have obtained a deeper plastic bath which the birds seem to like better. I was worried that the extra depth may have put them off but the contrary seems to be the case. The great advantage however is that very little water is thrown out on to the floor.

Deeper plastic baths with two shallow versions at the rear.

Lofts fitted with bays are very efficient in allowing bathing and one idea I admire is where the bath is slung under the floor of the bays, being revealed by the lifting of a false floor. The birds like this arrangement, as it is a simple extension of their use of the bay areas. There is no doubt that the aviary is even better and more convenient for bathing, again with the birds using their usual space and with the added advantage of being able to dry themselves in the open air. Whatever system is devised within any loft management system, it is far better that it is as simple and straightforward as possible. Like any chore within loft management, the easier it can be made, the better it is. Baths should be provided on a regular basis so the easier it is the better for both fancier and the birds.

I can round off by talking about bathing the show birds prior to showing them. I have always favoured the very natural way of presenting them with a bath of water - slightly warm if possible - and allowing them to bathe themselves. The question most asked is how long or how soon before a show a bird can be bathed. In my view, where birds are fit and ready to be shown, the condition will allow a bath to be given even the day before a show. I prefer a couple of days before but it is a matter of choice and convenience. The better the weather, the closer to the show date the bath can be given.

Some fanciers will individually bathe their birds using warm water and soap. Some use a soft brush and soft soap. The soap is massaged gently into the feathering before using plenty of clean water to adequately wash away any trace of soap finishes the job. The birds are then dried by allowing them to dry within the confines of a warm basket placed in a warm area, or by the use of a hair drier. I very much prefer the natural method but will individually bathe a bird where it manages to get soiled in some way.

It's elementary really

In exploring the fittings for a show loft, let me finish with something which is so simple that it hardly needs saying but the finest elements you can introduce into your show lofts are clean air and sunshine. These two factors are absolutely vital to produce show condition so when designing or fitting out a loft, have these considerations very much in mind. I am absolutely convinced on this observation and if the reader heeds this one piece of advice alone, a great deal will be gained in loft management and production of showing success.

Chapter 8

Requisites for the show fancier

THERE is obviously a great deal more to the art of showing pigeons than in simply possessing a loft of pigeons and the desire to get them entered in shows. In the last chapter I discussed some of the fittings which I felt were necessary in a loft designed for show pigeons so now we can move on another step to consider what the show fancier might need in addition to what is to be found in the loft.

Generally these items are not expensive and are of the type which might already be possessed within an average household although some like the necessity for good show containers might prove to be a major investment. Let us start therefore with the means of conveying birds from the loft to the show pen.

Baskets and show containers

Good baskets or show containers reflect the fancier and his birds. In Britain the most common are baskets made from wicker with cloth internal divisions. These are generally greatly valued and treated with considerable respect. They are not quite as easily stacked as the more compact aluminium show containers but in terms of comfort for the birds they have no equal.

I have been using a set of baskets for well over two decades. They look as good today as when bought thanks to a system of annual treatment which has maintained them in pristine condition. Every year they are thoroughly scrubbed in hot water to which is added disinfectant, soap and bleach before being hosed with a high powered hose. Following being allowed to dry in natural sunlight, they are then varnished every second or third year.

In Britain of course distances between shows are generally short enough to ensure that a normal show basket or container is quite sufficient. However, in other countries some of the distances are much greater so that a different approach is required. On page 64, I show a photograph of an American travel container revealing the extra space afforded to each bird together with the facility for food and water. It goes without saying that extra vehicular storage space is required for such containers. Therefore the correct type of vehicle is necessary for transport of the birds to and from the shows.

On that point it is worth mentioning some basic care when transporting teams of pigeons. Care should be taken to ensure that the pigeon bloom is not allowed to hazard the health of the fancier(s). Good ventilation with a free flow of fresh air from the outside and expelled - after passage through the cabin is a must. As an additional safeguard it is a good idea to cover the baskets or show containers with a blanket or sheeting to prevent the bloom spreading throughout the vehicle. I once saw an arrangement in the United States intended to cater for a lady who suffered acutely from Pigeon Fanciers' Lung. The vehicle used was a largish personnel carrier but the rear section had been completely sealed from the driver/passenger section to ensure that the good lady suffered no ill effects from the presence of the pigeons. The bulkhead sealing had been done professionally and with additional ventilation to the area designated for the pigeons.

Basket storage

Good and very expensive baskets and show containers

Safe basket storage in a steel cabinet

deserve proper care. They will last a lifetime if looked after so any steps taken will pay dividends for many years. For many years I simply stored my baskets on shelves in my garage, but from time to time would find that they had been a refuge for mice. Despite being emptied at the end of the show season and washed, they provided a warm haven for small numbers of vermin, which, sometimes gnawed at the cane causing irreparable damage.

English wicker show baskets: 2 x 6, 2 x 4, 2 x 2

Pigeon carriers for long journeys (U.S.A.)

Then one day I decided to purchase proper storage and bought two steel cabinets of the type used for stationery and files in offices. These can be acquired quite cheaply and can quite comfortably store quite a number of baskets. Since keeping my baskets in the cabinets I have had complete peace of mind in the sure and certain knowledge that my cherished baskets are absolutely well. It has proved to be a small cost for a huge benefit.

Of course there are other items which will need to be stored to keep the baskets/containers fresh and clean for the birds. There must be a good supply of sawdust and/or wood shavings or other materials for having in the baskets. I have seen all manner of materials used in addition to the two mentioned such as chopped straw, hay, wood chippings, paper-shreddings, grills, peat, cat litter - and so the list could go on.

Show pens

I discussed this in the previous chapter but as a show fancier, the need for a penning arrangement is an absolute must and I always urge show fanciers to find a way of having sufficient space for the erection and use of penning for the training of the birds. The pens will require shavings or sawdust as mentioned in the last topic, as the birds will need to have clean conditions for their training. Some pen cups for water will also be a useful training tool as in any show of more than a day, the penned birds will need water and of course food.

Clothing

Most fanciers are now aware of the dangers of breathing in dust from pigeons ranging from the bloom they carry to the feather dust and other forms of debris which go hand in hand with any form of livestock. The advice nowadays is loud and clear, that when in the loft, particularly when cleaning and otherwise working, that a loft coat, a loft hat or cap and a facemask be worn. These will keep dust off normal clothing and it goes without saying that they should be kept away from the loft and where possible hung up away from other normal clothing. Masks should be of sufficient specification to intercept microns of dust and manufacturers are now producing masks which are efficient, comfortable but above all extremely safe.

I would advise fanciers to purchase specialist masks through specialist suppliers and not the cheap versions which might be found in the average DIY store. Battery controlled motorised masks are now available which filter the air and keep dust away from being inhaled by blowing a constant supply of cleaned air over the face. These are obviously expensive but whatever the cost, health cannot be bought once lost.

Keen show fanciers will also be in possession of a judging/showing coat. These may well be white but will denote a certain degree of professionalism within the sport and are always to be encouraged. A telescopic judging stick completes the show attendance necessities.

Show preparation items

Although I will deal with these items in more detail in the chapter on show preparation it is worth reiterating here some odds and ends which are desirable to hold in readiness for the time-honoured session of turning a pigeon from the loft into a show candidate. A kettle, a sharp pair of small scissors, a nail file or emery-board, a nail clipper, some cleaning fluid, soft soap, a towel, a hair drier, a nail brush, talcum powder, chalk or chalk block - all these are items which will aid the show preparation process.

We then take the process a step further to the show itself. When the birds are taken from their baskets/containers just prior to being penned for the judging, they are often found to have soiled themselves during the journey, or having produced some other fault during the journey such as bending a feather or flight. A small kit ought to be carried with the birds to the show consisting of cotton wool, cleaning fluid, chalk and a pair of nail clippers.

Records – permanent and portable

Again, I intend to deal with this at more length in a chapter, but I have no doubt that every show fancier should keep proper and full records of all aspects of pigeon keeping and showing. I have a record, which is complete from the time I came into the sport, and which forms an important part of my planning, and just as importantly - my pleasure. However, to me, just as important is the small notebook I carry to the shows. Every bird in every class is listed therein and the details transferred to the permanent record in due course. This little book contains the details of the birds, their pen and class numbers, the judges, numbers in class and of course the name of the judge.

There is no short cut to showing pigeons. The work for the local show is just as great as entering the birds for the largest and most prestigious shows with a set procedure of detail. There must be a foolproof duplication of information to follow the birds from the loft the show container and on to the show pen - and hopefully to the winning rostrum! But more of that later.

Chapter 9

Food and Methods of Feeding the show team

OVER the years I have realised that the method of feeding pigeons is about equal in importance to the actual content of the food to produce show condition. In other words, even if the finest quality and highest price food is given, it counts for nothing if it is simply thrown down in front of the birds involving little time spent by the fancier with his birds.

A study of any book on pigeons will produce advice on how to feed pigeons with much of the emphasis being applied to food content quality and quantity. Most of the information provided is directed towards the racing side of the sport, but it is good to heed such advice and to read into the methods employed by the racing experts.

The fancier of today is presented with an astonishing selection of companies offering foods for pigeons with grains of the very highest quality grains. In years past the range available was fairly limited whereas there has been a greater awareness of the needs of the fancier and his birds. On top of this, there is a considerable increase in the quantity of peas and tic beans being grown more locally and dried and prepared using modern facilities on the farms. Quality products are now more available getting away from the previously dubious value of buying locally because of questions about the drying and cleaning of the various home-grown products.

In this chapter I would like to discuss the methods of feeding show pigeons because there are some differences from those employed by the racing fancier. However, I would always urge show fanciers to study the methods of the successful racing enthusiasts for it is very likely that in achieving their success they have established a successful method of feeding their stock.

As with any form of livestock keeping, there is no magical or even scientific formula which can be used to produce condition in pigeons. This would make pigeon fancying too simple and take away much of its interest and challenges. There are so many factors which determine the condition of pigeons besides food and methods of feeding. What works in one loft does not necessarily do so in another where the environment and other factors are so different. This is why pigeons taken from a successful fancier's loft do not perform as well in another and the expression often used is that not only do you need to buy the best but also to buy the skills of the winning owner.

Even the best and most expensive feeding mixtures will not necessarily produce show condition. That is a fairly short but conclusive statement but one which took me a long time to discover. There are so many other factors which have a bearing on the pigeons and their health. I have already mentioned environment within the loft in this and in other chapters, a situation affected by the success or otherwise of the ventilation system, the ability for sunshine to enter, cleanliness, the amount of time spent by the fancier and numerous other matters. Worm infestation, the presence of insect life on the birds, of rodents in or near the lofts, other illnesses, dietary deficiencies; all are features which will affect condition and no amount of good feeding or quality food will overcome them.

Pigeon management is very much an all-round system of work within the loft or coop with food and feeding being only one - albeit very important - aspect. With such a disparity on the size and type of breeds to be found in pigeons it is hardly surprising that methods have to be trimmed to suit individual breeds. The show racer is so much like its illustrious kin the racing pigeon to require much the same sort of treatment, whereas breeds such as the runt with its huge size will demand a different feeding regime to the tiny short-faced breeds. Birds which fly hard and long will need a different set of guidelines to those which merely sit about the lofts all day with the occasional trip to the floor or to the drinker.

Collective terms are difficult to use freely because of the terminology which differs between countries. For instance in Britain 'corn' means the general content of the feed and is a collective term, whereas in the United States and elsewhere, 'corn' refers only to maize in its many forms. Tic beans are common in Britain but much less so in other countries and the common term pea refers to so many types, size and colours. So, allowances will have to be made for my rather 'English' approach to the subject and awareness that local conditions and supplies will determine the management strategy to be adopted.

In most cases, pigeons for showing purposes are being kept in artificial conditions by being confined to their lofts or coops without a great deal of access to the outside world. In nature, wildlife has all the advantages of living in natural surroundings gaining food from wherever possible and taking from nature all the other ingredients of life as they can find them. Just as important as anything else however, they have bountiful supplies of fresh air and sunshine. We therefore have to recognise that we need to feed our pigeons to provide some of the deficiencies not available to them from the outside world such as grit and other minerals and by providing as much access as possible to the outside conditions.

Grain content

Reference is often made to mixtures as being 'light' or 'heavy' in nature depending on the protein content and I still feel that they are reasonable terms to use as a basis for feeding show pigeons. In racing circles great changes have taken place in feeding methods and here in the U.K. which has been by tradition a bean feeding pigeon fraternity for the distance racing, has been changed into one persuaded by European considerations to feed lighter mixtures to cater for shorter or sprint races. In other words cereal feeding has to some extent replaced the bean and pea feeding culture.

Success comes to those who feed nothing but the best, it comes to some who feed the cheapest foodstuffs from the farm, to some who feed little but turkey or fowl pellets, even wheat, barley and cracked maize, and to others who feed a very high content of beans. So, method and environment seem more important than the actual quality and type of feed. However, as the chapter is about the feeding of show pigeons, a look at a couple of typical 'light' and 'heavy' mixtures may be useful an insight into popular feeding methods by those who like to prepare their own mixtures.

Mixtures in measurements (parts)			
HEAVY		**LIGHT**	
Maize (Corn)	1	Maize	1
Kaffir/dari	2	Kaffir/dari	2.5
Peas/beans	5	Peas/Beans	3
Tares	1	Tares	0.5
Safflower	2	Safflower	2
Wheat	0	Wheat	0.8
Buckwheat	0.2	Buckwheat	0.2
		Barley	2

Any quantity can be 'made-up' using these 'part' measurements.

The guidelines for grain are quite straightforward. The best available should be purchased, not necessarily the most expensive, but the best available for the price which can be afforded. Neither does it means purchasing only sparkling, polished grains, for dust does not necessarily signify poor quality. Indeed some of the best farm grains which come with the presence of some other smaller seeds from other plants, even weeds, are often preferred by the birds over the polished and better presented grains.

Perhaps a look at some of the constituent contents of the most popular grains on offer throughout the world would also help. The following table can be used as a reference.

Comparative Table of Grain Constituents				
Grain	Protein %	Carbohydrates %	Fat %	Fibre %
Maize (corn)	7.1	65.7	3.9	2.2
Wheat	11.3	64.0	1.2	1.6
Barley	9.3	62.2	1.2	4.5
Tic Beans	20.1	44.1	1.2	7.1
Maple peas	19.4	49.9	1.0	5.4
Kaffir	7.7	60.5	3.0	1.9
Buckwheat	8.5	42.3	1.9	14.4
Tares (vetches)	22.9	45.8	1.5	6.0
Sunflower	14.6	10.3	30.7	28.1
Hemp	13.7	16.8	29.3	15.0
Safflower	16.3	29.8	29.5	26.6

Some Basic rules on grain selection

The choice of grain should include only that which is of good quality and free from mould, dampness or any contamination. The 'nose' test will always reveal a lot about grains and if there is the slightest doubt about the freshness, the grain should be left alone. A good sense of smell is quite an asset when choosing grain for the pigeon loft. Likewise the grains should be hard, especially the beans, peas and tares, the wheat and barley. It is very much a matter of experience and newcomers and novices are recommended to go only to reputable merchants or to take an experienced fancier along for his opinion. A good look should be taken also to ensure that there is no soiling of the grain by vermin. Any suggestion of mice or rat droppings should mean instant rejection of the sample.

Peas and beans should be uniform in size and appearance with no evidence of shriveling. Be sure to check that there is no presence of weevil especially in bean samples. Small holes will be an instant proof of this. Likewise peas and beans showing signs of a blue or purple coloration will indicate that they have been damp or improperly dried. They should be avoided.

Wheat, barley and oats should be as plump as possible as well as hard in nature with no visible evidence of mould or fungus marking. As far as wheat is concerned, the 'blue tip' on infected grain is typical of fungal infection. To test for fungus on the grain, place a handful into a large glass jar and cover it with warm water. After 12 hours pour the water away and cover the jar. Within 36 hours the jar and contents will reveal ample signs of fungal growth if any is present. Pigeons do not take oats too readily especially if it carries long 'ears'. The groat version is liked by the birds and is a good grain to use. Corn or maize likewise should be of good colour and free from any signs of mould or discoloration. The 'nose' test should be used for any purchase of corn or maize.

As to the age of the grain, whilst a certain maturity can be advantageous it does not pay to keep it too long as there is a gradual deterioration of food content. Very new grain can lead to some upset if fed to the birds when they are used to a settled mixture and any change of food should be undertaken gradually. I emphasise that this especially applies to the main show season for changes of diet can cause upset and loss of condition. The simple rule here is to have enough available at the start of the season so that no such changes are necessary unless to slightly change the balance of a mixture.

Pellet feeding

There are some very good pellet feeds available to fanciers. There was at one time a suspicion about the contents of some pellets but with reputable companies in the market place I have less fears about this. I have always favoured feeding pellets though not as a complete food for pigeons. For the same reasons as I advocate variety in the feeding of grains, I do so against complete pellet feeding.

I invariably feed pellets during the breeding season as a percentage of the total grain fed to the birds. They seem to enjoy the pellets which make a considerable contribution to the complete diet of parents and young birds. When pellets are fed the youngsters seem more full and happier and that seems as good a reason as any to continue the practice. I would also be prepared to feed good quality pellets right through the showing season as a means of providing the complete diet.

The same comment applies to the moulting period with an increased percentage content.

Turning grain into food

The actual choice of grains to be fed and in what proportion will vary from loft to loft and even from breed to breed. The large breeds of fancy pigeon will need a far different content to the little breeds with short faces. I hesitate to recommend any particular mixture but suffice to say that I always feed a mixture and do so as an analogy to the human diet. We would soon get tired of being fed one type of food every day and we enjoy variety. I am sure that the birds also enjoy a varied mixture rather than a boring diet of one grain such as peas or beans.

I therefore feed a mixture throughout the year and vary the content according to the season as follows:

- **Breeding season.** A basic mixture is supplemented with a fair amount of extra protein in pea and bean form, with additions as required of pellets, a calcium supplement using groats as a base and of course minerals.

- **Moulting period.** The basic mixture is enriched using peas and beans to make it a heavy mixture. I also use a mixture of smaller grains and a generous amount of linseed and other oil-bearing seeds.

- **Showing season.** Once the moult is approaching its end, preparations are made to produce the mixture which will take my loft through the showing programme. Again the basic mixture is used but is made richer with a higher concentration of peas and beans. I find that this adds body of a good solid type. Peanuts are also fed separately and are used as a top up after the main feed to ensure that the birds take this extra weight-inducing factor. I also make use of a depurative or cleaning mixture consisting mainly of wheat and barley with some safflower and smaller grains.

- **Prior to breeding.** The aim here is to treat the pigeons so that their show condition is quickly turned into a breeding condition. This will entail a loss of fatness and body weight, for over-fat hens will find it difficult to lay. A light mixture consisting of depurative, cleaning or even barley alone should be introduced gradually. Do not make the change completely at a feed but vary the food content over a number of days. Once incubation begins and there is proof that the eggs have been fertilised, there should be a build-up of 'heavy' content to prepare the pairs for the feeding work.

This is a rough outline of how I administer to my birds but there are always adjustments to cater for weather conditions and for other occurrences within the loft especially immediately prior to and after each show. It is quite non-scientific but experience in the actual feeding is the best form of guide. Whether my mixtures are heavy or light therefore depends on the times of the year. In the very broadest of terms the following seems to apply. The protein enables the muscles, skin, bone, feathers and other tissues to grow; the carbohydrates are the elements which keep the body warm and supply its energy and the same applies to the fats and oil. The other constituents include fibre, mineral salts, and vitamins and of course water. All will and should be present in the daily diet of the pigeons for show.

The contents of mixtures can therefore differ greatly and will to a large extent depend upon their availability. For instance, tic beans are plentiful and a staple provision in the U.K. but less well known in the U.S.A. but the reverse situation applies to kaffir, sunflower, and milo. The best available local supply will be the important determining factor of supply. It will therefore be for the fancier to produce a recipe for a mixture using whatever is easily available to him but including imported grains also.

Feeding methods

I made an assertion at the commencement of the chapter that the method of feeding is equal in importance to the actual content and quality of the grain. I most certainly believe this and recommend all fanciers to think about this and to examine their own methods with a view to improvement.

In basic terms there seem to be three ways of feeding pigeons:

■   Hopper feeding, likened to cafeteria, 'help yourself' style

■   Hand-feeding with stricter controls on volume and type of food

■   A combination of both.

Given the time I would always recommend hand feeding as the method to be used because it is a superb tool for the fancier to engage himself with his birds and to produce a trust and understanding with them. Properly done, it is a system which provides one of the best management aides available.

HAND-FEEDING

Although the best system, it is very time-consuming and one which demands a more rigid adherence to the times of feeding. It is a system not ideally suited to the busy workingman where time with the birds is at a premium. Likewise it is a system more suited to fanciers with small teams within fairly modest lofts or coops of two to three sections. For instance, as I both race and show my pigeons, I have three lofts with a total of eight sections. The time involved in hand feeding so many sections would be out of all proportion to the benefits, so I am forced to constantly modify my methods according to the seasons.

Hand-feeding systems do not entail the fancier entering the loft and scattering grains all over the floor for the birds to eat. I do not like to see food on the floors of lofts and recommend that any hand feeding be on to trays kept especially for the purpose. The mere use of the tray will act as a signal to the birds that food is about to be given. A tray should be of sufficient area size to cater for the numbers kept and should have a raised edge to prevent corn running off. After use the tray should be cleaned and stored.

Feeding the birds by hand allows the fancier maximum contact with his birds and should be conducted in such a manner to further this relationship. All movements should be performed in a steady manner without apparent haste and the birds should have to approach the fancier to be able to gain food. It is not necessary for the fancier to demand that birds take the grain from the hand but that it has to accept the human presence and thus build that important trust. It takes some while for this trust to be gained and hunger is the surest way of bringing the birds to the fancier.

The whole system, can become a 'play session' where fancier and birds are able to mingle. Apart from producing the tray, the fancier might use other signals to indicate that food is available. Some use whistles, bells or some other sound which is easily recognised. My own birds for instance know the sound of the peanut jar and gather immediately in anticipation of their best loved tit-bit.

Hand feeding is a method which can be used to keep the birds alert and on their toes. Whether this is done once or twice a day - or even more frequently is a matter for personal judgements. If the fancier prefers to feed once a day only - and for many years I favoured this - then regularity becomes all important for with such a period between feeds the birds will become quite hungry and also anxious if there is a marked variation of feeding times. Show birds which are anxious about their food supply will not achieve condition. Nowadays I tend to prefer two feeding sessions a day. The birds can be given an 'edge' by a slight underfeeding at one session so that their desire for food is heightened at the next one.

As to quantity, this is where experience comes in for the fancier should recognise when the birds have had enough. The general rule is that as soon as two or three birds indicate that they have completed their feeding and go to the drinker, then it is time to stop feeding. Of course some birds eat more than others do and some will tend to be fatter than others because of this. The fancier with sufficient knowledge of his birds will recognise this and be able to moderate the food intake of such birds.

Each feeding session can be very enjoyable both for fancier and birds. However, it can be very time-consuming and it is a brave fancier who undertakes to hand-feed throughout the year. I have no doubt as to the benefits but having gone through life with widely varying amounts of time available to me know of some of the pitfalls. It is far from ideal during the breeding season when old birds will immediately have to leave the nest to get food. This can lead to young bird losses and therefore I would recommend that hand feeding is not used during the times when birds are feeding young. A system of having food available at all times is necessary with a fair argument for small pots of food being kept in each nestbox.

The greatest danger in engaging in a rigid system of hand feeding is that it can become extremely demanding, making the feeding operation a chore rather than an enjoyment. This is to be guarded against because in this modern world there is only a given amount of time available to us all.

HOPPER FEEDING

Food hoppers should be covered to prevent the soiling of the food. They come in many forms, from the normal cone-covered vessels, to the wooden trough types and the metal reservoir types where larger amounts of feed can be put in but the corn is available for the birds to eat in small quantities. Indeed some hoppers can be sited so that the fancier can replenish them from outside the loft or section, thus not having to enter the area occupied by the birds.

For the fancier who is extremely busy or whose time is available at varying times of the day owing to shift work or other demands, then hopper-feeding in some form is probably the only way to feed the birds. The birds are usually happy with the system in that they have a constant source of food removing any anxiety as to when the next feed will come and the advantages during the breeding season are quite obvious.

There are modifications which can be worked into hopper feeding. For instance, a fancier may provide a staple diet of beans or peas, but likes to supplement the rather static method of feeding by providing additional grains at some stage during the day. These additional grains may even be provided on a tray quite separate from the hopper provision. This tends to avoid the wastage which can be encountered with a straightforward hopper system where a mixture is given. It is obvious that some grains will be preferred to others and birds will throw the some grains around to get at the chosen ones. Where the hopper contains nothing but beans for instance, the birds have no reason to be so wasteful.

The advantages to the fancier are many. Family life can be more normal without the fancier having to arrange the day to accommodate a rigid feeding system within the lofts. It allows holidays to be taken and where friends can simply top up the hoppers and drinking fountains to keep the birds living in their usual manner. It would be an imposition to expect a friend to hand-feed in view of the time involved

The biggest disadvantage is the possible waste of food, grains which are tossed around in the loft, which can then become soiled and which can then be an attraction to vermin. For the birds the disadvantage can be that they become overfed and listless and having the ability to get too choosy about what they eat. For these reasons, I tend to vary my hopper-system so that it becomes a modified one as follows.

THE COMBINATION OF BOTH BY MODIFICATION

For the reasons given I do not favour a strict system of either hand feeding or of hopper feeding on an all year round basis. During the height of the showing season I will probably revert to hand feeding considering it to be the very best way of feeding and controlling the birds. But at all other times I tend to favour a system of using hoppers but modified to the time I have available to me.

Hoppers will be found in my sections throughout the year. I feed on the basis of twice a day, providing a part feed in the morning and the more comprehensive amount later in the day. The amounts I provide are such that for most of the day there is a small amount of food available but that it will be all eaten by time the next feed time arrives. In this manner I am able to gauge the amounts to be given to provide a fairly constant source of good food, but to avoid any waste.

By feeding twice a day I can also make the birds come to me and the hopper for the food. They will quickly learn that they have to do this and will therefore place a certain amount of trust. For the fancier the advantages are quite plain to see for less time is required for the feeding arrangements and there is less of a tie to times and schedules.

The hoppers can be removed after the afternoon or evening feed and this provides an extra signal in the morning when they are re-installed prior to feeding. The great advantage of this modified system is that it can be modified day to day or season to season both to suit the fancier and the birds. For most of the pigeon year it is the system I prefer because of its extreme flexibility and lack of waste.

OTHER FEEDING NEEDS

Every pigeon loft should have a method where the birds can gain access to grit, minerals, clay blocks, green foods and other supplements. I prefer the use of smaller trays outside the actual sections where the various necessities can be provided without fear of fouling. It takes but little thought to devise such a system and I recommend all fanciers to make this provision. It should be coupled with some degree of regularity to ensure that birds kept in the unreal surroundings of captivity within their lofts or coops can get access to dietary needs. I once observed a world famous continental fancier who carried his feed to the loft in a bucket and at the same time, in a smaller bucket or container, was carried the grit. So, every time the birds received food, they also received a small quantity of good clean and fresh grit. This is a wonderful example of habit of regularity in fanciership.

And what of water? There should be a constant availability of good clean drinking water which cannot easily get fouled by the birds. As to specifics added to the food or drinkers, there are so many available to fanciers nowadays that it is quite confusing - and expensive. The result is that some fanciers hardly seem to provide clear drinking water. My only advice on this would be to make it simple and to use simple additions from time to time of such proven natural ingredients such as garlic, milk and the occasional tonic such as an iron based one.

ADVICE TO THE NOVICE

If asked by a novice or newcomer to the sport on how best to feed a team of pigeons I would recommend as follows. I would advise that he obtains a good clean mixture of proven quality to feed to the pigeons. If there is unlimited time - and there is so often when someone starts out - I would urge that a system of hand-feeding be used to build up a working knowledge of the birds and of their requirements and to create the mutual trust between fancier and the pigeons. There must also be a regular supply of clean water in clean, covered drinking vessels.

If the time is more limited I would advise the use of hoppers with a degree of supply and demand as described above as a modification between hand and hopper feeding. The main aim should be to self-instil regularity and system. This will be appreciated by the birds and will allow the new fancier to become aware of the needs of his pigeons. The closer the fancier is to the pigeons the better chance there will be of acquiring this knowledge and basic understanding of needs.

Coupled with this will be the need to have a system of administering the grit and other supplements and providing that these conditions are fulfilled, the novice is a long way there to -becoming successful and losing novice status. It is all very basic at that level but the final touches come with experience and time - at least for those who watch and study their birds and the successful practices of other fanciers.

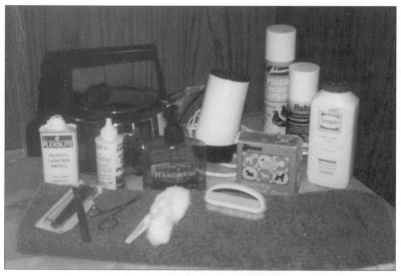

Suggested items for show preparation

Chapter 10

Producing a team for showing

Making a Start

So you want to show pigeons!

THERE is no foolproof method of making a sound start with pigeons but there are many ways of getting it wrong. I often reflect on my own introduction to the sport and wonder how I would go about it again or how I would cope with starting with a new breed. Although many years have passed since I first discovered the delights of keeping pigeons, closely followed by being bitten by the showing bug, it seems but only yesterday that I enjoyed those wonderful moments and started on the long journey to produce a good team for showing purposes.

Nailing my colours to the mast I would like to start by making the following observations or assertions on the subject:

- No pleasure equals that of winning with birds bred by the exhibitor

- What is required is patience, patience and more patience

- That a degree of good fortune is involved

- In general, success cannot be purchased for long term success.

- That your views as the keeper of the pigeons are as good as and probably better than many of the judges.

With those few general observations let us examine how the average pigeon fancier - or would-be - fancier can make a start. Of course, all advice contained in this chapter is done so in the realisation that so much will depend on the breed of pigeon required for showing. Some breeds are numerically strong with nation-wide interest while others are kept and shown by relatively few fanciers. It follows that in the popular breeds like the show racers and flying breeds there is a large reservoir of stock available and a large number of fanciers willing to help. In the breeds which are fairly rare, the sources are far more limited and it may be extremely difficult to acquire the correct stock to make a start.

In the majority of cases, the would-be exhibitor will know what breed is required to be kept for showing purposes so I will make no attempt to recommend particular breeds. The advice is intended to be the same whether it is for show racers, jacobins, pigmy pouters, Chinese owls, the popular flying breeds or the downright rare varieties of pigeons. Suffice to say however that for the absolute novice, some breeds are far more difficult to keep than others and those breeds requiring all the extra attention like the short-faced varieties, will require even more patience to produce them in numbers. However, the challenge presented by them is made worth while by these delightful pigeons.

Hopefully therefore the fancier will have a very set idea on what is wanted, the reasons for the choice and the aims within that choice. It is an excellent idea to set out with positive aims and goals I am sure that many fanciers start out as I did, wanting to keep pigeons, to have them flying out, then to extend the interest to either showing them or to competing with them as fliers.

Would-be fanciers who lean towards the flying varieties such as the racers, show racers or competition flying breeds will find them quite easy to acquire and to keep with plenty of advice available. These breeds are hardy and can be treated in and around the lofts or coops as creatures able to withstand wind and weather.

As for fanciers wishing to take on the more decorative breeds, they will do so in the knowledge that in general these breeds do not make ideal pigeons to have out on the wing, although some perform quite well and present an amazing sight when out in the fresh air and sunshine. These birds will generally require a more dedicated care within a loft establishment and ideally with an aviary in which they can display themselves to best effect. An aviary is another way also of keeping the hawk and falcon menaces from attacking the pigeons. However, every breed of pigeon will have its devotees, followers and admirers who will develop a sound knowledge to know not only the attractions but also the pitfalls which can also be offered. It is best to talk with some experts with knowledge of the fancied breed so as to gather an all round idea of what is involved in keeping that type of pigeon.

For those would-be fanciers who are still looking for a suitable breed, the advice for them is to attend as many shows as possible where there will be a wide variety of birds on display. There is no substitute for this, seeing some of the best examples of the various breeds on show having been prepared for the day's outing. Another source of information is to be found in the many specialist books available for reference including those with encyclopaedia references to all breeds. Monthly and weekly publications are also available where good information can be obtained on breed clubs and of course they will display advertisements of birds for sale.

Attending as many shows as possible is also the best advice to the more experienced fancier taking up a new breed. He will be in a better position than the novice as he will have a better understanding and knowledge of his aims within the breed and will also have an idea on where to go for his initial stock. The chances are also that he will know of some of the problems and difficulties to be able to plan to mitigate against them. However from this point on let us assume that the fancier has decided upon the breed to be kept and will be directing thought towards the acquisition of suitable stock.

Generally this will be done in one of the following ways:

- Acquisition of stock or breeding birds

- Buying birds for immediate showing

- Acquiring young birds, later-bred birds or even eggs

- Buying a whole or part team

Stock pairs or birds for breeding

In my view this is one of the best and safest methods of acquiring quality stock especially when obtained from a fancier who is well known and respected within the breed. The chances are that if such a fancier has retained older birds they have proven their value in some way. By buying such pigeons, in some ways the experience of the fancier concerned is also being acquired. Most breeders will be prepared to part with a stock pair or two at the end of the breeding season to make way for up and coming younger pigeons. This is an excellent way of getting a start.

Providing that such pigeons are not too old to breed, the chances are that they will produce some good rounds for the new fancier of acceptable standard. The new fancier is then on his way by showing young birds of his own breeding -albeit from the birds bred by someone else.

Stock birds obtained from clearance sales following a fancier's death or other reason, will most certainly provide good value. They had been retained for very good reasons and of course, generally stock birds can be purchased at far more reasonable prices than those ready for immediate showing. More patience will be required as I always state that any new acquisition is an investment in time, and as the results of breeding may not be known for some time.

Birds for immediate showing

It is always most tempting to purchase birds from a successful fancier which will be likely to win when shown for the new owner. It goes without saying that most will not want to part with their best winning birds and if they agree to let them go it will usually be at considerable cost. It is not as simple as that of course for when installed in a different loft, the chances are that the birds will feel ill at ease and lose condition, thus losing also the chances of winning top prizes.

Many fanciers will only buy the best they can with future winning in mind. However, it must be remembered that the best winners do not necessarily breed the best youngsters. I have seen vast amount of cash used to purchase winning pigeons from winning owners without really repaying the investment. Some people see this as being the only way forward but they stand the chance of losing out in a big way for by so buying ready winners they are displaying a sure lack of patience.

I made the assertion that success cannot be bought for long term success and genuinely believe this to be so. It is true that sometimes a fancier will win out of turn with the birds purchased from the success of others but they then start to fall by the wayside when they attempt to breed their own pigeons for show.

I love acquiring pigeons but my thrill is in winning with birds which I have bred myself. If there is a second pleasure, it is in winning and breeding successfully with a bird I have managed to purchase cheaply because the owner did not really appreciate its value. It is good to be always on the look out for good pigeons but to remember that the most expensive is not necessarily the best.

More mistakes are made at trying to purchase a ready-made show team than anything else. More money is wasted at this method of trying to build a show team than in all other methods put together. My approach is to be more patient and acquire for tomorrow rather than to purchase at high prices for today. However, in any breed there will be fanciers who, when money is on offer forget their role as fanciers and assume that of financiers.

Young birds, late-breds or eggs

Most fanciers of repute will gladly help newcomers by providing them with a start in the sport. After all, in thinking about the sport as a whole, its future depends on new blood coming into it and this is one way of giving some assistance to encourage people in. Most will breed on a few extra young birds at the end of the season when their numbers are satisfied, so as to be able to supply them to new starters. Some prefer to provide eggs but this is rather a difficult one to see through and having eggs depends upon the recipient having sufficient pairs of feeders available to sit and rear the resulting youngsters.

An acquisition of young pigeons throughout the season is also a good bet because the new fancier will not only be purchasing a ready made show team but also the experience of the breeder of the birds. Most fanciers will part with a selection of young birds from the second round onwards although will prefer to keep birds of his choice regarding colours and type. The late-bred situation is better in that these will be cheaper to purchase although not so straightforward in other respects. Much will depend on how late they are when bred because if too late they will fail to get right through the moult in the year of their birth and will carry nest flights through until the next moult. Even then the moult does not run true because flights will drop unevenly, often starting at both ends of the wing. However, apart from starting too early in the season, their ability to breed will not be affected.

Acquiring youngsters is a very good way of entering any breed of pigeons as good quality birds are more often than not provided. In most cases they allow the new fancier to be able to show them through the season. Thus experience of showing is gained as a start to showmanship and then as a special advantage, they are available to breed.

Buying a whole or part team

Sometimes owing to unfortunate events such as death of a fancier or in other ways leading to the disposal of a team of successful pigeons, whole teams come on to the market. They may be sold at auction, by tender or by advertisements in the fancy press magazines. This presents an ideal opportunity to break into the breed by acquiring the best birds in the team including the show birds, the stock pairs and the up and coming birds. No such opportunity should be lost even the outlay may be a considerable one. Not only are the birds as a team being acquired but much of the knowledge and skills of the previous owner also.

Providing that the disposal is a genuine one, and also a complete one, this is an excellent way of producing a top team in the shortest possible way. The main problem is that some of the best may already have been sold to other fanciers before the sale is advertised.

The chances are that more can also be acquired in the form of baskets, show containers and all the requisites to support the team. These opportunities are quite rare but they present the very best way to enter into the showing of a particular breed of pigeon.

Some additional considerations

I started out by asserting that in showing there is nothing more satisfying than in winning well with home-bred birds. Any win is good and should be appreciated but when wins are gained by birds bred by the efforts of others, there seems to be something of an anti-climax about it. The aim therefore should be to acquire sufficient birds of quality so that a good selection of youngsters can be bred which will start to win as home-bred winners. My top wins have been achieved both with birds I have bred and occasionally with birds bred by others. I know that I love the wins accomplished by my own products especially when the wins are under top and experienced judges of great knowledge of the breed. In years past I have exhibited teams consisting a hundred per cent of birds bred by myself and they were taken to the shows with great and lasting pride.

I also stressed the need for patience. I believe this to be one of the most important matters in the production of a show team. It all takes time, for while with a small and new team, the occasional win can be gained, it is only when there is true depth to the team that the chances of success are regular and consistent. In addition to patience there is also the need to be dedicated to the declared aims within the breed and not to be diverted when things do not go entirely to plan. All too often I have seen disappointment at lack of success at a show turned into panic with a culling of the team and attempts to purchase new birds. It is what I meant by my remarks that as the keeper of pigeons, your views on your birds are better than those of a single judge at a single show. Even the best champions do not win at every outing and neither do the best show winners always make the best breeding birds. Back judgements on your own birds for when you are repaid by success as a result of not being diverted, the pleasure is even greater.

It also leads me to the point that success of a permanent nature cannot be bought. A good team is more often than not based upon a core or a family of winning and breeding pigeons. The aim must be to produce such a family for then the flexibility is available to improve even more by careful introductions. I have no doubt whatsoever that the best chances of success are when they are based upon the success of a close-knit family. When I look for an introduction to my family of birds I generally seek it from a fancier with a family of his own especially if there has been some crossing between the two in the past.

It is far easier to put pairs together when the background of both is known than in taking two completely unrelated birds of doubtful origin and putting them together as a pairing. I am very careful indeed to sustain my family core and in many cases can trace it back over nearly four decades.

My advice to any newcomer is to make a thorough study of the birds on show and to establish an ideal to aim at. Then, having done this, to avoid the greatest pitfall of all to acquire birds from too many sources. It is far better to obtain birds from one or two sources than to buy here, there and everywhere. I have seen some examples of this where considerable sums have been used to attempt to buy a winning team. More often than not the purchaser ends up with a collection of birds unrelated, not similar and as such are not suited to the production of good winning pigeons.

In so doing they have broken all the rules by not having patience, in not bothering about the breeding of birds and by listening to too many fanciers. They also tend to heed the views of judges who are not necessarily the best able to determine the value of birds for both exhibition and breeding purposes. Instead of sorting out some ideals at the beginning and working towards them, they have thrown money at the problem and in most cases failed to succeed.

To sum up therefore the three basic rules I would pass on to a would-be pigeon show fancier would be:

■ Before starting, to make a thorough study of birds both at shows and at fanciers' lofts to establish an ideal at which to aim.

■ To acquire birds from as few sources as possible, mainly using fanciers with proven records of success and at breeding their winners within a true family of birds.

■ Be patient and not easily diverted from the original aims.

It is always good to listen to advice and to be prepared to act upon it but in the final analysis it is the judgement of the fancier on his or her birds which will determine success or otherwise.

Chapter 11

The Creation of a Show Family

THERE is nothing more satisfying than winning with pigeons which are home-bred from a true family. Likewise, it is very satisfying to own such a family of pigeons when they have been produced as a result of working to a prescribed plan over a number of years. The true test of a pigeon fancier is whether he or she is able to produce home-bred winners consistently. The chances are that if this is the case, the birds are being bred from within a family of pigeons. A visit to such a fancier's loft will reveal a specific type of bird and not a selection of all sorts of type, size and colourations.

In the preceding chapter I made reference to the desirability of creating a family of pigeons for showing purposes. By this, I mean that it is desirable to produce a strain of birds based upon family relationships within which good successful birds can be bred in a consistent manner. Over my many years in the sport of showing show racers I have tried to keep to a family of powder blues. Indeed my powder blues of today are quite closely related to the birds I started with some four decades ago. Today, I tend to keep a wider range of colours but the blues are still there and by pedigree and record can be traced back all through those years.

I started out with an aim to create my own family and would like to think that I have succeeded in this respect. Of course in a breed like the show racer, there are fads in colour which seem to affect the sport for a period of a few years at a time. As a result the blues have taken a back seat to other colours in the show winning, yet my heart has remained loyal to the colour and I still guard very jealously my old family and the birds and lines within it. I have often stated that even if I ceased to show, I could very happily keep a loft of powder blues for my own pleasure.

I often relate a story about my loft in my early days of my showing career. I received a visit from one of the top exhibitors of the day who was truly amazed when he entered my little loft for a good three quarters of the birds were blue bars sitting there like 'peas in a pod'. It wasn't a colour that he favoured and consequently he sent me a couple of hens of contrasting colours from his family, to blend in with mine. The results were wonderful and looking back I realise why. I had an established family as did my visitor, and when he sent me the two hens, he also sent years of his experience and skills, so little wonder that the 'cross' worked so well.

I use this example to show that the production of top class pigeons can be so much easier when they are produced from within a true family set-up. A good introduction, especially from another established family, is almost bound to work. So, my recommendation always is to a newcomer within the sport, to try to establish a family of pigeons.

To establish a family, the initial acquisition of birds becomes so very important. This is where good fortune can play a part in making an approach to a fancier of proven ability and standing who will want to see a newcomer or novice provided with suitable birds for such a good start. Looking back now, I was indeed very fortunate in finding such a fancier who provided me with my initial stock but also supplemented them by occasional offerings over the next few years. I think that I knew what I wanted to produce and within financial constraints managed to work my acquisitions into not only a winning team but one based upon a true family pattern. I was very fortunate in that my initial birds were also successfully shown. I often wonder whether I would have had the required patience had they been older birds for stock purposes only, instead of turning out to be birds which not only won well but then which bred well also.

Time and patience

It goes without saying that to establish a family of pigeons takes some time and plenty of patience. A few breeding seasons will be necessary to be able to judge the merits and values of the original stock although this time can be reduced by astute re-pairing of birds in the same season. You will therefore have the ability to judge breeding potential of birds when paired to more than one mate in the one year.

Although I warn about impatience, there is nothing depressing in attempts to produce a set family. It is an enjoyable feature of the year within any loft. Firstly there are the pleasures of breeding followed by the satisfaction of seeing the young birds develop as they pass through the moult. From this stage, planning can commence for the following year and so on, with the aims always to produce good pigeons for the show pen of the intended quality, type, colour and general appearance.

The biggest danger to patience is being diverted from aims by disappointments at the shows or by other setbacks. It is far better to work within what is available - perhaps with carefully chosen introductions - than to seek birds from all sorts of sources to 'buy' success. Whatever hobby, interest or sport indulged in, patience is necessary because it is simply not possible to start at the top. This is most certainly true about showing pigeons where it takes time to produce winners, but along the way, the pleasures are wonderful.

Pigeons for stock

How fortunate is the new fancier who is able to acquire good and proven stock birds of a particular breed. Such birds should be treasured. The ability to keep them however depends on the amount of space available for them. The fancier who is able to keep only small numbers may have to dispose of show candidates to make room for the producers.

The fortunate fancier is the one with either a separate section of even another loft or coop in which he can keep a few pairs of stock pigeons. Such a facility adds a new dimension to the ability to be able to produce a family. For those without this facility however, it is a delicate balancing act to maintain the stability offered by proven producers, and the showing potential of younger birds. Given a choice, I have always tended to opt to keep producers for after all, they provide the future of the loft.

A section of loft solely for stock birds is indeed an asset and as another example of its versatility I would also mention the following. When well into a breed, a pigeon is occasionally bred which is not a perfect show bird, but by its type, colour and general appearance seems to indicate that it will make a very good bird for breeding purposes. If the fancier genuinely believes this, it is prudent to find a place for it and if there is a stock facility available, it is far easier to put the potential breeder by for the breeding season. It is precisely the sort of thing which a fancier with a proven family can recognise - the potential of some pigeons to produce within that family establishment.

There is one further advantage of having a stock loft or section. It can act as a safety net to avoid those unfortunate mistakes that we all make in our careers at keeping and showing pigeons. We all dispose of birds which time confirms that we would have been wiser to keep. We make decisions which we would love to be able to change or correct at a later date. The availability of additional housing for stock birds would enable some of these mistakes to be avoided.

It would not necessarily mean the keeping of extra birds as space is also important but a breathing space can be provided to avoid the disposal of the golden producers.

Sources of stock – and the blending

The most important advice I can think of here is to acquire birds from only a few sources and not to obtain them from several lofts. Most fanciers will gladly part with pigeons but they will be the birds they most want to part with, possibly with doubtful origins. The best idea is to locate fanciers of repute and then to try to acquire birds with potential for breeding and if possible for showing success also. My chapter on how to make a start examines this subject but as we are addressing the possibility of producing a family, the fewer and better the sources the better.

Two of three lofts with a known family pattern will be more likely to allow the newcomer to establish success than having all sorts of pigeons from lesser-known sources. An introduction from one family to another is far more likely to succeed than the haphazard pairing together of two birds of unknown origin. When acquiring birds from trusted sources, there is the added advantage of also acquiring some of the experience of the fancier parting with the birds. The fancier will have used his experience and skills in producing his birds and these qualities will be transferred with the birds.

Although I advise a small number of sources I do not recommend a single source, unless it is one with large numbers where the chances of birds being too closely related are quite reduced. However, the small-team fancier will have birds which are nearly all closely related. The skills of the new fancier to be able to blend birds from other families to create a new - and if possible, a better family.

Family lines – advantages

There are many advantages of breeding within a family line but the most important seems to be that it is possible to know with a degree of certainty what will be produced from a certain mating especially pertaining to colour. With fancy breeds in particular, the type required is so important and it is within the family lines that it can almost be set and produced at will. With the lineage of both parents known, the type is almost determined at the time of mating the birds together. However, an imported bird can often produce birds out of type especially when it itself has been produced by a bird lacking in the required type.

Even within a fairly close family of birds it is possible to produce birds of different type for different purposes within showing. Think of almost any breed even with written standards, and there will be some judges who prefer a larger type while others prefer a more compact pigeon, perhaps with tighter feather. By astute pairing, the knowledgeable fancier will be able to produce birds for all purposes within his showing schedule, thus being able to use his skills to maximise the chances of showing success.

All fanciers dream of finding the valuable producer, the bird which produces pigeons of great type and potential. These birds occasionally come along and will breed good pigeons with almost any mate within the family. Occasionally, successful breeding pairs will reveal themselves and must be cherished. It is within a family that the chances are best of identifying such pigeons at an early stage in their lives. There are far more valuable breeders than are ever identified as such, birds which are sold or culled before their true vale or potential is recognised. Just as the family set-up offers the best chance of revealing such pigeons, they are even more enhanced within the small-team environment where smaller numbers kept enables the fancier to spend more time with each pigeon and thus to know them better. Adult breeders should not be disposed of until the winning potential of its progeny can be properly judged and once again patience is the key to this.

My attitude towards such successful pairings is to keep them together for several breeding seasons. The progeny blended into the existing family set up adds to the chances of proving the family pattern presenting an excellent chance to extend the lines of quality. This is what it is all about, the production of a complete and almost self-supporting family based upon lines of quality and related birds.

Chapter 12

Recording of Information for Showing

FROM the time I re-entered the sport in the early sixties I have kept comprehensive records of events in my show team. Even in those early days I could see the benefits which might accrue from recording detail. I am now extremely grateful to have made the decision for the information detailed in my record is one of great interest but more importantly of great value to me. Throughout my working career I was expected to record a great deal of detail and consequently keeping my pigeon record was simply an extension of that.

My advice to anyone in the showing side of the sport - indeed in any form of pigeon fancying - to keep an accurate record of birds owned, borrowed, sold, disposed of and of course the breeding and showing detail. The resulting record is a great source of information and knowledge to me and provides endless pleasures when time allows a look back over the years of enjoyment provided by my showing career. Even now, it consists only of two loose-leaf binders so the task is not, and need not be an onerous one.

Memory is fickle and the older one gets the more truth there is in that statement! My wife always reckons that whilst I can easily forget family matters like dates and so on, that I never err on pigeon information. Not true! My record often puts me right on fact and proved its value to me just about every time I have to research into birds and their showing.

Therefore in the early sixties when I thought about a suitable form of record, I decided on having a loose-leaf version, as it is far more flexible than a bound book. Current pages can be transferred to the historical binder so easily this allowing the current section to remain a manageable size at all times. I guess I thought quite a lot about the best way to produce and keep the record and fortunately, the system adopted then has stood the test of time. In those early days the main thought was in the provision of interest and enjoyment because there was so little to record anyway, but the aims changed somewhat when my showing involvement deepened and the need of accuracy became more important.

For fanciers who decide to produce a family of their own, the importance of records cannot be over-stated. It becomes necessary to be able to trace family line and pattern back through the generations to be able to add certainty of breeding arrangements within the loft. In my earlier days I produced handwritten pedigrees for my pigeons but nowadays use a computerised system which allows an instant recall of information and of course the production and printing of pedigree forms. The computer system can only produce information it contains so my written record proved invaluable for the inputting of reliable information into the computer programme. This has been the major development within my record system, something which I could not have imagined when I started it all.

With the added advantage of the computerised pedigree system I can very easily trace my family of birds back over the generations to those early birds I was fortunate to obtain in the sixties. An excellent blue white flight hen figured highly then and can be traced back with ease over a few generations. Fortunately for me over the years I have managed to possess some really good breeding pigeons which have anchored my family to the original foundations. These have birds which have originally shown well and which have then proved their value as breeders and as a result have remained with me for several years. In my chapter on the production of a family I made mention of the value of retaining proven pigeons and when they are identified as such, their value is great. Birds that continue to breed and rear good pigeons for many years prove their value because they are also indicating their vigour which hopefully will also be passed on to future generations. Occasionally four generations can be traced to a period of over twenty years.

There are many pleasures at highlighting such birds in the record system and to be able to recognise their contributions to the continuing success of the show team. A true value of an accurate record is in the ability to recognise the value of such pigeons as breeders. When glancing through pedigrees it soon becomes obvious when a certain pigeon's ring number keeps cropping up, that its value as a breeder can be recognised and preserved.

Recording information – notes made as they occur

The most accurate record is one based upon the recording of information at the time of it happening. Contemporaneously recorded information in the best available but in busy times I slip away from the best ideals and tend to update information from other temporary records carried with me at the shows, and of records held in the loft. So, nowadays I tend to use various reference sources but all are then used to update the main record from time to time.

Whilst I recommend any serious pigeon fancier to keep and

maintain a record I will not recommend that it should take an exact form. I will merely outline my own record aimed at the recording of show data and the pigeons in the show team within my own lofts and trust that it will help potential recorders to produce something to suit them and their available time.

As stated, my record uses a loose-leaf system and is contained in two large ring binders. One is the current record containing the records of all birds currently held while the other is the historical binder into which all records are transferred when the birds have departed from my ownership. In addition I use a small book which I carry to all shows and as stated I also use breeding cards within the loft to record all breeding details. A brief description of each is now attempted:

Current Record Binder (A.4 size)

■ Individual bird record. The first section is fronted by an index consists of a page for each pigeon currently in the loft. Each is given a number. The front of the sheet describes the birds by colour ring or band number and details of parentage. Any other information relevant to it is also recorded such as where obtained, from whom, cost, illnesses, when vaccinated and anything else relevant. The front sheet is very much an information sheet to provide detail on anything which is of interest to the fancier. For example whether the bird flies out, when transferred, any injury and wherever possible I display a photograph of the bird. In most cases, each page of the record is accompanied by a printed pedigree of that pigeon.

On the rear of the sheet is a tabulated record of all shows it has entered with date, show, class, judge, the number in class, position and prize money.

Birds are given their new page when they are considered to be part of the main team by way of showing successes or of breeding potential. So, a bird brought in for breeding purposes will be given its own page immediately and a young bird when it has been shown regularly and is then accepted as part of the team.

■ Shows entered. The next section lists every show at which birds are exhibited. It is an annual record of shows, providing details of the date, show title, judges, number of birds entered and details of prizes of note won.

Every show I have entered has been recorded in this section.

It is a form of diary of show attendance. It is revealing record as it indicates how over the years my showing habits have changed according to demands on life. In my early days I tended to show much more often than nowadays - and that was in times when the team lacked the depth of today, so that birds were occasionally over-shown. The railway system was used in the early showing times as the only way of getting the birds to some shows. Now I tend to be more selective at my showing and while a few years ago my showing was done almost exclusively at the main classics, whereas I now select the main classics and support as many local events as possible. I tend to travel fewer miles than in my earlier days so select shows accordingly.

■ **Acquisition and disposal of birds.** This section lists all birds I have bought, acquired, been gifted and have sold or otherwise disposed of. It has proved to be a most useful reference section. Generally, birds which are culled are not included under disposal but in retrospect it might have made the record even more useful had I started to record this aspect also.

The pages merely record the date of acquisition or disposal, the band/ring number and colour of the bird and the name and address of the fancier involved in the transaction together with any details of cost.

■ **Statistical.** The next section is merely a statistical exercise for me to be able to monitor the success of the birds at the shows. I record the prizes won at each show i.e. the number of specials, first prizes, second prizes and so on, as well as the number of birds sent to each show.

In reality it serves little purpose except as an added interest in comparing showing success year by year. It does tend to display periods of success or non-success.

■ **Breeding Section.** This is one of the most useful and most used parts of the record.

Each breeding pair is recorded in chart form so that the rounds can be recorded in detail. The full ring/band number of each bird together with colour is entered on the chart, and then as eggs are laid, checked for fertility, and hatched, the dates are inserted. When the young birds are rung the full ring/band numbers are recorded and prior to weaning, the colour of the youngsters.

The complete record of course is too bulky to be kept in the breeding section so I couple this record with a paper or cardboard chart of the breeding section in the same form as the breeding record described above. This is kept in the breeding section at all times and kept up to date on a day by day basis. From time to time throughout the breeding season or at its conclusion, the information is transferred from the loft chart to the main record.

Another equally good system is to use individually breeding record cards for attaching to each nestbox. This is another way of recording the information at source and as events occur. Annual studbooks also carry breeding record pages and many fanciers use these as their permanent breeding record. Likewise little loft pocket books can be purchased which contain spaces and charting for all the information most necessary to record.

The breeding record is probably used as much as anything with reference to it at all times of the year. It provides an amazing insight into the success or otherwise of breeding pairs or of individual pigeons when paired and re-paired throughout the season. This is why I regard a good record and a good pedigree system as being very important in spotting the best breeders.

Historical Binder (A.4 size)

When a bird leaves the team, its record bearing the same number allocated in the main record is transferred to the binder which contains all past records. In this binder will be found all the records of the favourites of the past as well as the breeding records of more than ten years ago. It builds into a fascinating collection of nostalgia. My historical binder is now bulging so I will shortly have to produce another and split the contents.

Concluding thoughts

For the sake of a few minutes at a time, a good comprehensive record of the loft and the birds will be built up. I am quite certain of its value to the serious show fancier - indeed any pigeon fancier - and recommend that such a record is kept and maintained.

I am quite convinced of its value as an aide to successful husbandry. However, in line with my original thoughts, I can confirm that the records provide endless pleasure in glancing through the records of departed pigeon friends and of the pleasure they provided during their time at my loft and in my team. Without apology I love my pigeons and love being able to remember those which were mine - and through my records - they always will be.

Chapter 13

The Selection of Breeding Pairs

SOME of the most important decisions taken within the loft and its management are those in respect of selecting pairs for the breeding season. On these decisions will depend the success or otherwise at the shows in the next show season and indeed in the foreseeable future. Having just discussed the creation of a family of pigeons, of course this topic is closely allied for in addition to finding the pairings, there is need to have regard to future family patterns. Fanciers need to devote great thought to this subject by planning the breeding campaign very carefully. The sceptical will say that good youngsters can be produced whatever the pairings used but the fact which stands out is that some fanciers are extra successful and are probably those who make a thorough study of their birds before pairing them.

For the racing fancier the decisions are somewhat simpler, being based upon racing performances, past production of winning pigeons and on the pedigree. Eye sign is used by some fanciers to determine their pairings while others use other theories and ideas. For many the use of the basket is their pedigree system although many think into the situation a little more. The same might also figure highly in the plans of the fanciers who specialise in competition flying for they will be influenced by flying ability as opposed to show potential. However for the show breeds, particularly those where handling properties play such a part, consideration for show success come to the fore.

There are of course the dual-purpose breeds such as the show racers and the exhibition versions of the performing breeds. For them it is important that they are bred to be able to fly or perform well, yet when the show season approaches to be of good enough type to win in the show pen. I often use the analogy of the dual-purpose breeds in the dog showing world such as the spaniels, retrievers and greyhounds when I have to explain the differences between the pigeons designed for showing such as the show racer, but which can also fly and race where properly trained. Because of their hardy nature and ease of management, many new fanciers are attracted to the performing breeds rather than the more conventional fancy breeds. They often use the flying breeds to obtain pigeon experience and then often move on to the demands of some of the fancy breeds with the need for more attention to standards and minor detail.

It would be impossible to present a chapter on the process of selecting breeding pairs as a guide to be faithfully followed because of the large number of separate breeds have rather specific considerations. Each breed will have requirements as demanded by the breed standard but nevertheless there are basic guidelines which should help or interest all fanciers. I will try to direct thought towards the average show enthusiast who seeks to produce good show quality pigeons within the breed to a quality as near to the breed standard or requirements as possible. In this way the advice will hold good for the enthusiasts of the hardy breeds such as the show racer and the flying breeds, as it does to the fancy and rare varieties in their many forms.

The breed standard for each and every breed will form a major part in any consideration of the selection of pairings. There is less room to be flexible under the dictates of a standard so pairings will have to be directed towards producing pigeons to suit that particular standard. On the other hand, the flying breeds and show racers may have no set show standard but will have a type of quality control, of requirements for showing purposes which will have to be borne in mind. Thought will be directed to body and handling properties, to the colouration and the other detail, in accordance with current requirements. Whether the standard is a written one or not, there is a vague and accepted norm in showing which all exhibitors will heed and work towards.

The good fancier will be thinking of and planning his breeding pairs throughout the year. With a sound knowledge of his birds and of the breed he will be thinking of pairing possibilities right through the seasons, using his skills and his intimate knowledge of the birds in his custody to bring them together to work for the future of the loft. Whether for a set standard or the more flexible breed requirements, the fancier will stand or fall on the judgements he makes in his selections of the breeding pairs. There is a degree of luck or fortune involved, but the most successful will make those judgements with a sound knowledge of the breed and of the pigeons available.

Some methods of breeding selection

It is generally accepted that there are three main systems of selecting birds for breeding purposes:

- **Inbreeding** is accepted as being a system of pairing closely related pigeons, such as mother to son, father to daughter and brother to sister. The aim is to produce birds which are very similar in nature to the parents, a method of being fairly certain of producing like within a family of birds. It is of course the quickest possible system of producing a family for all the birds so produced will become linked to the family pattern. It is suggested that birds so produced will only be equal to the parents and not better with the old adage that 'a barrel can only yield what it contains'. The danger of too much inbreeding is that it may cause a lack of vigour and virility in the birds so produced so that an introduction of new blood will be necessary at some stage. Another problem is that the use of closely related parents can occasionally produce birds with extreme faults and when this occurs there is a need for immediate changes to the pairings. However, when operating within a family, I am quite convinced that inbreeding can be used with considerable advantage to produce birds of a type or colour required. Providing that it is not over-used there can be advantages in trying this option to produce quality birds from within a proven quality family.

- **Line breeding** is a similar system of using a family line but using birds not as closely related. It is probably the best and safest method of producing good, sound and healthy youngsters with a good family pattern. It is more like pairing cousins, nephews and nieces and other birds which are related but which have a generation or more between them. It is a system of breeding in and around a family pattern thus assuring that the birds are sufficiently close to remain within type, but that they also have sufficient outcrossing. It is an ideal way to produce a family pattern but with added advantage of being able to use imported birds to change or modify type where required and to supply the vigour which is said to come with using outside bloodlines. It does not take long to absorb a new import into the family line to correct a fault or to add something better, with a general all-round improvement.

- **Cross-breeding** is almost the opposite of the above two systems, where use is made of pairings consisting mainly of birds which are unrelated and unconnected. For a fancier to adhere to this system in full would be quite extreme and in my view the system of cross-breeding should be used more in conjunction with line breeding and in breeding than as a separate and complete method of selecting breeding pairs.

These may be an over-simplification of the terms but I am not a geneticist and am content to leave the scientific explanations to those who are properly qualified on the subject. However, fanciers will gain a general idea so as to be able to plan pairings with some thought of method in mind. At a guess I would say that most fanciers use a system of line breeding accompanied by the occasional use of in breeding and of out-breeding by bringing in the occasional cross. I have used this as a broad idea for many years. Having a fairly close-knit family of pigeons I tend to breed to line within the family, but have no fears at using in-breeding from time to time and most certainly use birds acquired from other sources to blend in and to enhance my stud.

There was a time when my family was far closer than it is today. I would then have claimed that any 'imported' bird would be brought in for a season and then passed on to someone else. However nowadays I work on the theory that if the imports produce well, there is a sound reason for retaining it and to eventually make it part of the family pattern. In selecting birds to bring in to my lofts I am far happier if it is known to be from another loft with a substantial family pattern as I feel that these birds are far more likely to blend. An added advantage would be if there was some of my bloodlines within those birds, however distant, to provide a little added continuity of type.

By this flexibility my family of birds has broadened somewhat allowing me more of a choice of colours even within my blue based family. Yet, I still keep the blue family as pure as possible, occasionally using a very close pairing to ensure continuation of it. It is surprising sometimes how the loss of a single pigeon can leave a large gap in the family processes and steps have to be taken to either acquire back something very closely related or to 'set' the standard required by the use of a little in-breeding.

This is where pedigree is so important. I have always tried to faithfully record the breeding of my pigeons in written form. It is a subject on which I am convinced is worth all the work involved and in the final decision making, the pedigree often arbitrates on those decisions bearing in mind past family generations. Anyone keeping within a family of pigeons will find this a most rewarding occupation and one which will repay the work involved many fold. Indeed within the family, the pedigree production is made a lot easier especially when the records are computerised. Memory is fickle and I am convinced that we should all keep full records to assist in our decisions regarding pairings. I have referred to the subject more fully in Chapter 12.

There are many factors to be considered when trying to decide which birds to pair together. Much will depend upon the needs and demands of particular breeds for the breed standard is all-important. Reference to the standard or the ideal will have to be made to it at all stages. Thought will also have to be given to breed requirements even where there is not set standard. This especially applies to the performing breeds which have to be handled and where handling properties count for so much. However there are some matters which are common to all breeds and type of pigeons and I would like to examine them now.

- **Wild and nervous pigeons.** These have little value in a loft or in the show pen. Often the problem is one which is within the family and which is passed on from bird to bird. However birds which are wild and nervous will turn loft mates to be like themselves unless care is taken. It is quite uncommon for such pigeons to be tamed although the best chance is by taking them at a very young age and building their self-confidence. Temperament is so important within a show loft and breeding should be directed to producing good sound and quiet birds. In many cases the only way to improve the calmness within a loft is to dispose of the nervous or wild birds even though they may be excellent show candidates. The only way they can or should be kept is to house them separately, then to work hard on the young stock to try to tame them to be able to live happily within the main team of birds.

- **Size.** Size is important within any breed. Even in breeds with a set standard there will be variations of size. I have never found that pairing birds of extreme sizes produces youngsters of average size so pairings generally need to be made to produce minor adjustments in build to suit a breed standard or to meet the requirements of the show judges.

- **Feather quality.** Some birds carry an abundance of quality feather while others are less so endowed. It is a good plan to breed for quality feather for such birds are easier to condition and always seem to look so much better. Initial impressions count for so much during the judging process.

- **Eye colour.** This is a more complex subject and in most cases needs to be addressed in line with breed standards. Within breeds with no set standard, there are fashions in the type of eye required and fanciers will need to breed towards what is generally wanted. Breeds requiring a light eye will have to be paired to produce that type and generally, whatever the breed, the main fear is to produce birds with 'bull' or broken eyes. Eye clarity and brightness are matters which are important especially as an indication of good health.

- **Expression.** Years ago I might have dismissed the importance of expression in winning pigeons. However I am now convinced that the top winners have that little extra something, which often amounts to a bird having a pleasant expression. That word covers a number of matters which can affect expression overall such as eye colour, size and type of head and even the colour of the cover feathers on the head. Whatever it is, the birds with the sweetest expression generally please the judges most especially in hens. To many, expression means only that a cock should look like a cock and hen like a hen but there is a little more to it than that

- **Vigour.** I always try to breed for vigour especially in my racing loft. In the show loft however, we must learn to identify vigour in pigeons. These are the birds which are active and attentive, live longer and produce youngsters much later in life and manage to feed them well. Some birds are the opposite of this, languid and generally lacking in personality. I try to breed strength and vigour into my birds and it is yet another consideration.

- **Temperament.** This is an extension to the nervous or wild birds. There are birds which are poor rearers, poor at laying and which do not sit well. Where possible breed these traits out and instead use birds which enjoy the breeding operation. Breed for character, the birds which are always noticed within an average loft.

- **Colour.** Breed standards often dictate the colour to be aimed at but in the non-standard breeds the colour required must play an important part in the pairing process. Almost any colour will go with another colour but there are safer colour matings than others and I find it very wasteful to breed birds which are poor or indifferent in colour. The presence of white is a danger to some breeds and some fanciers avoid it at all costs.

- **Type.** Type is something which probably embraces all the other considerations listed above. It is something which is almost beyond description, yet within any breed it is recognised for its quality or lack of it. Some birds have it, some do not and like size, it is something which is not produced by pairing birds of extreme types. I therefore recommend that 'type' be a major consideration in the pairing process.

- **Show personality.** Yes, as unusual as it sounds, there are birds which enjoy being in a show pen and which attract interest by their expressions of pleasure. Such pigeons can gain a little advantage with a judge for most fanciers admire tameness and character. Astute pairing can produce them and as a show enthusiast, it is a trait in a pigeon that I tend to admire.

Those general observations direct me into one other aspect of breeding pairs. When a successful pair of breeding birds is discovered the obvious question is whether they should be paired annually. Some fanciers make it a rule never to pair two birds together more than once, believing that it is better to strive for something better than to settle for success so far achieved. My own feeling is that I will always pair successful birds together for years on end and have some pairings which have been together for several breeding seasons. It is a great pleasure to re-pair birds of former 'love matches' for they really take to each other so well and indicate their joy. A pairing which produces excellent show candidates should in my view be kept together for at least a few seasons. That is not to say that such birds should not be paired to other mates, for astute re-pairings can prove so much in the breeding season. It should indicate whether both cock and hen are good breeders or whether it is one or the other producing the standard of young birds required.

The final consideration is the judgement of the fancier for on them will be determined the success of the show team and the reputation of the owner as a breeder of good pigeons. There are no easy answers to this subject just as there are no easy short-cuts to successful pigeon fancying. Much care and consideration must be applied to every decision for it is quite true that every fancier is judged upon the quality of pigeons produced during each breeding season.

Chapter 14

Preparing Birds for the Show Pen

PREPARING show pigeons for shows can sometimes seem like an art form. It manifests itself as the fancier working in harmony with the birds to produce them for the pen at the very peak of their condition. It is more often strived for than attained, but when success is the result, it is all very satisfying for all concerned. In my many years in the showing side of the sport I have been asked on numerous occasions how show fanciers manage to produce such condition but in all honesty it is not an easy question to answer. For a start, many show pigeons being bred for the show pen, almost condition themselves, so it is just a matter of adding those final touches. However as we all know, hard work and experience coupled with an ability to heed advice and listen to the experts does help.

Take the greatest show champions whether they be Jacobins, Owls, Pouters, Rarer Varieties, Flying Breeds or Show Racers or of whatever breed, colour or type, and exhibit them when they are out of sorts, and they will be seen as an ordinary pigeon. However, to present that pigeon in the very peak of condition results in an almost breathtaking picture of perfection. This, even more especially, applies to the breeds which also have to be handled, for if not in condition outwardly, they will not handle as they should. The handling breeds therefore have this extra ingredient to consider when striving for that elusive peak of condition.

I also assert that in order to produce condition, there is required a system of management which should be present at all times of the year. It would be futile to neglect the loft and the birds for most of the year, failing to clean them, to offer bathing facilities and to be irregular with food and water, then to expect to be able to change all when the shows approach to have any prospect of showing success. The same would apply to the racing enthusiast, for racing success depends upon all-year effort.

This is my basic message on this subject. I believe that management in the loft and with the birds is an almost full-time occupation, a task which should be consistent but also enjoyable. If pigeon keeping ever becomes a chore, then it is time to part company with the birds. In all my years with my birds, I have never gone to the lofts without anticipation of enjoyment. Every longer absence from the lofts such as a holiday or vacation doubles this anticipation. I have always been a lover of pigeons with my pigeons always receiving every consideration and good treatment.

Having said that, I have rarely been a man of absolute habit. Most of my working life was spent working unusual hours so I like to think that the birds became used to my unsociable routine and together we adjusted our system of pigeon fancying. Within reason the birds are fed at fairly regular times, kept clean and I try to spend a good amount of time with them. This must be the minimum aim of any would-be pigeon show winners. It is the minimum amount of management to reduce stress in the birds by giving them anxiety about when they are likely to get food, water, grit and minerals. How can birds relax and condition themselves if they suffer constant anxiety about these necessities of life. I will deal with environment a little later on but now I would like to take a look at show condition and would divide my thoughts into three stages as follows:

- **The day to day, week by week management**

- **Pre-show routine at home and at the show**

- **The Post-show period.**

Each is as important as the next in terms of adequate management of a potential show team and I would advise anyone interested in showing their pigeons to take heed of this and to inspire themselves to positive effort to produce good showing condition. However, to take things in turn I will first deal with normal routine management as from this hopefully will emerge showing success but more importantly the satisfaction of possessing and managing an excellent team of pigeons.

Day by day, week by week . . .

ENVIRONMENT

I mentioned above that I would be discussing the environment within the pigeon loft or coop. In my view, one of the most important aspects of pigeon keeping is the production and maintenance of a settled, pleasant environment for the birds. It will never be maintained if there are too many birds for the space and it will never be managed if the pigeon fancier rushes in and out of the loft, depositing food and water and little else of himself. Contrast this with the fancier who spends a great deal of time with his birds, mingling with them, handling them and generally enjoying them. The chances are that his movements within the loft will be unhurried, they will be positive and constructive with a degree of conversation with the birds and the chances are then that there will be a degree of mutual trust. The birds appreciate that there is no threat from the presence of such a fancier and feel happy and settled as a result.

As to space, this is well worth looking at. One of my 'bibles' of the fancy has always been Barker's 'Pigeon Racing', a book I have owned for most of my years in the sport and one to which I constantly refer. Dr Barker advised a cubic footage of 27-28 for each pigeon in the loft. Therefore, a loft or compartment of six feet by eight feet and seven feet high would accommodate six pairs of pigeons allowing space that few, if any fanciers would be able to devote to pigeons. I now believe this to be a luxury and think that nineteen to twenty cubic feet is a more reasonable and I work this out as follows. The sections in my main show loft are six feet (180cm) by six feet (180cm) with a height of seven feet (210cm) at the front and six feet (180cm) at the rear. This provides a cubic capacity of just under 240 cu.ft. In each of these compartments I have six nest boxes for six pairs of pigeons and it seems all very reasonable for them.

However, from time to time numbers increase quite a lot and I know that I 'breach' my own guideline. I would prefer that readers take this as a recommendation and use it to compare the situation within their own lofts. It is no bad thing to work out the cubic capacity and then to divide it by the number of pigeons housed in it. It need not mean a great deal but it is worthy of consideration. Of course there are many additional factors which will affect the air space such as the degree of ventilation, the light and the amount of furniture i.e. nest boxes, perching space and so on. There are many other ways of ensuring that overcrowding is avoided such as restricting the number of perches and ensuring that a quarter of them are unoccupied.

Much goes towards the provision of a settled and healthy environment within a loft. It is something which money cannot buy but which can be attained by sometimes a degree of luck, but mainly by a fair amount of working experience. Think of a settled environment on those magical days in the early spring when the sun shines after a long period of inclement weather. Think of the birds and their reaction to it, for suddenly the loft breathes life instead of being fairly quiet and unexciting. Add to that the chance for them to bathe - and their reaction is one of contentment at being in their home.

SCIENTIFIC TESTING FOR HEALTH

The sport is constantly on the move, developing from one phase into another. This is perhaps personified in the modern trend of using microscope examination to detect health attacking internal parasites in the pigeon droppings and in the crop. Such parasites are usually carried but can be most harmful to young pigeons and manifest themselves in older birds when some other external pressure allows them to multiply in such quantity to adversely affect health. The main problems are to be associated with worms in their many forms, canker and coccidiosis.

Beyond that I will say nothing for I am no expert on diseases, and prefer to use the services of an expert if the situation arises. Kits are now provided allowing the use of such equipment to be relatively simple if the instructions are followed to the letter. In addition, some laboratories offer services to analyse sample sent to them and will provide the correct equipment for the gathering and packing of such samples. The more progressive fanciers now use such services routinely as well as at any time should they suspect that all is not well.

GOOD HEALTH

Good health is important to the production and continuance of condition in pigeons. It is onward going and needs to be addressed at all stages of the year. I am against routine treatments on the basis that 'there may be a problem'. This attitude tends to build up problems, as the birds will become immune to some of the benefits of the treatments. The only routine treatments I will use are those for worms and canker before the breeding season commences and I like to treat young birds for canker soon after they are weaned. If a young bird is seen to have canker, the chances are that it is often too late to be treated. That is my very unscientific reaction to this particular ailment.

One treatment I firmly believe in however is the inoculation of all birds against paramyxovirus and I now choose to do this as soon after weaning the young birds as possible. Having witnessed a complete young bird team wiped out in a loft while the injected older birds remained untouched has left a lasting impression on me.

Birds should be handled fairly frequently as a health check. Any birds looking even mildly out of sorts should be examined to ensure that there are no obvious symptoms or injuries. If there is any doubt then the best plan is to isolate that pigeon until it seems to regain a satisfactory state of health. The obvious things to look for are the eye which should be bright, the wattles which should be clean and white, the breast area which in a fit pigeon should be light coloured and not bluish, and the final check is with the feet which should be warm. I often associate cold feet with the presence of worm infestation.

Most of it is quite basic stuff. There are enough potions on the market to build up enormous stocks to quell any problem. My approach is more simple that in that condition has been achieved for many, many years, before the inception of the potion philosophy with the old time fanciers using a few but effective ideas on health. They would use garlic, cod liver oil, good grit and minerals, an iron supplement and a de-worming treatment. Perhaps when money allowed a tonic would be purchased based upon quite simple but good ingredients. I will not condemn any of the present day potions for some are excellent although based upon the most simple ingredients which can be purchased from chemists and greengrocers at a fraction of the cost.

CLEANLINESS – THE BASICS

■ **Clean food.** One of the most basic requirements of health in pigeons is in the provision of good clean food. By this, I do not mean food of the highest quality or cost but food, which is sound, nutritional, and above all, food which does not smell of mould or other impurities. Pigeons will thrive on almost any good food whether it is the cheapest barley, right through the spectrum of the highest priced grains. The soundest advice I can give is to smell the grain offered. If there is any suggestion of an aroma of mould or of rodents having been near it, then do not feed it to your pigeons.

The rest is up to you as the fancier to determine what you want to feed to your pigeons. A high protein diet perhaps, one containing a high level of carbohydrates or one high in fibre. It will depend what you the fancier, the one paying the bills will decide is best for your birds. You can take your pick on the vast array of grains and mixtures available. But whatever the cost, just make sure that it is free from smells as bad grain can lead to a dramatic loss of condition and even illness.

■ **Clean water.** Pigeons require more of a constant supply of drinking water than it needs to be sparkling clear. Indeed there are very good arguments for allowing drinkers to remain uncleaned or unscoured for periods of time so as to allow a natural anti-bacterial environment to be created. Over the years I have read about successful fanciers who claim that they change the drinking water placed before their birds on a number of occasions a day. In some cases it may be true but my guess is that this is more often claimed than is true. Take for example the racing pigeon which is taken from its loft, marked and placed into race panniers with many other racers, all of which have to drink out of the same drinker for sometimes a matter of days. The dangers of cross-infection of disease is great in any case, but for birds used to a sterile drinker every day, their resistance is bound to be less than that of birds which have built up their own resistance to the spread of disease. Again, my claim is a very unscientific one, but it is one I believe in. You can equate the racer to the show pigeon being taken to a show and having to rub shoulders with other show candidates, and in some cases to use drinkers which have been used by other pigeons at various times.

I do not like to see dirty drinkers or dirty drinking water but in my view water is best left and topped up for two or three days especially where any form of supplement or tonic is being administered. From time to time I then thoroughly clean the drinking vessels and use bleach to ensure cleanliness, but this is done weekly rather than on a daily basis.

■ **Clean air.** To some extent I have dealt with this under my notes about environment in this chapter and in my chapter on pigeon lofts. However, the importance of good ventilation cannot be stressed enough in modern-day pigeon fancying. In basic terms it is allowing clean air in to take the place of stale air which owing to its lightness is removed at a higher level in the loft. It does not have to be a draught of cold air, but a system which allows a natural circulation of air in any conditions.

A warm loft is the best one to encourage a natural change of air. Therefore clear glass openings at ground level allow not only sunlight but also the warmth of the sun in. This rises and allows the natural function of good ventilation by allowing the used air to free out of the loft at ceiling height. Of course the air to be clean also has to be free from dust and bloom (pigeon protein), so any loft should wherever possible have a system of allowing dust to escape so that it is not constantly on the move within the loft owing to the turbulence caused by the birds flying about. Grill floors are widely used nowadays both as a way of keeping the birds clean but also allowing the dust to drop through. Vacuum cleaners are also good at dust removal and my attitude is that dust removed from the loft is troublesome no longer.

- **Clean Lofts.** Without making a chore out of it, the cleaning of any pigeon loft is important. In my earlier days I used a floor covering of sand which could be sieved regularly to keep it looking good. However, nowadays we are much more aware of the dangers of breathing in pigeon bloom so any form of dust is to be discouraged. I have tried all manner of floor coverings such as sawdust, shavings, straw, chemical agents - such as cat-litter and so on, but I have now returned to the basis of having clean floors which are regularly scraped.

The other alternative is to use a system of grills so that droppings and other debris fall through on to the floor below where it can be systematically removed. I may well try this in due course though at the moment am content to use grills underneath each row of perches as a halfway stage. Each fancier will devise a system to suit the management process chosen. Apart from the removal of waste products, there are other considerations such as the cleaning of the walls of the loft to remove a coating of bloom, the removal of cobwebs as they appear, and the cleaning of loft windows and so on. A clean loft reflects the method and expertise of the fancier and as such should be considered at all times.

- **Clean pigeons.** Show fanciers must be especially aware of the need to be able to produce clean pigeons. Outwardly this will be achieved through providing a clean environment and by offering frequent bathing facilities. However, that is but half the story for the quest to keep insect life at bay is a constant one. How demeaning it is to have a show bird rejected because it was found to be carrying insect life. It has happened to us all and despite all the care, is bound to occur again.

I constantly watch out for insect life on the birds. Every time I handle a bird I look for it but of course as the years have passed so has the efficiency of my eyes and I am quite sure that I often miss the occasional 'tic' or mite. In days of advancement within science to produce better products, there are also penalties, so that products which seemed to have worked for years, suddenly no longer seem to do so because regulation has determined that some ingredient has had to be removed or its use varied. Likewise, the insect life seems to build up its own immunity to some of the products. I would therefore advise an array of products including powders and sprays, but also a product for dipping the birds, and for spraying the loft interior, but just as importantly, the new product which when applied to the bird's neck area, will protect it against parasites for many weeks.

I believe this problem to be one of the hardest to combat within the average pigeon loft and there needs to be a constant vigil to keep all such insect life at bay. I briefly referred to the subject in the Chapter on breeding because one of the biggest curses within the loft is an attack by red mite so my remarks about being vigilant at all times regarding insect life are pertinent at all times. Even when writing this, even today I have discovered a bad infestation of red mite in one of my lofts. It is April the 2nd - normally too cool for red mite to be found. I have therefore spent most of the day combating the problem and by coincidence, have been informed that another fancier friend has discovered the same problem in his loft. I have included this piece of information to reinforce my advice on the subject and as I mentioned earlier, it was only when I donned my reading spectacles that I discovered the problem.

Preparation in the pre-show period

Providing that the loft management system is in place and that the birds are being looked after in good surroundings, the chances are that the birds will be in good condition. The idea of show preparation is to produce that extra bit of condition to turn them from card winners into class winners. It sounds easy but needs a fair amount of thought and planning.

For many years I was solely a showman. All effort was directed towards showing success with my little team of pigeons. I entered the sport as a showman and have never lost that urge to present pigeons for the judges in that very peak of show condition. During the years when I kept birds just for showing, due in no small part to the fact that my occupation forced occasional transfers from area to area, I always maintained an interest in the general sport including racing, and of course the flying breeds and the showing of the fancy breeds.

However, when circumstances allowed, my yearning to get

further involved in the sport took me into the racing sport and this taught me a great deal about food and feeding. Any show person should read just about anything available on the care of pigeons. Some of the enlightened fanciers who are winning out of turn at racing have produced methods which provide them with something extra for racing performances, and in my views, many of their methods have merit for show people.

Many show people feed quite a 'heavy' mixture of grains with a high protein content and while this will produce good weight, it is sometimes the wrong sort of weight, body which feels a little more like pudding than the muscular type. The widowhood fliers need muscle for their method of racing and they achieve this by a system of breaking down the weight of their racers by feeding a lighter depurative mixture earlier in the week. They then return their birds to the heavier mixture towards the race basketing day so that the muscle blows up and is ready to return as energy on race days. The depurative mixture is sometimes described as a cleaning mixture, in that it allows the system of the bird to get cleansed to prepare it for better food which will produce muscle.

Looking at the show pigeon, the system works very well for them in that as an important show approaches, their heavy body can be cleansed by feeding them the depurative which is mostly carbohydrate in content, barley, wheat with some safflower and perhaps some other small grains. The timing of this for the show pigeon is quite important because to reduce the weight too much may make it impossible in the time to get the muscular weight put back on.

However, when this is done properly, the result is quite startling because the pigeon carries good body which is not heavy in nature but gives the impression of body with a corky feel. In other words the body is present but does not feel heavy.

A further idea to boost good body after a short period on a cleaning mixture is to treat some corn or grains in a quantity sufficient for one feed. Take the grains and moisten it with pure lemon juice. To this add some beer yeast - about a tablespoon per half kilogram - and allow the mixture to dry naturally. When fed to the birds, they will simply burst into energy and condition but it is to be done infrequently only and not on a weekly basis.

Another lesson that show fanciers can learn from the racing specialist is to use pigeon herbal tea as a means of cleaning the blood and to tone the system in a natural manner. About a week before an important show is a good time to allow further preparation in the ensuing period.

This is all well and good for birds which are fairly normal in body weight, responding to the good management, but what about birds which are in the other two extremes, i.e. those carrying too much weight and are fat, and those which are too light and which require more body.

For birds carrying too much weight, the old idea was that such pigeons should be shut away for days on end in a basket. I do not, and have never subscribed to this cruel way of treating pigeons and prefer a kinder approach. A show pen is an ideal aide for this because the fat bird can be installed in while the main flock is fed. The bird in question can be supplied with a small quantity of grain of the non-fat type such as barley, wheat, beans but just enough to keep its gizzard active. The small amount of grain it is to receive can also be moistened with pure lemon juice. Once the food has been taken up from the main feed, the bird can be returned to its compartment.

For birds which require more weight, the work can be quite intensive. If the bird is an isolated example of lack of weight then it can be treated as an individual, but if the flock is tending to lack good body, then the lot will have to be treated. The first consideration is whether there is something causing the bird to fail to put on weight and thoughts which come to mind are firstly worms, canker and then coccidiosis. An examination of specimens from droppings and throat swabs will determine this.

Providing that the health is satisfactory, then a system of fat feeding will generally pay dividends. Generally pigeons enjoy eating peanuts and also small seed mixtures, both of which contain plenty of fat. They will enjoy eating their way to added weight in this way - almost as they would enjoy a few tit-bits. This must not be overdone because the wrong sort of heavy body can so easily be gained. A good tonic in the water is also a good idea to tone the system to require more food.

Actual preparation

The process of taking a bird from its loft or coop and actually preparing it for transportation to the show is of course very important. The imprudent fancier will simply do this, install the birds in their baskets or show containers and convey them without the work of physically checking each and every detail of the birds entered. The chances of success are thereby greatly diminished because many minor blemishes will be missed and many of the entries will be disadvantaged.

The first preparation is one of having the baskets or show containers properly prepared. All traces of dropping should have been removed and fresh sawdust or shavings added as required. The baskets should be clean, dry and where possible warm to receive the birds.

The actual checking procedure should then commence. A room set aside is the most ideal for this especially with the advantage of running water. I would say that the following items would be most useful:

- A kettle of boiling water for feather steaming
- A hairdryer
- Insect powder
- Insecticide spray
- Chalk block or in loose form
- Cleaning spirit
- Cotton wool or other soft cloth
- Talcum powder
- Sharp scissors
- Nail clippers
- Emery boards or nail files
- Soap
- Small brush
- Towel

Reference might be made to my chapter on advanced showing methods, as some of the detail is included there. However, each pigeon having been basketed in the loft, and brought in to the preparation room is removed gently from its place in the basket. The hands of the fancier should ideally have been coated with talcum powder or powdered chalk so that there will be very little friction between the hands and the cover feathers of the bird. The checks then commence with the handling properties and then a good look at the head and eye including the wattles, eye-ceres and feather sheen. Any small blemishes can be rectified using the chalk block. Each wing should be checked flight by flight and secondary by secondary. Hopefully all will be in good order but any requiring a slight trimming can be treated using the scissors. As each wing is opened there must be a special look for the existence of insect life and it is always a good idea to spray or powder the birds at this stage.

The tail feathers should then be examined for any form of blemish and where appropriate use made of the insect powder or spray. The feet and legs should be examined and properly cleaned. This is where the use of the small brush and the soap and water come in to use, with attention also being given to the rings or bands. In my early days in the sport I was encouraged to scrub the legs and to add vinegar to the water so as to make the legs look red. Nowadays I would guess that a more natural appearance is what is required so cleanliness is the most important factor with emphasis on clean feet.

Small stains in cover feathers can be dealt with using the cleaning agent or in most cases simply by stroking the offending area with a dampened, clean cloth or cotton wool. Bad soiling may entail an individual bathing and use of the hairdryer but in most cases if the bird is in such a state as to require this, it may be best left at home to bathe naturally.

A fair amount of time must be set aside for these checks. It is impossible to estimate the time to be taken, as most birds will require little or no work while the occasional bird can demand quite a few minutes. The more time available the better the checks are likely to be and the chances of faults being missed greatly reduced. I have always regarded this session for every show to be most important.

Once finally basketed, the birds will benefit from being kept warm by being placed in a warm room and the internal areas of the baskets covered in paper to keep heat in. The only check left is the one immediately before going off to the show, to ensure that any droppings are removed to prevent soiling.

Training for the shows

As part of the day to day management systems within the show loft, there is an ongoing need to train the birds to prepare them for the actual ordeal of being shown. Wherever possible the show fancier will have some pens available for this purpose. In my own loft I have two sets of two always erected in the corridor of my loft, right alongside the young bird compartment. It is therefore very easy for me to pop some youngsters into the pens for their first taste of being behind bars! When I have visiting fanciers I invariably have birds in the pens and I then invite my visitors to judge them as a further taste of being shown.

I play with them in the pens and also feed tit-bits and provide a water drinker for them also. It is also a good plan to place young birds in show baskets for a few hours also. It is not only a case of training either, for thought will be directed to defining the birds which seem best for the shows. Some birds are 'naturals' for the pen, looking the part both in colour and type and while it is difficult to define, they have a little something to attract the judges. On the other hand it will become apparent that some birds just do not have what is required and it may be better to dispose of them sooner than later.

Fanciers may get away without going to the trouble of working at the pen training but in my view every minute spent in training birds for the show pen is time well and productively spent. Show pigeons endure a great deal of stress during every show and everything done to prepare them for their ordeal is good for them.

Preparation in the pre-judging period

I suppose that the best piece of advice is to arrive at the show in plenty of time. Not only is the time quite special for social purposes in meeting up with friends and fellow competitors but it is important to allow for the final checks and preparation to be done. To arrive late and to have to rush through the penning procedure renders much of the previous preparation as being wasted.

At the show hall, each bird should be carefully removed from its carrier and thoroughly checked for the final time. A small kit should be carried to the show consisting of 'first-aid' articles to deal with any problems discovered. Contents might include the following, cotton wool, a cleaning agent, chalk in solid form, talcum powder, wet wipes, nail clippers and scissors. The bird may have managed to become soiled during the journey so some cleaning will be necessary using either the wet wipes or the cleaning agent. The talcum powder should be used on the hands to make them smooth for the handling of the show candidates. The chalk can be used to cover minor blemishes to the wattles or even eye ceres. The clippers and scissors are not often needed at this stage - but better to be safe than sorry. I could almost add insect powder to this little pack but the chances are that even if discovered at the show, and killed, insect life will still be seen by a discerning judge. However, it is surprising how often insect life can be discovered having emerged in the warmth of the basket.

Small matters can be considered even at the very moment of penning. When placed in the pen, the bird will often defecate and the dropping should be removed where possible to prevent the bird walking through it and possible fouling itself. Also, in classes in which the fancier has more than one entry, the actual pen position of each bird can be controlled to provide that extra little chance for success. For instance, if your entry is a blue show racer and its pen is one in a row of four or five other blues, the blue may be better penned elsewhere and its place among the other blues given to a bird of a contrasting colour such as a chequer, red or mealy. These are small matters but they can make that little extra difference to the chances of success or failure.

Post-show routine

In all my years as a show enthusiast, I have been absolutely convinced of the value of having a set routine after each show to settle the show birds back into their lofts and back into their routine. As fanciers we can so easily forget the stress involved for the birds in being carted off to shows from the time of being caught in the loft, to the basketing, the penning, judging and then the return period of re-basketing and the journey home. The racing pigeon in his racing days is subject to even more stress but how many racing fanciers really apply thought to this, sending their birds to races week after week. You only need to think of yourself in journeying to shows, the travel, the timing and so on to appreciate what is involved for our feathered friends. An analogy I often use is to remember our dogs when they returned from the shows. They enjoyed being shown very much, liking the car journeys and the canine company at the shows, but after an outing, they slept for most of the following day.

However, there is much which can be done to alleviate the situation. Whatever the time of day or night that I arrive home from a show with my birds they are returned to their loft where they can have some food and water. Their sheer joy of being back is quite obvious and is one of the great pleasures of pigeon fancying. Even in the middle of the night I return them to their loft or coop using lights to allow them to settle. A most useful aide in this is to have a timer/dimmer switch which will reduce the lighting gradually over a set period to suggest to the birds a normal dusk to darkness routine.

I prefer to provide a light feed for the returning birds, usually some of the cleaning mixture, though to be fair, I am less concerned at what I think they need to what I believe that they enjoy. The drinking water can be treated by adding some electrolyte salts, as these will quickly return energy. Some honey or glucose will be just as useful in this respect.

Where possible the following day a bath is offered to the birds as a certainty that they will enjoy this and derive great benefit from it both physically and mentally. The mental attitude of the birds is so important, for if they feel happy and contented, they will restore themselves to peak condition much more quickly. Likewise, on the day after the show, I try to check them through to ensure that they haven't picked up stray insect life at the show, and I also tend to use a pigeon tea in the drinking water.

These are all relatively simple matters which will be varied depending upon the style of management within the loft. However I am confident to advise that consideration be applied to the post-show period, as it is so important to the birds. After all, show preparation for the next event begins immediately after the current show and the quest for show condition starts here!

Concluding thoughts

I have tried to offer a few considerations throughout this chapter as a way of stimulating the mind to think ahead and to be constantly aware of good management to encourage the show team to maintain good showing condition. I would recommend also that the season's showing campaign be planned in some detail with a plan being committed to paper. Certain birds will be required for certain shows and this will result in them having to be rested for other shows.

The interior of Jim Kerstner's van, adapted to convey his show entries in comfort for the long journey from Florida to Louisville, each bird having its own box with food and water containers

119

A good racing fancier, for instance, will do this, deciding which birds he will want for certain races and will use the early racing programme as a method of training and preparation for the main prestigious races. He will decide which birds will be prepared for the long distance races and those which will be used for the sprint races and which will be lightly raced as a means of preparing them for subsequent seasons. Such a plan will prove to be very beneficial for the show fancier, charting when and where the shows are to be held and deciding entries by reference to the strength of the showing team.

The birds cannot maintain top condition if they are shown week after week at each and every show. For the fancier the greatest satisfaction is in winning at a show where the planning has directed good chances of success. This will apply to any breed of show pigeon, matching the team to the requirements of the show calendar. If there is any doubt, then give it to the pigeons so as not to over-stress them and to provide them with the sort of programme with which they can cope. Some pigeons will withstand a hectic show programme better than others will and this is where the fancier's knowledge of the birds will be valuable to manage each bird as an individual rather than as a flock. If that sounds like an over-simplification, then it is not, for time spent with the birds is the way to achieve this knowledge and understanding as a relationship between fancier and pigeons. And that, is what show preparation is all about.

Chapter 15

Advanced Showing Methods

THERE is a great deal more to pigeon showing than entering them, and taking them from their lofts before depositing them in a pen for the attention of a judge. That hardly needs saying but what I intend to do in this chapter is to discuss certain procedures which can help gain success both from the preparation and treatment of the bird but also in preparation by the exhibitor. Both are important aspects of the sport to attempt to gain some advantage over competitors in a planned but lawful manner.

Some of the topics I intend to discuss in this chapter have been considered as 'taboo' or something better not talked about. However, as we are talking about the showing of pigeons, let us take a full and frank look at the subject with a view to increasing our expertise within the sport. There will be some items here which are not normally discussed with fanciers feeling that they are best left unspoken. Let me make it clear, that I do not regard any of the items contained in this chapter as being illegal or anything approaching cheating. However it will be necessary to have regard to the regulations under which shows are held as some rules may prohibit the use of some of the adjustments I am going to mention.

Always operate under the relevant rules because otherwise there is a danger of falling foul of the authority of show organisers or controlling bodies.

Let me first look at some very simple matters which are in fact show preparation

- ■ **Toenails.** These should be kept trimmed. Some birds, especially hens grow them quite quickly so the use of good scissors or a clipper is necessary

- ■ **Bent flights or tail feathers.** In any loft situation birds occasionally manage to bend flights or other large feathers. The easy solution is to steam the relevant flight using the stream from a kettle but in some cases which are not severe, the flight will return to normal if gentle pressure is applied in the opposite direction to the bend. In extreme cases, where the bend has developed into a fracture, it may be necessary to splint the flight for a few days to enable nature to allow re-growth but in the vast majority of cases steam is the answer.

- **Wattle marks.** Damage caused by another bird pecking at the wattle can affect the showing of a bird. White chalk can be used to mask the mark as can white correction fluid though I have always regarded this as a last consideration.

- **Greasy wattles.** The same remarks apply though unless there has been a physical cause of this, the chances are that a greasy wattle also indicates general lack of condition in the bird.

- **Fraying to flight, secondary or tail feather.** Mainly owing to faults in growth caused by stress, some feathers do not finish off with a good sharp edge. Sometimes the problem is caused by damage, for instance a moth eating at a feather or owing to being rubbed against or caught against something sharp. In simple cases trimming of the end of the flight will eradicate most of the problem.

- **Pipy vent feathers.** Some birds, especially hens - seem to carry feathers around the vent, which have not fully cast away the sheath protecting them. In other words, the feathers have a 'pipy' feel to them. Birds provided with plenty of baths normally cast the sheaths naturally but in some cases remedial action is required. In most cases a gentle rubbing of the affected feathers will free them from their covering but steam can also be applied providing that great case is taken. Steam is scorching hot both for bird and fancier so extreme care should be taken. Probably a bathing of the feathers using warm water is a better all-round solution.

- **Extended beaks.** The top mandible of some birds tends to grow longer than it should and for showing purposes should be trimmed or filed back. A sharp clipper is best for the purpose with a nail file or emery board used as the final touch to ensure that the resulting shape is quite natural.

So far, so good with little or nothing said so far that is controversial or worthy of argument. To proceed however, let us examine the staging of pigeon shows in general and to make a very simple observation. **In an ideal world all shows would be fair, all judging would be fair and unbiased free from prejudice, bias**

and favour. In all my years in the sport I have believed this and while from time to time little incidents occur which can knock that simple faith, I firmly believe that in the vast majority of cases, matters are fair and properly done. Those who seek favours merely cheat their friends and cheat themselves. In general they come unstuck and lack genuine friends.

Many years ago when some fanciers were winning shows with show racers possessing race certificates. An old friend made a most telling statement to me. He said that while we are drinking in one room, those so-called friends are in the show hall cheating us by using dubious means of gaining advantage. I have never forgotten that statement and have always tried to live by standards which cannot ever be questioned.

So, assuming that all shows are fair and the judging unbiased, let us take a look at ways of enhancing our chances. Firstly, knowledge of the sport, of the shows and of the judges is a great help. Keep notes of judges and their methods of judging together with their preferences and ultimate choices. The clever fancier will have a memory of such matters or better still a little record system or card system in which he records such information. For instance, did the judge favour a particular colour, a type, large or small, did he display prejudices or fads, did he appear in total control, did he select birds carrying weight or did he prefer them on the lean side.

Showing should be an art and never a lottery. Named and competent officials who know the job and more importantly know what is required as far as the birds are concerned should judge every class. Throughout the showing world this is the state of affairs which exists in the showing of any form of livestock. There are one or two terrible exceptions where the judges are not named with their classes and this has created a dreadful and unacceptable lottery aspect.

Having spent a lifetime in the sport of pigeon showing, I am more and more convinced that the greatest pleasure is in winning under a top judge, known for his or her knowledge and utter competence. If this win is then accomplished with a home-bred bird which was expected or backed to win then so much the better and more memorable and pleasurable. It takes a lot of work in building a thorough knowledge of shows, judging and judging. Through my experience in the sport I have a good knowledge of what a judge looks for, and can therefore use some skill to anticipate what that judge will go for in the future. For instance, many years ago I entered a little show racer hen under a well-known and respected racing judge. She failed to score and when I met him later in the show, I thought I might just mention her to him. However, when we shook hands, I immediately knew the reason, for his hands were huge, the large hands of a working farmer and quite obviously he tended to like birds slightly on the larger size.

I could go on and on with such examples but it does indicate that a fairly comprehensive database can be established to enhance chances of showing success. Some judges have dreadful colour fads almost verging on prejudice. This should not happen but it does and where it does, it is far better to be aware of it for future use. This can be seen with every breed of pigeon and of colour variations within the breeds.

Having made some general remarks in respect of both pigeon preparation and of extra work which can be undertaken by the exhibitor, let us now take a look at some more slightly more advanced ideas in bird preparation. I will deal with these in list form with brief comments on each section as appropriate.

■ *White or light coloured beaks.* In show racers this is a constant point for discussion. Birds with pied markings often carry a lighter beak and in some birds this is revealed even where there is no obvious white present but where pieding is being carried. In some colours the lighter beak can be excused - almost taken as normal as in reds, mealies, yellows, creams and silvers. However the lighter beak in a blue or chequer is frowned upon. To treat or not to treat is the question and over the years I have seen a large assortment of 'cures' tried, ranging from boot polish, dies, styptic pencil, coloured pens and pencils. I believe that the styptic pencil has proved to be the best overall solution but care must be taken because it achieves colour change owing to slight burning.

■ *Badly damaged flights.* These can be replaced by splicing a better but matching flight in its place. This is done in three stages. Firstly a replacement flight will have to be found. White flights are the easiest but other colours will have to be found from existing birds and in my experience, the role is often down to a favourite stock pigeon. Stage 2 is to cut the old flight off using sharp scissors. The exposed end is best left for a few days and the length remaining will depend on the position in the wing (or tail), because a discerning judge should not easily discover the joint. Retain the piece of feather removed so that it can be matched to the new 'implant' both for size and colour. A good glue is required, also a flexible piece of wire - such as a straightened section from a paper clip. One end of the wire will be inserted into the stump while the other will go into the 'implant'. When the fit is regarded as satisfactory, glue will be used to make the join permanent. The flexible nature of the wire will allow a certain adjustment to make the 'new' flight lie correctly with existing flights. I have never tried this exercise with a tenth primary, as the chances of the join remaining undetected are slight.

■ *Single sided white-flighted pigeons.* Certainly in show racers, it is quite common for good birds to be reared carrying a single white flight in one wing only. Strangely enough, this white flight often disappears and is replaced with a normal coloured flight during the first moult. Where it reappears it begs the question of whether the white flight is better cut and replaced with a normal coloured flight, or whether a white flight is implanted in the other wing to provide balance. The instructions contained in the preceding paragraph apply to this exercise but I would couple it with some further advice. Do not attempt this too close to a show. The amount of handling involved is not good for condition so a few days at least should pass. Another tip is to keep a supply of good flights for such uses, flights collected during the normal moult within the loft.

■ *Minor flaws in feather ends or slight fretting.* Although I dealt with this briefly in the opening preparation factors, I now do so because in some cases the work involved is quite considerable and which requires good eyesight, a steady hand and good sharp tools. Often where there is fretting, more than one flight end can be affected so more than one flight will have to be trimmed. Likewise where only one flight is fretted, the amount of trimming involved may involve the trimming of neighbouring flights in order to produce balance. The aim of the trimming is to make the affected flights look as normal as possible.

■ *Thin bars on barred pigeons.* One of the main drawbacks in the breeding barred pigeons is that it is very difficult to produce them with thick, wide and dark barring. The lighter the colour the more likely it is that the bars will be lacking as mentioned so powder blues are very prone to this. It is accepted that in most cases of a thinning of the visible barring, that the normal covers feathers are hiding some of the bar colour. Therefore a careful trimming of the cover feathers will often reveal more bar colour.

It goes without saying that such a job requires a steady hand, good sharp tools and plenty of patience. It is not always successful especially where the bar is very thin and unless done well, any judge with reasonable eyesight can spot the 'job'.

- *White feathers elsewhere than in flights.* Quite frequently a bird will carry one or two white feathers in the hackle detracting from its general appearance. The 'offending' feathers can be removed in the easiest manner by plucking them out – ideally using a pair of tweezers. However I advise against this practice as immediately they are removed, new ones will commence to grow and the new feather will first appear in 'spiky' form. My advice is that if it is necessary to remove a small number of feathers, to use a sharp pair of scissors removing anything white in sight, but leaving the base of the feather(s) in place.

- *Raised or twisted feathers in the hackle.* Some birds even when in show condition will suddenly show a feather which seems out of place or even twisted out of its normal sleek position. This is most noticed when the birds are subject to some stress – such as being shown for instance. These can be dealt with by carefully catching hold of the feather in question and gently pulling it – not so that it comes away but so that it can turn naturally back into its proper place. Sometimes it is necessary to twist the feather gently but if the problem cannot be rectified gently, then it might be necessary to cut the feather as described in the preceding paragraph.

- *Filing of wattles of older birds.* Some cocks begin to get coarse in appearance at quite an early age. The most apparent signs of this are a coarseness of the wattles and a growing of the cere. In the case of wattles, the safest way is to gently file them to a smoother state using either a nail file, emery board or a pumice stone. In more extreme cases I have known a razor blade used to trim off the worst of the coarse growth though I would never recommend this. If this is to be undertaken I would advise great care and also that any such work is done a fair number of days in advance of a show.

I feel certain that this list will give cause for discussion but as we are talking about showing for the more advanced fanciers, I feel that it is well worth mentioning. Although I will be producing a chapter on show preparation I thought that I would end this one with some ideas which are closely associated with both subjects.

With shows approaching, particularly the important and prestigious ones, every care will have to be taken to ensure that the peak of condition is achieved at exactly the right time. A bird when in the absolute peak will maintain this for some while and it is not quite like an athlete who requires his maximum output at a certain minute for a certain race. So, what about bathing the birds prior to a show. I believe that there are two points here. If one uses the bath to encourage condition, then the bath should be presented at least two weeks before the show. A good bath makes the birds feel good and they can start to pick up in condition both physically and mentally. A further bath will then be offered nearer to the show. However in the case of birds at their peak of condition, the timing is less important as a bird in that very top order will enjoy the bath and its bloom will cause the water to disappear without loss of bloom. I often bathe the birds the day before a show though prefer two to three days lapse between the water and the showing procedure.

When actually preparing the birds for the show, do so in plenty of time and make it without rush. It is surprising just how many little defects are to be found at basketing time so plenty of time is the best way to do the checking properly. I prefer to do this the night before the show, leaving the birds in the baskets overnight to settle. It is also said that the warmth from the baskets will improve the bloom and condition. Many people actually have the birds in their baskets in a warm place indoors overnight and my first introduction to showing included the advice to do this. I was told that the Welsh fanciers of the day brought the birds indoors to share the fireside for the evening prior to the big show. The warmth in the baskets can be maintained better by placing some layers of newspaper or brown paper between the internal covers and the lid of the basket/container. I would also couple this with the advice to warm the baskets prior to use, as when stored in sheds and garages, they can become quite damp.

However before travel to the show, be sure to clean the baskets to remove droppings which might soil the birds en route to the show. It isn't a bad idea to cover the tail of the birds with either a little polythene bag or to wrap some tissue around it. This will keep the tail from becoming soiled and as we all know, some birds seem to manage to do this on every journey.

As for the journey, some thought might be given to the transportation. Some fanciers arrange their baskets so that the birds travel looking in a 'forward' direction. This will depend upon the available space but is a matter well worth thinking about. I would urge any show fancier not to use a trailer for conveying the birds to shows. I have known many to try this but it has always ended in failure because of the fact that the birds are thrown about more in the confines of a trailer and I am never satisfied that the ventilation can be made right. Indeed I have always had a great fear of the effects of carbon monoxide and for this reason never allow birds to travel in the boots or trunks of cars. My attitude is a simple one – that if the air is good enough for me it is satisfactory for my pigeons

As for the arrival at the shows, plenty of time should be left for this. It can be a time-consuming matter to pen a number of birds, for once again routine checks should be carried out on each bird. This will particularly apply to cleanliness to ensure that the bird has travelled without soiling to the feathering. Enough time should be allowed for this and for the birds to settle. I have always believed in trying to get my birds settled to their pens and find the best way is to provide them with a small pinch of seed which they like. This will quickly be devoured and will allow the birds to feel more at home in the unusual surroundings and provides something for the crop to work on. Care must be taken with this as too much seed may lead to allegations of an attempt to 'mark' a pen, but when done properly is nothing but beneficial to the bird. In my earliest days in the sport, the greatest pigeon show I ever knew, always provided penning in which there was a drinker containing a small amount of water and each pen contained a small quantity of good quality maples. Each bird was therefore able to settle, to eat and drink and this simple procedure allowed a fair competition in that every pigeon, whether they had travelled one or a thousand miles were thus allowed to settle. I am afraid that nowadays there is not enough thought for the birds.

So, with that thought I will close on this chapter which contains some contentious thought on the showing of pigeons. However I do so with one closing shot. That whatever, it is the pigeon that deserves every consideration and fair treatment. Showing involves them in a great deal of stress and discomfort and anything we, as fanciers can do to alleviate this, we must do and prove to any casual observer that as fanciers we genuinely love our pigeons.

PART 3

Chapter 16

Lofts for Racing Pigeons

Racing requirements

FOR most of my early years in the sport, all thoughts of loft construction were directed to the needs of show racers. When ever I raced birds - and often these were show racers trained up for the purpose - I raced them to my show loft. I guess that most of my interests were in just seeing the birds arrive home rather than in speedy trapping to win races.

However, when I moved to my current address in a more permanent mode, I found more interest in the racing side of the sport and joined my local racing club. Involvement with the membership and their birds led to have a racing loft constructed so that I could maintain a small team of racers - and this has grown so that the racing side has equal status to the show team - and possibly a position of precedence.

My initial racing loft was a three-compartment structure with an uncomplicated front which had sputnik traps to allow birds to enter and leave. Then I had two large bays fitted to the front for each of the end compartments although the central compartment only had access by the front door. This compartment was the one I mainly used for racing the adult birds, so the door was fitted with a small flap and wire traps of a size of only fifteen inches (54cm) by ten inches. (25cm). There were trees immediately in front of the loft so that the returning birds had to negotiate these before finding the little flap. Despite these problems I enjoyed some remarkable successes. These whetted my appetite and led to further loft changes to accommodate more serious racing. Plans were made to make the loft more suitable for racing but also more convenient for me.

The main alteration was the construction of a corridor running along the entire front, the roof of which is made of plastic glass to allow more heat and light in. Trapping is by stall traps and these have proved to be ideal for my purposes. More on that later but it illustrates the fact that many racing enthusiasts spend much of their time seeking improvements and ideas to enhance racing performances - and there is little wrong with this.

Variety

There is probably no typical racing loft. I have seen many lofts in my travels in the United Kingdom, in Europe and the United States of America. I have seen lofts in tiny back yards where the birds had to drop very steeply between the roofs, large, elaborate, purpose-built lofts set in large gardens, roof top lofts in America, house top lofts in Europe, small home made structures and almost anything which fancier and pigeons can use in some sort of harmony.

The immediate question of course is whether it is the fancier or the loft which is mainly contributory to success and having seen so many varieties of pigeon homes I am bound to say that it must be the fancier, his skills and his management that is the driving force. The only addition I would make to that claim is that wherever possible, when lofts are being designed or built, the comfort of the fancier can be most important because if he or she feels at home, the attention to detail is likely to be so much better. Therefore, the addition of the corridor to my racing loft has made it a better home for the pigeons with more air space, but it has made it much better for me to be able to attend to their needs.

Changing Fads and Fashions

In all my time as a pigeon fancier I have been an avid reader of all pigeon material including books and the weekly and monthly magazines. As a showman I have therefore been able to keep abreast of the racing scene and to witness and understand how things are constantly changing. Indeed, only by making such a study could I ever manage a successful show team, for what is good for one side of the sport is often right and good for the other. For instance, in the early days there was a fashion for fresh air. Lofts were constructed so that there were openings on all sides of the loft so that the winds could blow through.

I once visited a most successful show fancier who had his pigeons housed in single breeding pens which were almost completely open to the elements being clad in wire netting, and the only shelter was a small box-like structure situated at a high level at the rear of each pen which the birds used for sitting and rearing. My visit was made during a period of sub-zero temperatures, yet the birds - all show racers - were quite happily sitting eggs or young birds.

The situation changed somewhat abruptly when the racing turned to the widowhood method which was being practised on the

European mainland. This called for warmer lofts with controlled forms of ventilation and in many cases a fairly dark interior to keep the inmates quieter. Clay tiles were being used more and more on loft roofs, copying the continental fashion, and grills on the floors both to ease cleaning duties and to aid both ventilation and reduction of dust levels. It is probably no coincidence that cases of 'pigeon fanciers' lung' have multiplied owing to the more closed type of loft whereas in my early days of air and wind lofts, this problem was hardly known.

As I mentioned earlier, it never pays to stand still. The successful fancier is the one who is always observing, learning and yearning for more success. He will be constantly reading about his sport, studying the methods of the successful and considering what changes can be made to loft structure to enhance winning chances. Therefore my advice is to continue to study the lofts of others and to watch developments in construction. Do not change for the sake of change, but always be prepared to do so.

The Roof

I had always favoured a one way sloping roof on the basis that it took all the rainwater and deposited it at the rear of the loft. I was persuaded that pent style roofing with tiles is superior in the control of air, ventilation and warmth. When I bought a stock loft it came with a tiled pent roof but it was not entirely to my liking. The roof space soon become thick with dust and bloom made even more visible by cobwebs which seem to attract the dust. I never did find a method of disposing of the dust and bloom in the roof area and as this was a racing loft so goodness knows how much extra bloom there would be if my show racers had been housed in there for they carry far more bloom than the working racing pigeon.

I am inclined to recommend the use of a pitched style roof with clay tiles if this can be afforded. However, the lean-to type of roof is perfectly adequate. It is most important that whatever the shape of the roof, that it be waterproof for dampness of any kind spells disaster in the conditioning of pigeons. I like as much height as possible - within reason for the more air that there is the better, though height has to be balanced by control over the birds. If the birds are provided with too much space and they can become wild and unmanageable.

I am becoming more certain that the roof should allow sunlight in through clear tiles or through the insertion of clear glass or Perspex in the roof covering up to a quarter of the total roof area. It is not wise to have too much light. Nature's goodness is thus used to produce health and vitality. There are many products on the market to enhance the amount of light and warmth in the loft including double-skinned plastics which not only produce the light but also prevent condensation. This is yet another area where fashion is changing and where it is well worth watching what the most successful fanciers are doing in this respect. It is no new idea of course and reference to Barker's *Pigeon Racing*[1] will show that Dr Barker in the early years of the 20th Century advocated glass roof panels.

The Floor

Grilled floors are now quite popular and have much to commend them. In the large professional studs the floors are grilled and this seems to have been adopted by the most successful racing enthusiasts. They save on cleaning time in that the droppings fall through to a lower area where they can collect and dry, they allow the dust to drop through out of harm's way, and the pigeons themselves remain cleaner as a result.

If I have a reservation about them it would be that food is bound also to drop through because birds tend to throw their food about and it thus becomes a haven for rodents unless cleared regularly. This can be avoided to some extent by having the feed trays on a wider tray with a raised edging, so that most of the food is caught on the tray area

Air can be allowed in through the under floor grill area to flow up through the loft to the roof where it can escape through the tiles or through high level vents. One very good idea I have seen is to have a boarded area immediately under the perches so that this air, whilst flowing at all times, does not actually flow against the birds on their perches. It was likened to someone in the windy street standing back in a shop doorway to be out of the draught, yet still enjoying the freshness of the air. The boarded area under the perches can be a straightforward board which will need to be regularly scraped clean, or it can be a tray into which is added either sand or sawdust or provided with a grilled covering.

For those who cannot afford floor grills, then good quality boarding is essential. Gone are the days when many had to use old floor boarding salvaged from other sources which resulted in an uneven surface for cleaning purposes. One of the best investments is a good quality boarded floor - preferably of exterior quality ply boarding which then makes its scraping and cleaning an easier matter. I also favour a double skin with insulation between to facilitate

---

[1] *Pigeon Racing* by Dr W. E. Barker

a more even temperature. It is essential however to have any floor well up off the ground so that rats and other vermin are unable to find shelter underneath. If they can shelter underneath the chances are that they will attempt to gnaw an entry to a lucrative source of food within the loft. Rats are deterred by creosote so a good coating of both sides of the flooring and all supporting joists is thoroughly recommended.

Floor covering

Over the years I have used all manner of litter on the floors of my loft. Indeed, litter seems a good description term for whatever I have used has failed to provide satisfaction and has looked untidy. In my early days I used sharp sand on the floors to a depth of a few inches. I liked using the sand and kept it looking clean by sifting it regularly. Nowadays I have a mild to moderate allergy to pigeon protein and I blame the use of the sand, for in those days I did not wear a mask or other protection when doing the sifting and therefore breathed in much of the resulting dust. Indeed deep litter was another of those fashions for at one time - and it was when open lofts were the vogue - we were being encouraged to allow the dried droppings to remain to form a mat or layer of dried droppings which required little or no attention.

I then used a chemical 'stay-dry' material similar to that used in cat trays but the dust was unacceptable. I have tried sawdust and wood shavings and also straw but nothing has fully satisfied me as keeping the floors clean by scraping them and adding some lime or floor-white. It can be tedious but at least it is satisfying to see a clean floor in the knowledge that a clean loft reduces the risk of infections.

The walls including windows and doors

Good quality materials should be used in the belief that the best is always the cheapest in the long run. A good thick tongue and groove or weather boarding covering should be used or else, exterior quality ply board. I have insulated the walls on my lofts by having an inner-skin of a wipe-clean wall covering and between the two layers have a layer of insulation. I have this in two lofts while in the other I just have the outer boarding. In all honesty I have found little difference to the birds and their performances.

As for windows and ventilators, I have always been an exponent of the use of adjustable glass louvres. They allow light in, they allow air in and yet can be closed up to prevent both winds and rain or snow entering. They can be used to control the warmth of the loft and are just about ideal for the modern pigeon lofts. They have many advantages over fixed areas of glass or plastic in their very flexibility. I have yet to find anything as good and useful. In the front of my main loft I have nine sets of glass louvres and over nearly two decades they have provided me with a warm, light and dry loft. It is very important to use clear glass through which both light and the heat from the sun can pass, and that it is kept clean.

If possible, the lofts have glass panels at floor level so that the morning sun can get into the lofts. The result is that the warmth will dry any dampness from the floor and the heat will rise and assist in the ventilation. Clear glass is necessary for this for while obscure glass will allow light in; it does not allow the warmth of the sun through.

Trapping arrangements

The biggest difference between the racing loft and the lofts for show pigeons is the requirement for a good system of trapping for the birds. I have tried all sorts of traps ranging from the simple hanging wires, the wired shaped traps, simple drop in traps, the sputnik traps I mentioned, the open door or window methods. I have finally arrived at the use of the American style stall traps which I have found to be the best system I have ever used. The birds can be trapped without the fancier having to go into the loft to catch and handle the birds to remove the race rubber or counter mark. The rubber can be removed from the foot quite easily and the bird is then allowed into the loft. It is the fastest system I have ever used.

However, methods of trapping depend upon the system of management enjoyed by the pigeon fancier and there is no right system for all. I have simply quoted my own experience as a busy person who enjoys pigeon racing and who, along the way has tried a number of methods and options.

Aviary for stock pigeons

The stock racers require extra good treatment and access to the outside world is one way of providing them with the quality of life they deserve. Often the birds housed in the stock lofts are too valuable to be risked out flying and fanciers should therefore attempt to arrange an aviary or flight so that they can enjoy the open air in safety. There are many advantages to this in that the birds can be provided with baths out there and benefit from the more natural form of living.

Loft Appearance

The pigeon fancy as a whole is often judged upon the appearance of a 'local' loft. One, which is smart and cleanly presented, presents a good advertisement for our sport, whereas one which is neglected and 'tatty' does little for our standing.

Lofts - even for racing purposes - do not need to be painted in bright colours. The trend in the last few years has been away from paint and more to the more natural looking products. Some of these look really smart with a finish which is equal to the appearance of painted surfaces, yet, which protect and last well for several years. Older products such as creosote are extremely cheap and practical and maintain wood in good condition for many years with a minimum of fuss and hard work.

The average racing fancier puts great thought and effort into the structure to which he races. While we can argue whether it is the loft or the methods employed which lead to success, there is little doubt that all work directed to the dwelling place of the racer makes a great deal of difference to it and its desire to return there in the shortest possible race time. Always bear in mind that, though the loft is just a loft to the fancier, to the birds it is their home,, and as their home it has to be the most desirable place on earth. If it is not the birds are unlikely to return to it as if it were so. If the structure is crowded, airless, damp, smelly, uncomfortable, draughty, noisy, a place of tension, then the birds are unlikely to have little loyalty or affection for it. The moment they discover something more congenial they will forget all about the place they have just left. 'Home is where the heart is' applies as much to the pigeon as it does to man, perhaps even more so. Fanciers forget this at their peril.

Chapter 17

Pigeon Racing for the busy fancier

I HAVE raced pigeons for many years but it is only in the last decade that I have been able to treat my racing as seriously as it demands. Over the years in the pigeon fancy, my main interest has always been in the showing side, an interest which was born in me within a very short time of having been introduced to pigeons. However, as the years past, and my involvement in the sport became more involved, I found myself more and more in contact with pigeon racing enthusiasts and of course found myself attracted by the performing nature of the racing pigeon. So I made a decision to go into racing seriously and arranged for a loft to be built from which to race.

Over the years in the showing side of the sport, showing was the only way I could properly compete because I was making my way in a profession which entailed changes of address so that the main consideration had to be to keep everything portable. A race team as well as the show team under these circumstances would have made any such removal very arduous at both ends of the move, and of course the race team would have to be started all over again in the new location.

Such decisions were made in view of a demanding job with irregular hours and days off, much time spent away from home and because of trying to provide for a growing family. The latter part of that statement of course is a very important one for whatever else happens in pigeon fancying the family should always come first. Pigeon racing with its incessant demands on weekends is not the ideal situation in which to plan for family enjoyment on outings to the beach and other pursuits. I have laboured this to make a special point; that pigeon racing is time consuming as well as expensive and this aspect needs to be addressed before the commitment is made. To try to run two teams, one for the showing and one for racing is even more mind-bending.

Let me say here and now that I get great pleasure in racing the birds. The sight of a bird returning to its loft from a long distance race is one of the greatest sights in pigeon fancying. I never fail to

EYE SIGN

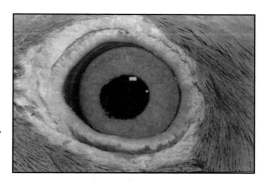

This is a 9.00 racer
and a 9.00 breeder

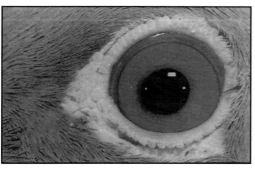

This is a 9.05 racer
and a 9.00 breeder

This is a 9.15 racer
and a 9.15 breeder

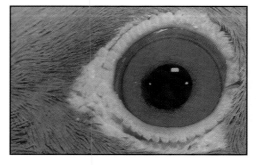

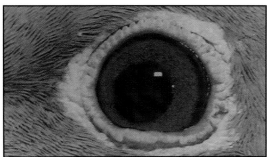

This is a 9.15 racer
and a 9.15 breeder

This is a 9.25 racer
and a 9.15 breeder

This is a 9.25 racer
and a 9.15 breeder

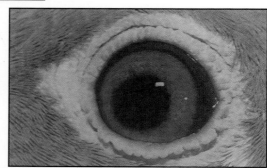

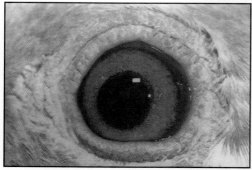

This is a 9.25 racer
and a 9.15 breeder

This is a 9.25 racer
and a 9.25 breeder

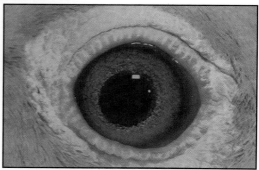

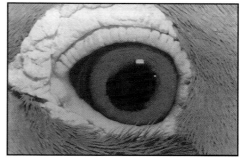

This is a 9.35 racer
and a 9.15 breeder

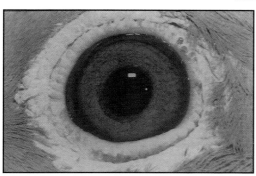

This is a 9.35 racer
and a 9.25 breeder

This is a 9.35 racer
and a 9.25 breeder

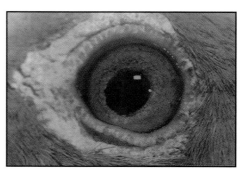

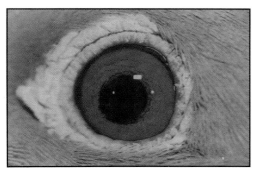

This is a 9.35 racer
and a 9.25 breeder

This is a 9.35 racer and a 9.35 breeder

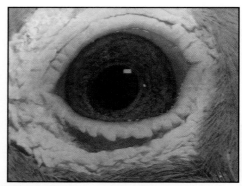

This is a 9.50 racer and a 9.35 breeder, just look at those speed lines going across the circle of correlation

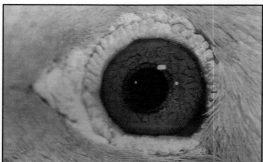

This is a 9.50 racer and a 9.50 breeder

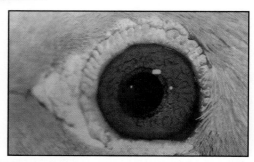

This is an inbred eye, Lo Nipus 9.25 racer, notice distance lines, this is a 9.25 breeder ready for a cross

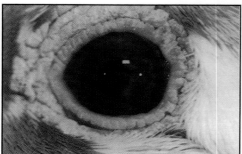

A SELECTION OF PIGEON BOOKS

*German Olympiad
Show at Dortmund*

*Doug McClary's
Mealy cock*

*The author judging in
the United States*

The author judging at the National Show, New York

Judging at the Blackpool Show

A top German Show

Douglas McClary outside his lofts which face south and allow sunshine in when doors are opened

Author's loft corridor. Note ability to feed and water from this area; also show pens

SHOW RACERS

Opal chequer pied hen, owned by S
Sauvary, Guernsey

Lavender WF cock, owned by S Sauvary,
Guernsey

Beautiful red Show Racer cock bred by
the author

Young Show Racer mealy hen, BYB
Midland Show

Right: Medallion cock, top winning mealy
cock, BO Sex Blackpool Show of the
Year, two Regional award wins

Left: Powder blue Show Racer hen, owned by M and Z Morrison, bred by the author, BIS at Blackpool Show of the Year

FLYING BREEDS

Below: Yellow cock of F Humphries, Best Flyer at Cheshire County Show

Left: Andalusian Baldhead Birmingham Roller, breeder D L Darbyshire. Photo: Robert Bennion

Above: Competition Tippler of J R Brocklehurst, Best Flyer, Cheshire County Show

Left: Champion Print Tippler hen, owned and bred by Les Dawson

FANCY BREEDS

Right: Copper White Flight Gimpel hen, BIS Royal Lancashire Show, owned and exhibited by T. Edwards

Above: Red Voorburg of B Rennison, winner of Best Young Fanciers' Trophy, Doncaster

Photos: Feathered World

Right: Modena – Tom Crane's young Yellow Schietti hen, Runner-up to BIS at Doncaster

White Self Chinese Owl of Hayes & Poole, Best Fancy at Cheshire County Show

Felegyhazer Tumbler, blue ganzel, Special Show Hamburg, hv Band. Breeder – Holger Pilz, Plavam See.

Photo: *Ingolf Zungnickel*

Left: Old Dutch Capuchine, an adult Yellow cock, bred by Richard Kaesler, Menden. Photo: T. Hellmann

Above: Young White Fantail of M Richardson, BIS Doncaster

Left: African Owl of B & R Glew, Best YB Juvenile Doncaster

Below: Capuchines, section winners at Doncaster for Shore & Hankinson

Left: Norwich Cropper, Best Young Bird at Great Yorkshire Show, owned and exhibited by R & K Rennison

Above: Modena – Best Opposite Sex Fancy at Doncaster, exhibited by G Duggins

Photos: Feathered World

Left: M Purdam's Blue Bar Genuine Homer cock, BIS Otley

Above: Short Face Tumbler of E Hampson, Best Fancy Cheshire County Show

Left: Best Juvenile Flyer at Doncaster, G Duggins' Exhibition Print Tippler

LOFTS

The author's show loft showing extensive use of glass louvres, also three large doors to allow in maximum sunlight when opened

An American loft for racing and showing

Conventional box perches

Left: An aviary provides a perfect environment for pigeons

Right: Two types of perches: on the left with pull-out trays; on the right, easily made DIY perches

Lofts suitable for fanciers who suffer from pigeon fancier's lung or pigeon allergy. Pictured are lofts of Keith Mott of Surrey – 6 x sections for long-distance natural pairs. Also on the right, double loft for ten young birds each season

Lofts of Dick Lipski, Milwaukee, U.S.A., maximising the natural sunshine

Above: Aviary set up for each single flight nest box. Note plastic protection against cold winds

Right: Single pair nest boxes showing exit door to individual flight

feel humbled by it, never fail to marvel at it and never to forget the sheer effort and endurance of that bird to get home. These are the rewards and pleasures of all the hard work and what makes it all worth the effort.

With my particular background in mind I thought that my chapter on pigeon racing would be better addressed to the busy man because that is how I have been throughout my racing career. I have enjoyed good successes with my little racing team but would prefer not to call myself an expert, more one who is experienced at arranging my racing programme to fit in with other busy schedules, including of course managing my show team. The result is that in my present circumstances I can never be a hundred percent committed to pigeon racing and have therefore adjusted my input to suit my own circumstances. I know of many others who are committed to both sides of the sport and who manage to achieve good success at both, so the problems are most certainly not insurmountable.

The easy advice to anybody would be not to try both sides at once but that is rather too easy to say and if total year-round commitment is sought or preferred, who am I to criticise. The fact is though that either or both efforts will suffer somewhat in the attempt to excel at both but providing that winning at all costs is not the only aim, the sheer pigeon enjoyment will be great. It will amount to maximum enjoyment from simply owning and using at least two teams of pigeons.

Before describing my way of racing designed to fit a busy schedule, perhaps some description of the main methods of racing will be of assistance. In the time and space available I cannot hope to provide a précis of every detail of each system but a few words on each will at least provide a general idea. It is generally accepted that the following are the main methods of racing pigeons:

- Natural system
- Widowhood
- Roundabout
- Celibacy system
- Young Bird racing

As a final comment on the general situation of pigeon racing, I would like to add one final observation. It is, that pigeons race well in many cases despite their owners! In other words they seem to be able to turn in performances even when their treatment and management leaves a lot to be desired. Many fanciers imagine that these valiant little birds are flying machines whereas the truth is that they are little beings which require persuasion and plenty of looking after to be able to really give of their best. Many fanciers fail their birds in these respects.

Natural system

At a guess I would say that the majority of racing fanciers still use the old, time-honoured method of racing by using the system which best describes itself, as the natural system. In the briefest of terms, the birds are raced while paired and when both cocks and hens are raced during the incubation of the eggs and of the rearing of young birds. Unpaired birds are also raced naturally. I am bound to say that while I assert that most still use this system, it is not necessarily true that the majority of top winners come from use of this system. It has been overtaken by other better and faster ways of racing the birds.

However in terms of enjoyment the natural system has much to commend it. The best results would appear to come when the long distance races are held for both cocks and hens turn in some wonderful performances at the distance. In the early shorter races, a naturally flown pigeon will not often beat a top performing cock raced on the widowhood or roundabout system. Under the natural system, the birds are paired and allowed to rear either one or two youngsters in the first round. It is when they have been sitting just over a week on the second round that they come into form when the first primary flight is thrown. So, the date of pairing is arranged so that the first flight is thrown just when the main races are scheduled, generally the medium to long distance events.

As many of those who use the natural way of racing enjoy winning the distance races, they almost use the earlier and shorter races as a training time for their birds and when the occasional win occurs, it is quite gratifying. However, it is a time for building muscle and for equipping them with the right stamina and mental attitude to cope with the longer distances. Although described as the natural system, it is not an easy one for a great deal of care, attention and observation is required. Individual birds will perform better under certain conditions such as a hen returning to her nearly hatching eggs or another while feeding a youngster of a certain age. Each bird is different and notes need to be made of each performance to detect when the bird is most likely to perform well. Watching the birds is the key to it all, especially in noting exactly when eggs are laid and so on.

The birds seem to enjoy being on this system of racing in that they are happy and contented when paired and strive to get back home to their mates. They are also happy when exercising together around the loft and in general there is far less strain on the birds when treated in this natural manner. There are drawbacks of course. For the fancier who wishes to win every race, the system is not really an ideal way, having been superseded by other racing methods. Also, fanciers can inadvertently cause great anxiety to their birds, especially to hens when sending them in the wrong condition, or wrong phase of their breeding. Hens which are forced to lay in transport crates can never be expected to perform well - indeed to get home even. Good observation and attention to detail should avoid this situation but I am afraid that it happens all too often. Likewise a hen should never be sent to a race within four or five days before or after laying eggs.

For the average fancier who enjoys average success, this is a good way of keeping, managing and racing pigeons. The fancier who enjoys simply seeing his birds returning to the loft and to their mates, this is indeed a most rewarding system of racing. Normal lofts can be used with normal breeding arrangements. Those who are able to keep and race their birds on this most natural of systems, especially those who can allow their birds to enjoy an open loft style of living, will gain maximum enjoyment from their racing pigeons. If pigeons perform best when they have a love of their homes, then this is surely the system for the pigeon and for the best all-round enjoyment.

Widowhood Racing

I have seen this method of racing, as being the fastest system that there is. It has become increasingly popular and seems to be practised in most countries of the world. In basic terms it is a system which uses only the cocks after their young bird season. There are many variations to the system as fanciers continue to experiment and try different motivations so as to make themselves even more successful.

The system is well suited to the small-team fancier with limited space and providing that a suitable system can be devised to ensure that the widowhood cocks perform well and that suits the management at the loft. Widowhood racing to the vast majority means the racing only of the cocks but if one reads Rotondo's 'Pigeon Racing' he asserted that both sexes could be successfully raced on the widowhood system and had many wins to prove it. However, for the sake of simplicity, I will refer only to the racing of cocks. The pairs are mated early - probably in December and are allowed to rear either one or two youngsters. Some fanciers replace the eggs with pot eggs so that the pairs do not have to rear youngsters with the attendant strain.

When the pairs go down on their second round of eggs, and have been sitting for a few days, the hens are removed, leaving the cocks to incubate the eggs - at least until they tire of the task in a few days. The cocks will rear on the young birds where appropriate. The cocks are then kept quiet and on their own for the period between the leaving of the eggs and when they are re-paired prior to racing. It is generally accepted that there are no perches in the widowhood loft so that the cocks have to use their own nest boxes as perches thus making them extremely defensive towards their own bit of space.

When the races start, the hens are introduced back into the loft with their cocks and allowed to mate and lay. The pairs are allowed to sit the eggs for about ten days before once again, the hens are removed. During this period the cocks can be trained lightly. The cocks will sit the eggs for a couple of days only but when they leave them, the eggs should be removed and the nestbowls cleaned and overturned where it can be used as a form of perch by the cock. The cocks will probably sulk for a few days and are best left quiet but then training can commence.

Only light training is required because the cocks will fly and exercise so well around their loft when liberated. The sight of a really fit team of widowhood cocks is a wondrous one as they tell all about their good fitness and condition by their very appearance and flying. The cocks will exercise independently of each other displaying exuberance and sheer fitness.

Hopefully the time of the second pairing, the laying and the sitting will bring the cocks into form just when this is required. The fancier will know his racing programme and when he wants to start his racing seriously. Just prior to the birds being basketed for the race, the nestbowl is placed the right way up and the hen is shown to the cock briefly to convey the message to him that when he returns from the race, she will be there waiting for him.

That, in the briefest of terms is the widowhood system. It is a simple system once the fancier has taken to it and has managed to get the facilities right to support it. Fewer birds are required under the method but the drawbacks are plain to see. The hens are not raced so that much talent within the loft is lost and of course thought will have to be applied to keeping the hens happy and in condition during their periods of absence from their mates. Some are confined to little pens or boxes but the best method seems to have an aviary for them so that they can live as happily and naturally as possible. They should be prevented from pairing together and restrictions on the amount of food will normally remedy this.

However, the widowhood system has revolutionised pigeon racing as properly practised, it is indeed the best and fastest method of racing pigeons at present known. However, knowing racing fanciers and their ingenuity, it is highly likely that something even better will emerge in due course.

Roundabout system

This is slightly more complicated but has the considerable advantage of having both cocks and hens racing on a semi-widowhood manner. The basic requirement is to have two identical compartments, each containing the same number of nest boxes and other fittings so that each closely resembles the other.

One compartment is the main one and is used for pairing the birds and for the rearing of a round of youngsters. Indeed, the start of the campaign is almost identical to the commencement of the widowhood season. The date of pairing is flexible though later than the widowhood pairings, as many fanciers like to have their pairs together for the opening race or two. The first round is reared as usual and when down on their second round of eggs, the hens are removed from the cocks and placed in their identical boxes in the second (identical) compartment. They will be kept confined in their boxes and fed and watered in there, preventing them from pairing to each other. Once they have left the eggs, the cocks can also be kept in their boxes.

The system then is one of system and habit. The hens are allowed out for exercise first and while out, their section and boxes are cleaned. The cocks can then be driven into the second compartments and will enter their identical boxes. The hens are then allowed into compartment one, and will enter their own boxes, trapping easily thinking that their mates will be waiting for them. The cocks are then liberated from compartment two and while out; their hens are transferred into that compartment. After their exercise period, the cocks are allowed back into their own compartment.

In basic terms, both sexes are allowed out from the loft via the compartment number two, but gain access only through the main breeding compartment number one. On race basketing days, the system is very much like widowhood in that the cocks are provided with their bowls prior to the hens being allowed back in with them for a few minutes prior to being placed into the shipping crate. This is a fairly labour-intensive period and cannot be done in a hurry. Both cocks and hens can be shipped to the same race and should return fast as widowers, expecting to find their mates awaiting them in the nest boxes.

Once established this is an excellent system allowing full use of both cocks and hens for racing. There is slightly more work involved in the transferring of birds from compartment one to compartment two but when up and running the birds keep themselves in excellent form. Also, properly worked and the sexes kept separate there is little problem of hens laying eggs right throughout the racing season.

Celibacy

This is probably the easiest of all racing systems. It is practised throughout the world, especially in the Southern Hemisphere, yet is often described as something else. It is the racing of both cocks and hens from different compartments when they are kept in such a manner as to be unable to see each other or to be able to communicate in any way. The basic requirement is two self-contained compartments to which the inmates race.

It is claimed that the birds on this system maintain form for much longer periods and do not experience the stresses of the natural, widowhood and roundabout systems. The moult commences later and the result is that the birds carry better racing feathering throughout the racing season, yet moult out fully by the end of the year.

There are three ways of using the system. One is to pair the birds and to allow them to rear a round of youngsters in the normal manner. Three or four weeks before the first race, they are separated and do not see each other again through the race series. The cocks fly to their nest boxes and the hens to their perches. The second method is not to mate the birds at all and to keep them separated throughout the season. It is suggested that having no stresses caused by the rearing of youngsters, the birds can perform even better and for longer periods of sustained effort. Thirdly, a compromise between the two systems outlined above is practised, in that the birds are paired but allowed to sit their eggs only for ten to fourteen days before being separated and raced in the celibate manner. Exponents of this way claim that the mere sitting enhances condition and can be used halfway through the racing season to promote another wave of racing condition.

This is an extremely simple and straightforward system of racing and is well suited to the newcomer to the sport as a means of gaining understanding of the needs of the birds and of obtaining practical racing experience.

Young Bird Racing

I have included young bird racing under the list of systems although the actual racing of young birds is not a system or method. However, some of the systems mentioned can be and are used to promote better young bird racing which is becoming more and more sophisticated. At one time the racing of young birds seemed to be done more for enjoyment and for providing the birds with experience, than as a serious form of competition. Then the rewards started to become more attractive and the top fanciers started to apply deeper thought and effort to getting the best out of their young birds.

For the serious fancier, there is a great deal which can be done to promote better performances from the youngsters. In the main to enable this, the young birds have to be bred earlier to hatch in early January with pairing commencing in December. This also helps the widowhood flier in that it provides the widowhood pairs with a longer period of rest between rearing the young and the commencement of racing.

The early youngsters can then be prepared in a number of ways. In chapter 4 I mentioned the uses of light and darkness to promote or delay the progress of the moult and this is now an acknowledged way of enhancing performances. By keeping the early-bred young birds in additional light, they will complete their moult in time for their racing programme. In the case of birds kept on the darkness system, their body moult is completed quite quickly at the expense of the primary flights. Therefore at the end of the racing season in time for the main classic races, they are in a good bodily state and available to race.

Young birds not treated in these manners are fully into their moult just when the maximum performance is required. Some fanciers send young birds to races in a deplorable state of body feather and would most certainly not dream of sending an old bird to a top race in such a state. To get the best out of the young birds, the darkness or light systems can be or should be coupled with other systems. These would include racing them paired so that they are sitting eggs or rearing young birds, having them on the widowhood system or using a system of celibacy coupled with jealousy. Young bird racing is developing all the time as the clever fanciers invent or try methods and systems to further get the best performances out of birds in their first racing year.

And for the Busy Person

I hope that the brief descriptions of the various racing systems will assist anyone looking for a method suitable to themselves for the racing of pigeons. Of course in such a few words it is impossible to do justice to the systems mentioned so my advice is therefore to read as much about them as possible. There are books in the libraries and of course the weekly and monthly pigeon magazines carry a great wealth of knowledge. The real experts are the ones with the ideal background to fill in the detail for the newcomer to the sport or to the fancier seeking a change of direction.

As someone who has raced in varying ways owing to the changing demands of career and of family life, I have at least tried all of the systems mentioned, while at the same time maintaining my team of show pigeons. All have much to commend them and can provide ample rewards in racing success as well as in sheer enjoyment. My racing methods have had to adjust to the time I have available and my advice to anyone would be to do this because after all, the main career comes high up in terms of priority as do family considerations. Too many fanciers spend large sums on their lofts and birds while keeping their family short of cash and of their time and attention.

So, I can now describe how I race my pigeons and some of my philosophy in arriving at my present system. My racing team is a small one, designed to fit into a three section loft some fifteen feet (460cm.) by eight feet (245cm.) including a corridor running along the front. The loft was designed and constructed to these dimensions because of the space I had available at the top of my garden behind my garage space. I have nest boxes in two of the sections while the third contains only perches and is used for the young bird racing. Trapping is by stall trapping, a system I like very much and I can honestly say that I have found no better way.

Both racing sections are designed for widowhood racing and contain nine and eight nest boxes respectively. One section houses the most experienced cocks while the other is used mainly for the yearling team. I do not enjoy sprint racing, preferring the middle to long distance races at classic and national level. As my team is a small one numerically I have to be quite selective in my entries and consequently I rarely enter many birds for races - normally two to five in number. I genuinely try to manage the team, taking them from the young bird racing, through the yearling stage into the two year and above phase when I believe them to be at their best. Some ideas I have on this are as follows:

- Every bird introduced into the loft is an investment in time. It will take some years before its value is fully appreciated.

- Extra care is taken of yearlings. Most stray birds are at the yearling stage and I firmly believe that the yearling suffers far more in the colder early-season winds and weather than the older, more experienced racers. I therefore refuse to send yearlings until the weather is warmer and even then I race them quite lightly.

- Long distance strain pigeons need to be treated with far more patience than the sprinters. Therefore as young birds they are raced but not excessively and as yearlings they are used sparingly. After that they have to work for their perches.

- Young birds are raced and trained well although cocks tend to be stopped when they have shown signs of promise so as to provide some yearling strength. Good hens are raced hard to provide proof of their potential for breeding purposes and the best are then paired to the yearlings.

- New introductions are accepted for their potential as racers and breeders rather than on pedigree or strain description.

- Stock birds are carried when known as breeders of successful birds.

- Observation is necessary at all times. Any bird which seems at all restricted in its flying is rested. It is amazing how many take knocks or minor injuries while in flight and are then ruined by sending them to races while unfit.

Although I race on the widowhood system I do not pair as early as many. I do not try to race the entire racing programme, preferring to be selective in my choice of races. I prefer to start a little later, avoiding the cold winds and to prepare my birds for the middle distance classic races. My birds are paired, often using pairings from previous years in the belief that such pairings perform better. Both compartments are paired at the same time. The yearlings are provided with the best of the yearling hens from the previous year's young bird racing. I usually breed my young bird team from the widowhood pairings, taking a youngster from each pair only.

Once the birds have been separated while on their second round of eggs, the hens are placed in another loft while the cocks are allowed to fly as freely as possible - at least as freely as the raptors will allow.

I re-pair the birds about three weeks before I intend to commence racing the cocks. After they have been sitting for about seven to ten days the hens are removed so that training can commence. Training consists of a few fairly short tosses designed to get the cocks back into the ways of being basketed and racing back to their loft.

The early races are used to provide the stamina necessary for the longer races. However the yearlings are treated quite carefully. They are raced for about three races before being stopped so that they are available for their two-year stage. When they have been retired for the season, I then commence to train and race their hens - the best of the hens from the previous year. They are raced on the natural system with the hens sitting eggs and sent when in that condition. In rare cases I race hens to a single young bird in the nest. The advantage of this is that the yearling cocks are experienced enough to be suitable for following years while use is made of the best of the hens to further judge their potential as breeders of the future.

In this way I usually have anything from three to six yearlings put by for the following year. I believe that far too many yearlings are ruined in their first year of adulthood by firstly being raced too early in the season, and then latterly by giving them far too much racing. I appreciate that yearlings put up some terrific performances and I stand to lose some of these by my system of management but I will not destroy their willpower by thoughtless over-use. These comments would especially apply when the yearlings are later-bred birds from the previous year or are birds which have been only lightly raced. Too many of these are ruined by thoughtless fanciers who race them as though they are more experienced birds, so losing them or ruining them in the process.

As for young bird racing, I do not enjoy the experience very much. I treat it more as a necessity than as an enjoyable side of the sport. The situation with raptor predation is becoming worse and worse making our birds run the gauntlet of attack every time they are in the air. When a kit of old birds is attacked it is serious enough as they have the experience to get home after being scattered. However the young inexperienced birds scatter in all directions when attacked and in many cases are so scared by the incident that they are lost for good.

146

For my young birds I train them from their first liberation just up the road, up to distances of about twenty miles (30km) and race them according to weather conditions. I apply the darkness system as I find that it provides me with a team of moulted pigeons for the main races and as I have found no problems with its use. I tend to race the young hens more than the cocks to provide them with the chance to show their value, while the cocks are given experience of training and racing them kept back for their yearling stage. I do not have the facilities to use the youngsters paired up or on the widowhood system so they are simply raced to their perches. Despite claiming not to enjoy young bird racing I work at it quite seriously to ensure that the birds are given every possible chance of being properly equipped to race. Unless they have been properly trained they are not sent to races. I must say also that the young birds return to their loft with a certain exuberance which makes all the effort worth while.

The young bird darkness system is used only in the one compartment I have for the young birds. I prefer the use of dark blinds or curtains of the reed/plastic reed type as they allow the air to circulate. **Absolute** darkness is not needed for the period required, in my case from 1700hrs to 0900hrs the following morning, merely that it is dark enough to keep the birds quiet. If it is not sufficiently dark it may not prevent the wing moult in all birds.If shuttering is used to induce the darkness, then I would urge the use of fans to keep the air circulating otherwise respiratory problems could occur. It is not a difficult thing to manage, merely to have a certain regularity to apply and remove the darkness at the given hours.

Health and Fitness

Only the fittest, healthiest and best birds win. It goes without saying that every racing fancier needs to try to ensure that his birds enjoy the best of health throughout the year and especially during the racing season. I am not a subscriber to the philosophy that one should treat the birds routinely for worms, canker and coccidiosis. However, I am a believer that birds should be tested routinely for any problems revealed to be treated. The services of a good veterinary will ensure this as will access to a testing laboratory. The fancier himself can do much by avoiding excessive stress for his birds and by administering a good diet, as well as ensuring a supply of green foods and of garlic in the water at least once a week.

147

So, why not have a go?

That, really is it. I concentrate on a few races a year with all other club racing used as a means of preparation for them. Of course as the races entered are mainly classic and national races, the competition is always of the highest quality and it is easy to finish a season with little or nothing to show for it - except certainty that the best has been done for the birds and their chances. Geographically I am very dependent upon suitable winds and have little or no advantage from the main drag of the birds. Yet, despite all, the enjoyment is intense and the spectacle of a pigeon arriving back home from a classic race is one of the great rewards in pigeon racing.

I trust that I have shown that even the busy person can enjoy pigeon racing providing that he or she adjusts any systems to meet the demands of work and the needs of the family. It is not necessary to change a way of life in order to enjoy the birds; their performances and the contacts made with other fanciers. The hobby/sport is a most rewarding one and well worth the effort involved in producing a racing team to fit in with the other domestic arrangement.

Chapter 18

Showing Racing Pigeons

WHEN the racing is over for another year, the average racing fancier is faced with a long period of little action within the loft. The birds will quickly fall into a full moult and will have to be properly managed to enable the stock to be fit and well by the end of the year. The breeding season will then come round by way of preparation for yet another racing season. But in between the racing season and the breeding season there is the 'close' season, the quiet time, the time for reflection and planning. To fill this period and to remain involved with the sport, many fanciers are turning to a few winter shows to add to their pigeon enjoyment and social contacts. This can be either at a strictly local level of club shows, or by taking on the added incentive of showing at open and classic events.

Some racing enthusiasts have made the showing of their racers almost an art form and win prizes galore at top shows. Along the way, apart from the sheer pleasure at winning, they are enjoying the added advantages of social enjoyment and in meeting fanciers from all walks of life. This article is intended to cater for any racing man who wishes to have a go at the shows, to make suggestions on how chances of success can be enhanced by some basic rules and groundwork.

My first advice would be to be unafraid to have a go at any level, because at most shows catering for racing pigeons, the birds are judged by successful racing men who are looking for racers only in the genuine mileage classes. So, as far as can be determined, there is a level playing field for every entry and I believe this to be particularly true in Scotland. Therefore, the chances of winning say at the most famous show of all, the Old Comrades, will be virtually the same as taking honours at local events. I appreciate that the usual advice is to start at the bottom and work the way to the top, but when showing racers, I genuinely feel that the chances are as good nationally as they are at local level.

That is not to say that some of the racing showmen of the day do not win out of turn. This is because they have the ability to recognise the type of pigeon that most judges will accept. However in most racing lofts there are birds which are good enough by way of looks and type to take on anything else. So the advice is to have a go. By all means start off at the local club shows but do not stop there, think of having a go elsewhere. Don't let lack of success at local level deter thoughts of taking on the 'big boys' for they are all there to be beaten, and knowing the circuit, they will accept and appreciate being beaten by a better bird on the day.

What type of racer is required?

This is the most often asked question, for it is the start of it all. I wish that I could describe that in a few well chosen sentences but it is simply not possible. There are however, factors which most racing fanciers, and thereby racing judges - will accept. Those of us who enjoy showing, and especially the few dual-purpose fanciers who do battle at both sides of the sport, would dearly love to have a family of pigeons which not only perform and race well, but then can be role-changed to win in the show pen. We have seen a few succeed with strains such as the Delbars, the Dordins, the Jo Nipius/Jan Aardens and the Kirkpatricks. Whilst there are still some examples of lofts containing numbers of such types, in the main strains have changed particularly towards Continental strains where performance is more important than appearance. And let's face it, on race days the best looking racer is the first one across the garden and through the doors!

There was a time when those lovely blue and mealy Dordins, some with white flights, could catch any eye at the shows. It was suggested that the late Pierre Dordin had introduced show strains to improve the looks of his family of birds. I don't know the truth of that, but certainly the Delbars and the Dordins were beautiful pigeons and seemed to carry that extra beauty. Along came the chequers and chequer pieds of the Ko Nipius/Jan Aarden families and most fanciers will admit a regard for good lookers. As to the Kirkpatricks, they seem to have done it mainly on handling properties though some of the reds and red pieds are so very attractive in appearance. The first time I ever saw the beautiful grizzles of the Berlangee Delbars, I was transfixed.

Identification of type. Type is the short word which has a multitude of meanings and showmen use it to cover a number of facts which make a show racer acceptable and likely to win. It might cover factors such as handling including balance, general appearance, colour, feather quality, head and eye and stance in the pen; so let us look at these in turn.

Handling and balance. For racing pigeons in racing pigeon shows judged by good racing fanciers, I believe that this is the most important matter. I have always believed that most decisions made by a Judge are made in that split second between a bird being taken from the pen and before it is held up for visual examination. Therefore, a cracking looker, which is short in keel, wide in front, too fat or too thin, will be marked down because the balance is not acceptable. The place to start therefore is in the loft by handling each bird in turn and trying to determine in a detached manner, those which 'come to hand' best. Indeed, the best time to do this is to go into the loft in the dark and handle the birds for balance, marking each out of ten and noting those which seem to have the qualities of good handling and good balance. You will be disregarding those which are too deep, too short, too shallow, too small, too large, coarse feathered and those with obvious physical defects - e.g. damaged keel. The start has been made however, for at least you will have produced some starters for your line-up to take to the shows. The numbers may be small, but this matters little, for it is far easier to work with and handle a small team than to swamp the event with numbers.

Appearance. The next step is to take a look at the candidates so far found to make sure that they also look the part. Good looks count for much in the show pen and even the most ardent racing judge will take to a bird which looks good. After all, his skills as a judge will be assessed on the looks of the bird he selects. What is beauty after all, but something which possesses properties admired by the majority. It does not mean a stunning red chequer, or a yellow or a dark chequer white flight, but can mean a normal coloured bird with a rich, strong eye colour and an intelligent expression. One of the best and most successful racers I saw at the shows during a recent season was a hen of ordinary looks which possessed a lovely rich dark eye, which set off the intelligence she seemed to exude from a most attractive head and face. To catch the eye of the judge is a fair way to success. Just look at any sale, and the chances are that the best prices will be paid for the best looking pigeons

Feather. The quality of the feathering will count for a great deal. The smooth, silky feathering is sought and will add much to the bird with the balance and the overall looks. It will also need to be major blemish free. By this I mean that there are no missing or broken flights secondaries or tail feathers, no gaps or bald patches and nothing too much out of the ordinary. The most important feature however is the texture overall, because like in the handling operation, the judge will mentally assess feather quality at the first touch.

Head and eye. I have already partly covered this aspect. The eye should complement the head. Eye colour is not always the most relevant feature because birds with pearl coloured eyes can win in the show pen as can birds with the light coloured eyes associated with certain families, especially the Jannsens. The overall impression should be of intelligence on the part of the pigeon, a head which suits the body and an eye which complements the head.

Stance. I have listed this last because it is found out only when a racer is placed in a show pen. It needs to stand well, so that its other points are shown to best advantage. Some pen training is desirable to get the bird used to being penned and not unduly frightened by the occasion. Make no mistake about it, a fair amount of stress is involved in taking a racer from its normal environment and placing it in a pen in a warm and smoky room to be viewed by many people. Many racing men will have no access to pens prior to a show, but a lot can be learned about the stance of a bird by using a nest box instead, or even getting it to stand in or on a perch. Wild pigeons never show well so try to ensure before entering them that they are calm types and not likely to provide any judge with a headache when he comes to the handling.

The above guidelines all pertain to the pre-entry, pre-show period. It is best to apply time to the preparation like this so as to select candidates which can stand a chance at the shows. The work can be done alone, standing by ones own assessment of the birds, or by inviting a racing or show colleague along to cast an eye over the birds. Two heads are better than one in this respect, but whether solo or aided, the work to select a likely team can be described as the most important part in producing a show team. Let us now look at the show preparation work.

Condition and Cleanliness

These are the two most important matters necessary for success of your chosen candidates. The best looking pigeon in poor condition cannot win so now is the time for the skills of the fancier to come into play to produce the good condition - and of course cleanliness. These cannot be produced overnight and the message is a simple one that good management and care throughout the year is the easiest way to success.

Good food, clean water, grit and minerals in regular supplies are the way to this. They will not necessarily produce the sparkling condition which might need some other inducements to be brought out. Even the best food and water will not condition a bird suffering from worms, coccidiosis or canker. Most birds will be carrying some, if not all of these maladies so thought must be given to treating or supplying the means for the body of the pigeon to suppress them. It is little different to finding form for the race team. It needs to be borne in mind.

However, when there is good, consistent management, the chances are much greater that good condition will be present. There might be a need to tone up the body, by use of pigeon tea, breaking them down slightly through a reduction in food quantity or by feeding a cleansing mixture before bringing them up to sparkle in time for the show. As I said above, it is so similar to establishing race condition except that for shows there is need for a little extra weight. Lack of surplus body weight in racing is desirable, but for the showing, enough weight to aid the proper balance is something which must be present. Some judges will like the birds to be fairly lean but in my experience that bit of body does help the overall balance of a good pigeon.

As to cleanliness, it is a fairly simple matter but must be addressed in two ways. Firstly, birds must be free from body parasites. It is no use whatsoever spraying for this just prior to the show, as it should be done a few days before. When done close to the show, there is the likelihood that dead insect life will still be seen in the feathering.

Birds must be bathed a few days before the show to enable all dirt to be removed from the feathers. I will deal with the immediate pre-show checks a little later, but there is nothing to beat a good bath for birds to clean themselves and to be provided with an invigorating session in water.

Judging Considerations

It is a good idea to discuss how judges perform their task as a means of making decisions to stand the best chance under them. Exhibitors may be lucky enough to know what a particular judge looks for, whether he favours a particular type or colour, or size. However, generally this sort of knowledge is not freely available so the exhibitor will have to try to anticipate the fads and fancies of the judge. Some of the issues judges will have differing views include the following:

■ **The Moult.** I have always believed that birds which have raced and worked hard will be delayed in the moult. Any racing judge worth his salt should make allowances for the moult and while non-working show racers might be expected to be clear of the moult, the working racer should have an allowance made for it.

- **Frets.** Birds which have worked hard at racing might be expected to carry badges of their courage in the form of frets. Racing men as judges who look for fret marks to discard show candidates are not doing themselves or the sport of pigeon racing any favours. I believe that small frets should have allowances made and the experienced judge will always do so.

- **Cleanliness.** Birds presented in the show pen should be clean including feathering, beaks and feet. Basic checks will safeguard against this but dirt on feathers will render a bird likely to be left out of the cards. The same can be said of body parasites which should be absent and any judge is entitled to disqualify a bird carrying them.

- **Wildness.** This is less easy to overcome on the part of the exhibitor unless he has the time to engage in some pen training for his birds. Of course birds which are quiet and tame in the loft will be likely to be tame in the pens. Judges do not like having wild birds in front of them and will generally favour a more docile pigeon which is quite willing to be handled without fuss or panic.

- **Condition, type and balance.** It goes without saying that these factors are necessary for a bird to succeed in the show pen. They are self-explanatory and need little further description except that it is good to know whether a judge favours birds thin at racing weight or whether he prefer them carrying a little body. There must be balance in that the bird should settle into the hand and not be either too heavy in front or carrying too much length behind. The weight must be suitable for the size of the bird so that the overall impression is one of glowing health and of a bird suitable for the show pen and for the judge's attention. If any racing fancier is in doubt about which birds are balanced, he should handle his birds at night in total darkness so as to reduce the chances of being influenced by colour or other considerations. A session of just handling the birds with no other persuasions is extremely revealing and an excellent exercise in getting to know the team better.

Show Preparation

The chances of a good racing pigeon in a show will be greatly enhanced by proper and careful work by way of show preparation. This work will not produce a swan from an 'ugly duckling' but it will enable a pigeon to stand a better chance of showing success. One thing to remember is that a pigeon which is supremely fit will require little assistance, for somehow the fitness seems to charm away any stains or other deficiencies.

A minute or so spent in checking for small defects and hopefully remedying them will be time well spent. The basic equipment which should be available is as follows:

- kettle of hot water for steam

- soapy warm water and a small brush

- towel

- source of heat e.g. hair drier

- sharp scissors

- insecticide

In case this makes it all seem complicated, it is not necessarily so. All items will not be required, indeed, with luck hardly any will be used. As a showman, I tend to look at things with a 'belt and braces' attitude, knowing that on average, some birds will require a fair amount of cleaning and it is better to be prepared for it.

The first check is for cleanliness. Check that all feathers are clean and free from any staining and that they are free from insect life. It is important to spray the birds for this problem a few days before the show for even dead 'tics or lice' continue to cling to feathers and thereby be visible. Most stains can be removed with a dampened cloth, using light stroking motions the way of the feather. Be very careful not to press too hard as tail feathers are very easily removed. The chief source of problem is the end of the tail feathers in cocks where they brush as a way of showing off. Stubborn stains may need to be washed out but if this process is used there must be a thorough rinsing prior to drying, otherwise a drying stain will be left. A towel must be available to keep the hands dry, again to prevent cover feathers being inadvertently removed and it is even better to use talcum powder to ensure smooth handling. Small stains can be removed by the use of a liquid spirit based cleaning agent and often cigarette lighter fuel will serve the same purpose when applied with cotton wool.

Any feathers which are bent will need to be straightened using steam from the kettle. Flights and tail feathers are the most likely to require steaming. Some feathers may carry damage to outside edges and a careful use of sharp scissors can remove most of the damaged area without changing the outline or nature of the feather concerned. Neck feathers may also be standing out and these can be put back into place by carefully pulling them so that they twist back into their normal position. It is better not to pull such cover feathers out because they will regrow with quill which can be felt or seen.

The obvious check is to ensure that there are ten flights and twelve tail feathers as the most visible source of fault. The same applies to secondary flights because missing feathers will leave gaps which can be faulted by a judge. Smaller checks are also advisable. Make sure that the beak is clean and has no extra growth to make it 'hook-like'. A file or emery board may be needed to smooth or shape the beak. Check that the wattle carries no damage such as peck marks as the result of fights in the loft. White or French chalk will hide most such minor blemishes.

Some of the checks will also be necessary at the show prior to placing the bird into the pen. During transportation there is often some staining especially the tail feathers, so some observation at this stage will be helpful. Many showmen will be seen with a tin of lighter fluid to cope with such minor stains.

It is all basic and quite simple but all such checks will repay the exhibitor by enhanced chances in the show. However, having used the pre-show period to prepare the birds, it is pointless unless the birds are carried to the show using suitable divided baskets of containers. The use of race baskets should be discouraged as they allow fighting by the birds and cause superficial damage.

* * * * *

My final piece of advice is a very simple one. It is to enjoy the show and enjoy the showing. It is a matter of pride to produce for the show pen an example of the birds to be found in your loft, a matter of being proud of your pigeons. The two sides of the sport are very different though both are enjoyable and offer satisfaction to the keen pigeon fancier. It is a great pleasure to win with ones own pigeons, whether at racing or at showing. The latter is available to all and the little effort involved can be made very worthwhile, not only from winning prizes but from the social side which goes with shows and showing.

Therefore, the showing of genuine, hard working racing pigeons can be a very rewarding sideline to the overall sport of pigeon racing. Do not be fearful of it, but be prepared to have a go. It is rather like racing at top levels of competition - you can't win if you don't enter!.

Chapter 19

Evaluation of Racing Pigeons by Eyesign

(The Brian Vickers system)

IF ever there is a subject in pigeon racing circles which will provoke discussion and controversy, it is that of judging birds by their eye-sign for racing and breeding capability. It is a subject which is followed and believed by many, but totally disregarded by others. There would seem to be little common ground in the study of eye-sign, either it is accepted and believed or else it is something treated with disdain.

For many years as a racing enthusiast I was a doubter until one day I met Brian Vickers. I had purchased a copy of his book on the subject and found it to be entirely readable and understandable. (Reference to Eyesign Evaluation in Racing Pigeons by Brian Vickers). I discussed the contents with Brian and consequently he called at my lofts to examine the eyes of my racers. I was extremely impressed with this at the time and even more so in the fullness of time when his assessments of my little racing team proved to be absolutely correct. I also took him to my pigeon club and invited members to bring a few birds for his examination and assessment.

Nearly all those who submitted their birds were sceptics at the beginning of the session but by the conclusion were anxious to learn more having been convinced of the accuracy of the assessments given. These were not only of the pigeons I may add, but also in some cases of the methods of their owners. I also saw Brian examine the eyes of some pigeons from a top loft and positively identified one bird with top marking and assessed the bird as being capable of founding a dynasty of winners. The bird had already done that having made that fancier a most respected and successful racing enthusiast.

I was privileged not only to watch this expert at work but also to be shown in some detail his methods of evaluation. He has kindly allowed me to reproduce some of his thoughts in this chapter. I have read many articles and books on eye-sign and its value but I can honestly say that I have never seen it stated so lucidly than in the work by Brian Vickers. Eye-sign experts have all had their theories, many of which were concerned with the colour of the eye and the number of circles which could be seen and identified. The Vickers method ignores the colour and once this was out of the way, the rest seemed to fall in place making the assessments simpler, basing them on five aspects only.

Equipment required for assessments

There are two basic requirements in order to be able to assess the eyes of racing pigeons:

- An eyeglass similar to those used by jewellers with a 10x magnification. It follows that some practice will be necessary to be able to use the glass while handling the bird.

- A light source. The best is strong natural sunlight but artificial light is quite satisfactory especially when directed towards the eye.

Method of marking the value of the eyes

Racing Ability		Breeding Ability	
Top Racer	9.50	Top Breeder	9.50
Federation winning Family	9.35	Breeder of Federation winners	9.35
Good Racers	9.25	Good Breeder	9.25
Inconsistent racer	9.15	Inconsistent	9.15
Doubtful ability	9.05	Doubtful ability	9.05
Unsatisfactory	9.00	Unsatisfactory	9.00

Birds can be assessed with a mixture of marks such as 9.25 for racing and 9.15 for racing, which means that it has the ability to race well, but should not be used as a breeder. It follows that in many cases where fanciers breed their best racer to best racer, consistency can suffer because the breeding ability can suffer. It is asserted that the value of eye-sign is sex linked, with the sire passing it down to daughters and hens down to their sons. Brian states that his ideal breeding pattern would be to pair a champion sire to his daughter, taking a son from this pairing and outcrossing him to a top marked hen; with a daughter from this pairing paired back to the champion grandsire.

Brian Vickers is certain that the great advantage of mastering the assessment system is in being able to asses imports for breeding potential instead of purchasing pigeons merely because of the pedigree they possess. It should also enable fanciers to be able to cut down on numbers, to reduce losses by identifying potentially good racers. The eye should be taken as a measure of the brain to improve on their homing ability. The better the eye the better the ability.

The Five Checks of Eye-sign

- Iris
- Pupil
- Circle of Correlation
- Distance Lines
- Speed Lines

The Iris

The main criteria of measuring the quality is the Iris. The iris should be consistently chunky in appearance with no breaks or patches because these will render the bird as unreliable. It is important not to confuse a change of colour near the circle of correlation with patchiness. A patchy iris is one with raised patches of cloud-like formations with flat areas between them instead of a consistent thickening of the iris cover. Birds with good breeding eyes should be paired to others with good breeding eyes so that the odds of breeding quality is considerably improved.

The biggest temptation is to look for too much in an eye. To look for distance, dust, star clusters, serration around the circle and other fanciful ideas is a mistake, so the concentration should be on the iris which contains ninety per cent of the ability factor. Colour counts for nothing so it is safe to ignore violets, racing greens, yellows, pearls or other colour ideas, also to avoid thinking about the laying sign or the standing sign.

The eye-sign evaluation is made up of the actual physical appearance of the iris. The circle of correlation is important yet a minor matter when taken with the importance of the iris. The main qualification for quality birds is that the iris is complete and unbroken from the outside edge through to the circle of correlation. This is the start of racing ability and as the iris builds in density, so the racing ability increases. The more chunky and unbroken the iris, the better is the racing ability.

The breeding ability is seen in breeding lines running through the iris. The better they stand out in definition, the better the breeding ability of the birds. The best of the breeding lines contained in a genuinely chunk and unbroken iris will make a bird top quality at both racing and breeding. They are rare.

The Pupil

The pupil should be as near round as possible and the smaller it is the better.

The Circle of Correlation incorporating speed and distance lines

The circle of correlation is a smaller consideration in the evaluation of eye-sign although more important in a potential breeder. Its importance is in the fact that it houses the speed and distance lines. The distance lines go around the circle of correlation while the speed lines go across it. The more defined these lines are, the better.

In the best pigeons the circle seems to drop down to a lower level from the edge of the iris. The line drawings show this and it is quite noticeable in the eyes when more experience if gained of reading them. The width of the circle is not critical as has been believed in

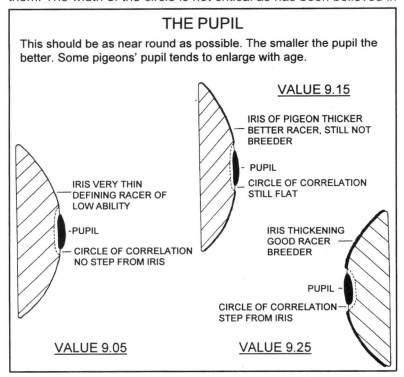

THE PUPIL

This should be as near round as possible. The smaller the pupil the better. Some pigeons' pupil tends to enlarge with age.

VALUE 9.15

IRIS OF PIGEON THICKER
— BETTER RACER, STILL NOT BREEDER

- PUPIL

CIRCLE OF CORRELATION STILL FLAT

IRIS VERY THIN
— DEFINING RACER OF LOW ABILITY

-PUPIL

— CIRCLE OF CORRELATION NO STEP FROM IRIS

IRIS THICKENING GOOD RACER — BREEDER

PUPIL -

CIRCLE OF CORRELATION — STEP FROM IRIS

VALUE 9.05

VALUE 9.25

the past, the main consideration being that the speed and distance lines can be read. When the circle narrows it is necessary to pair the bird to one with a wider circle. A better-defined circle of correlation is a good pointer towards breeding ability.

It will be seen therefore that the Brian Vickers system is an uncomplicated one with the main emphasis being placed upon the quality of the iris. It removed all the complicated nature of eyesign as described by the earlier writers on the subject who seemed to want to make it almost an 'art form'. Brian Vickers on the other hand uses a simpler approach and brings it all down to a basic one capable of being understood by the majority.

There is one other consideration which cannot be adequately described by drawings or descriptions, and that is that of the eye carried by birds which are too in-bred. When a bird gets too inbred, its iris seems to flatten and to lose character. A good outcross to a bird with a high marked eye is required to remedy the situation and this needs to be done as early as possible as if the inbreeding gets too marked it is very difficult to deal with.

The reading of eye-sign is an enjoyable sideline to pigeon racing and when this system is mastered it can save a great deal of effort,

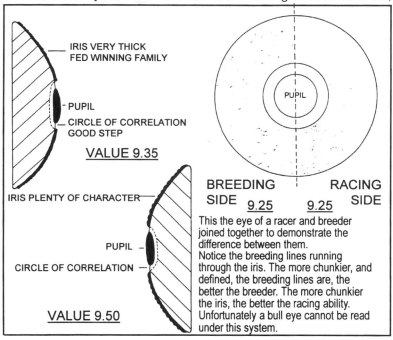

IRIS VERY THICK
FED WINNING FAMILY

PUPIL

CIRCLE OF CORRELATION
GOOD STEP

VALUE 9.35

PUPIL

BREEDING SIDE 9.25

RACING SIDE 9.25

IRIS PLENTY OF CHARACTER

PUPIL

CIRCLE OF CORRELATION

VALUE 9.50

This the eye of a racer and breeder joined together to demonstrate the difference between them.
Notice the breeding lines running through the iris. The more chunkier, and defined, the breeding lines are, the better the breeder. The more chunkier the iris, the better the racing ability. Unfortunately a bull eye cannot be read under this system.

time and expense in developing a sound and progressive team for racing. It enables a fancier to determine his breeders and to identify the birds with racing ability. Just as importantly it allows him to spot the duffers. The answer is in constant practice with the eyeglass and not to over-mark the birds. From the assessments, the breeding operation can be planned with much more and more rewarding certainty.

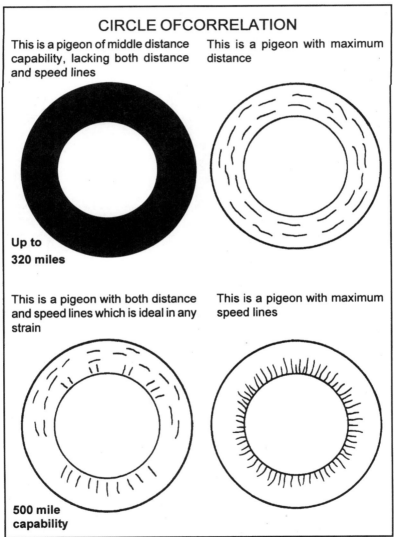

CIRCLE OF CORRELATION

This is a pigeon of middle distance capability, lacking both distance and speed lines

Up to 320 miles

This is a pigeon with maximum distance

This is a pigeon with both distance and speed lines which is ideal in any strain

500 mile capability

This is a pigeon with maximum speed lines

Chapter 20

Starting with Racers, Stocking the Racing Loft

YEARS ago, the methods of stocking a racing loft were comparatively simple as a study of old books will reveal. Sources of supply were to be found in the weekly or monthly magazines or in the year books, or from local lofts. However, in the last couple of decades a great change has occurred in most countries where pigeon racing is practised, and that is in the formation of professional breeding studs. The studs offer a great array of pigeons for racing and breeding in a manner which makes them a most attractive proposition. Once the fancier has decided on how he intends to race, he can obtain all his stock from a stud and can even tailor his purchases to the prices of the birds on offer. In most cases the fancier is able to visit the studs and to view possible strains and types before making purchases. An examination can be made of the claims and records of the birds at stock so that a judgement can be made about where to make a start within the racing fancy.

However, in yesteryear, there were hardly any professional studs although one or two fanciers offered themselves as a point of contact, offering good quality stock for racing or stock purposes. However, these were the exceptions and most stock changed hands on the basis of one fancier to another, or in auction sales or charity auctions. The numbers of strains were much fewer in number whereas today great emphasis is placed upon strain which seems to take precedence over almost everything else.

Before we can discuss some options on how to build a stud of successful and serious racing pigeons, certain decision have to be made by the fancier, decisions which will require considerable thought and research so as to avoid costly changes of direction later on. Decisions will have to be made about the type of racing to be adopted. For instance is the racing going to be aimed at the shorter, sprint races, say up to 250 miles, (400 km), or to the intermediate distances appeal, i.e. races between 200 and 450 miles, (350 to 700km}, or to aim for the extreme distance events. In short, the considerations may be listed as follows:

- Sprint racing

- Medium distances

- Extreme Distances i.e. over 450 miles (700 km).

- Whether to concentrate solely on club racing

- To club race but also to enter for Federation/Combine competition

- To join the Classic and National clubs and organisations

- To concentrate on Open races

- Whether to race for cash or simply for carded positions

- Whether to pool or bet on entries.

- The direction intended to race including whether to use inland or cross-water races

- Whether racing is to be done at weekends or in mid-week - or both.

- Whether to go it alone, or to seek friends to work together for training etc.

- The method of racing to be used i.e. widowhood, natural, roundabout

Much will be decided by one's locality. Pigeon racing varies considerably from one area to another, dependant upon the numbers of fanciers, clubs and organisations and the type of racing involved. In some areas very few will race in the Nationals, preferring to use available Federation or Combine competition, whereas in other parts, the Nationals and Classics play a dominant role while in some areas the majority of competition is at club level.

So, the locality will determine in most cases the type of racing to be undertaken, although the fancier may well wish to shape the intended programme to suit his or her way of life and the time available to him and the family. The fancier will however be talking to fellow fanciers to ascertain the local moods and 'politics', the movers and shakers in the area and where the best type of racing is to be found. This will decide where to seek membership of a club or other organisation and this alone will relay the type of racing, by having to endorse the existing aims of the organisation concerned.

164

The novice or newcomer should try to make his aims clear as early as possible particularly on the type of racing to be used, for the biggest mistake to be made is to attempt to do all types of racing with a young and inexperienced team of pigeons. This is a sure recipe for disaster. Hence, if long distance racing is to be the aim, then it must be accepted that a waiting game will have to be played, using birds with 'distance credentials' which are unlikely to perform well against proven 'sprint' families in short races.

Within pigeon racing circles there are distinct families aimed at particular functions. It is a 'horses for courses' situation where sprinters rarely win at the distance, and the distance pigeons are rarely fast enough over the short distances to beat the short distance specialists for speed. It is possible to keep some birds of several strains or type but this will require a large establishment and a great deal of work to try to cater for races from the first to the last in old bird racing. Young bird racing can be a little simpler but the above comments on types for certain races apply even to the racing of youngsters.

The best idea is to visit as many lofts as possible, many in the local area but also a few from other locations to take a few soundings on the methods employed by the successful and to form a personal opinion on why the unsuccessful are not. Time spent on this exercise will be time well spent as a form of research into pigeon racing and where one wants to be within the sport. It should be coupled with reading all about the sport in as many books and publications as possible.

Of course into this equation will enter the methods of racing also - whether to use the widowhood system, natural racing, roundabout or some other way as already discussed in Chapter 17.

Where to acquire racing stock

Within the sport today there is a great choice. Perusal of the weekly pigeon magazines will reveal numerous advertisements offering birds for stock and racing. Advertisements will appear in every edition throughout the year and as will be seen a little later, the time of year might well affect the manner of obtaining stock. For instance it is quite easy to purchase young birds for racing purposes in the early months of the year, but at other times of the calendar, birds on offer will be mainly for stock purposes because many will be too young to race in the year of their birth. Most of the popular strains will be on offer, presenting a feast of possibilities for the would-be purchaser.

The studs will also be present in the advertisement columns

offering the products of top quality and proven stock. Obviously not everything on offer from the best of parentage can be winning champions or top producers, but the chances are always there. Visits to the studs are very rewarding experiences and I recommend them to anyone starting out.

These two sources are supplemented by sales. The sales are mainly of two types, the early season sales are mainly for young birds for racing - often as buyer/breeder events, and later in the season when racing finishes, the main sale season commences offering a vast array of stock. Sales take on many forms and the buyer will have to beware of the skills of carefully worded advertisements which are designed to embellish the past and the potential of the birds on offer. There are reduction sales, birds shipped in for sale from other countries, and probably the best are the sales which are clearance sales following the demise of a fancier or of someone leaving the sport. Such sales are well worth visiting as good pigeon occasions and as a means of making an examination of the sport and of its members.

These are the many sources clearly available and obviously there are many more which can be established by enquiry. Fanciers in the immediate locality are generally willing to part with good birds and those in other areas can be approached for stock and for advice. In conclusion therefore, let us add to the information with some thoughts on the time-honoured ways of acquiring stock.

Young Birds

When I sat down to write this chapter my thoughts were directed to myself and how I would make a start back into the racing side of the sport should the need ever arise. I felt that this was the most practical approach I could make to the problem and so advise accordingly. Depending on the time of the year, the purchase of a team of young birds straight out of the nest would figure prominently. The advantages are obvious:

- Within days they can be settled to the new loft and have frequent flights around it

- There is no need to keep unbroken birds

- A limited young bird racing programme can be entered

- Those which come through the training/racing, can be used to breed from for the following seasons.

- The strain or type of bird can be considered in the purchase

The birds can be sourced in any number of ways. Some of the studs offer packages at set prices of birds for racing purposes and will also offer birds with pedigree details for a little more. Young birds can be purchased at sales or from advertisements and offer the fancier a ready-made team on which he can build a future. The advantages are plain to see in that the team can soon be flying out and providing their pleasure as they do so. The principle removes some of the impatience often associated with newcomers who want to see instant progress and the acquisition of a young bird team is one method.

There are downsides of course. The young birds are unproven and have no background of success so that all of their future is dependant on them and their racing ability - and perhaps more importantly on the ability of the fancier to be able to manage them properly and to get the best out of them. If they are sprinters then some evidence of this should be seen in their limited racing careers as young birds, though it must be stressed that the prudent fancier will not ruin them by giving too much work. If they are longer distance pigeons then they will need more care and patience for their young bird experience is but a part of the knowledge and muscle-power they will require in their later years.

I would also mention the acquisition of teams of late-bred racers. This is an art in itself for late-breds require a great deal of patience to guide them from juvenile form in the year of their birth into good racing birds either as yearlings or as two year olds and beyond. They can be a cheaper source of stock but they demand so much care and attention to take them into successful adulthood that I would always prefer to have earlier bred birds.

All in all the purchase of a team of racing youngsters is an attractive method of acquiring an instant racing team and it is one that I think I might employ should the need ever arise.

Old Birds

After the young bird season has finished, the most usual way into a racing team is by the purchase of a team of birds for stock purposes. In this way, birds can be purchased which most closely fit the aims and requirements of the fancier. In other words, if the birds bought have either raced and won well, or have been responsible for breeding winning pigeons for others, the advantages are plain to see.

More patience is required for taking on a team of older birds for things do not happen overnight. However, for those who prefer to breed their own youngsters then this is by far the best method, for with their newly acquired birds they can breed a team of youngsters which can be raced from the loft. Also, if the birds purchased cost a great deal of money - as they can - then effort will have to be directed to their security - and by this I mean that they are unable to escape by accident. The ideal is to have a stock area or compartment - ideally with an aviary - so that expensive purchases can be kept safely without fear of escape or accidental liberation with other birds. For the serious racing enthusiast, a stock section is a great asset for hopefully; from the breeders will emerge all the best of the racing candidates.

It is possible of course to purchase old birds to race but this is fraught with difficulty. Firstly they have to be settled and then liberated to their new abode. If they have raced elsewhere they are likely to want to return there, so the problems have to be anticipated. My experience is that I have rarely succeeded with 'broken' pigeons unless they have been brought in as young birds. I much prefer using either young birds which are homebred, or which have come at a young age and only been raced to my lofts.

Old birds can also be acquired from several sources including locally, from sales advertisements, from auction sales and of course from the breeding studs. They can be bought according to strain or type with many strains being almost descriptive of the sort of racing for which they are best equipped. However, I would sound a couple of warnings when viewing birds ready for purchase and eventual breeding:

- Do not become too bound by strain. The best pigeon is the one which is first back to the loft from a race, so the best idea is to identify the best and to breed from them. Indeed there are examples of strains which in some circumstances have become quite inbred and therefore might have lost some of their racing ability.

- The same thing applies to looks. As a show enthusiast I enjoy looking at good looking pigeons but of course in racing parlance, it is obvious that the best racers are most often not the best lookers. The best racers are the birds which possess vigour, vitality and a degree of character and this may mean that good looks come way down in their attractions. I would rather have a team of poor looking pigeons which perform and win well for me, than a team of good looking show types which are almost always among the also-rans. Having said that, all racing fanciers like to have something unusual in colour, or something good looking in their teams. This can be borne out by the fact that in an average auction sale, the good looking birds, especially those with striking colours such as the yellows, blacks, creams, silvers, opals will find the most buyers.

The biggest challenge in pigeon racing is to find pigeons, especially pairings that can produce good winning pigeons year after year. These will really become 'golden pairs' worth their weight in gold. Many lofts have such pigeons but few fanciers have the experience or ability to identify them for their true value

Eggs

This method of acquiring stock has almost disappeared as an option thanks to the success of the professional studs and their ability to offer such good stock at attractive prices. The authors of most of the older books recommended the purchasing of eggs as a means of getting top quality stock from top fanciers. It was probably true then and to some extent has merit today.

For the new fancier however it provides additional problems and uncertainty. For a start there will be a need to have feeders in place, i.e. pairs of pigeons acquired simply to rear the young birds of others -all ready to incubate the eggs and to rear the young birds. It demands a great deal of good timing to have the feeders ready to take on the eggs which have been brought in for the purpose. There is also the uncertainty as to the exact parentage of the eggs brought in. My guess is that few newcomers have the patience or experience for such a venture and the ability to purchase teams of good quality young birds is a more attractive proposition. However, it can be done and some of the breeders of the short-faced fancy breeds are great experts at it being able to match feeders to egg supplies.

Patience

There is one piece of advice that I would place above all others, and that is to have patience. The racing of pigeons is a craft, which has to be worked at. Short cuts can be taken by carefully obtaining as much information as possible by word of mouth and through the written words of experienced fanciers. However, there is only one real experience and that is in doing the work and experiencing both the hard work and the sheer elation of success. I have seen new fanciers gain sudden and speedy success but in general this turns out to be by sheer chance and rarely is it a continuous or sustained one for them.

Mistakes will be made and that is for certain. Any pigeon fancier will confirm that whatever their experience, so the newcomer will know that he faces hard work and will hope for good fortune along the way. Many mistakes can be avoided by heeding good advice when contemplating the start into pigeon racing and as stated above, research will pay dividends for those first important steps.

PART 4

Chapter 21

Fancy Pigeons

I F you feel that you have enough challenges in life, fancy pigeons are not for you! If however a fancier seeks a challenge involving a huge amount of commitment, study, work and involvement, then to establish a successful team of fancy pigeons is a most gratifying and rewarding hobby. Indeed for many it is more than a hobby - it is a way of life, an obsession, an all-absorbing love of the pigeon as a domestic companion. Pigeons have been kept and promoted for hundreds of years and for those who decide to keep a few, they are but continuing a tradition of centuries.

In all my time in the sport I have been privileged to know many fanciers who have kept and enjoyed keeping fancy pigeons. Some of the happiest have been those who have kept a few of a particular breed in a shed in the back yard, tending them with love and care, striving always for improvement, and from time to time exhibiting them at the shows. On the other hand there have been the specialists - those who operate in a much larger manner with lofts of pigeons of various breeds and applying great care to each charge and somehow managing to cope with those huge demands. Indeed the manner in which pigeons are kept and enjoyed varies as much as in any other sphere of sport or hobby. We all have our commitments, aims and strictures on time and have to operate within those constraints.

The obsession in those who race pigeons is fairly obvious in that they seek to produce pigeons that will win races. Some will want to win every race they enter whereas the more patient will concentrate on particular races or events in which to win awards or money, for often the rewards are considerable. With those dedicated fanciers who keep fancy pigeons however the rewards and incentives are less well prescribed for the outlay on food, entrance fees and travel expenses are fairly certain, but the rewards are almost non-existent in financial terms at the end of the day. What therefore drives the fancy pigeon enthusiast on? It must and can only be the personal satisfaction of producing within a standard, a pigeon which is special and which will be admired by other enthusiasts in that field. It is the joy of being a show person, by attending shows and in seeing one's own pigeons competing against the best on offer from fellow enthusiasts. That, in essence is what pigeon fancying is all about and nothing personifies the fancier better than those dedicated to fancy pigeons.

'Beauty is in the eye of the beholder' comes to mind when one thinks of the wide range of fancy pigeons, from the best known to some of the very rare varieties. Each holds a special fascination for some, while others might consider some of the more unusual breeds to be extreme and un-pigeonlike. Fortunately, every breed possesses its own devotees who seek to perpetuate and improve their choice in the vast array of fancy breeds.

For many years I have been on the periphery of the fancy pigeon hobby and have kept some breeds for periods of time. I believe most sincerely however that some of the top fanciers are master breeders devoting long years into breeding colours and types into their chosen breeds, developing a profound knowledge of genetics and colour/sex linkage. I have nothing but admiration for such fanciers and as fancy pigeon enthusiasts they rank with the best of the flying breed competition winners and in the racing sport, with some of the top fanciers who produce top winners year after year.

So what is a fancy pigeon?

If a hundred fanciers were to be asked this question, the likelihood is that there would be a like number of answers. We all have our own views on what such a pigeon is and that applies to non-fanciers as well as those who keep pigeons. Most will easily identify a racing pigeon but would have more difficulty with a show racer. They would know about fantails but beyond that would be hard-pressed to name a fancy pigeon or flying breed. This was the sort of problem facing me when considering a chapter on fancy pigeons - how to put a subject across in the space of a chapter when a book devoted to the multi-breed hobby would be quite possible.

There are hundreds of breeds of fancy pigeon and it would take a large volume to even attempt to describe them all. However I have decided to select a few breeds which I consider to be the best known in British shows. These can only act as a random sample of my choosing but readers will get an idea of the vast scope of interest presented by fancy pigeons in general.

One problem was in how to sub-divide the large number of breeds and types. I have seen various descriptions and divisions including:

- Blowers
- Fantails
- Wattle breeds
- Table pigeons
- Homers
- Colour breeds
- Toy breeds
- Muffed Varieties
- Rare Varieties
- Tumblers
- However I have decided to bring it all down into two main categories, namely
- Long-faced
- Short-faced

All breeds of pigeon fit into one category or the other and under each there will be sub-categories such as the blowers. In simple terms, the shape of the head and face decides the distinction. The short-faced breeds have more rounded heads with shorter beaks resulting in feeders being required to rear their young birds properly and are therefore more demanding to keep and breed. The long-faced breeds are capable of rearing their own youngsters and are also used as 'feeders' for the short-faced varieties.

The Long-faced Varieties

- **English Pouter.** This pouter is one of the oldest known of all fancy pigeons having been mentioned in the seventeenth century as having its title because of its ability to blow up its crop so. The Pouter is a large bird standing sixteen inches in height but with a slender body set on the longest possible and slender legs, which are 'stocking-legged' . The crop or globe should be large and should have a crescent of white. The birds are coloured but with white flights and a mainly white underside.

- **Pigmy Pouter.** This is virtually a much smaller version of the English Pouter, being about half the weight. It is a delightful, friendly little bird.

- **Brunner Pouter.** In size it is similar to the Pigmy Pouter but it does not have feathered legs and no crescent on its crop. It is found in self-colours and in various other colour combinations including pieds. It is a quick flier and in a group presents a wonderful spectacle.

- **Norwich Cropper.** The Norwich is a wonderful breed which should boast a very large crop. It is medium in size and carries most of the markings expected in the English Pouter. Balance is very important for the carriage of the large crop and the legs are clear of feathers. This is a friendly breed which is said to fly with grace.

- **Holle Cropper.** This is a very old Dutch exhibition breed which is short, round and erect with its breast as broad as possible. It is a vivacious and active little pigeon which should have its head and neck thrown well back in a neck-shaking manner. It comes in many attractive colours and it is little wonder that it has such a following.

- **Fantail.** The Fantail is probably the best known of all fancy pigeons. In appearance and build it is not unlike the Holle Cropper, but with the magnificent tail from which its name is derived. This is a very ancient breed and has always attracted a considerable following as a purely exhibition breed. The body should be small and round with the small plain head resting on the cushion formed where the tail meets the body. It should face directly ahead and not with the head cocked to either side. The tail is all-important and should contain anything from 30-38 feathers but there can be more. The bird should appear as though standing on tiptoe and there should be a shaking movement. It can be found in many colours and also in lace form.

- **Garden Fantail.** This is the fantail known to non-fanciers as the white birds to be found in gardens in dovecotes. They are now being exhibited and remain extremely popular in their white form and as good fliers with homing ability.

- **Indian Fantail.** Not as rounded as the exhibition Fantail, this attractive breed is growing in popularity. It is a larger bird with a large and long tail which is not held as close to the head which carries a peak crest, with legs which are grouse-feathered.

There is no shaking movement.

- **Long-faced clean-legged Tumblers.** These come in several forms and in levels of popularity they are, Self-coloured, Bald-headed, Beard, the Barred, the Mottle, the Rosewing, and Whiteside. The shape of the head, body and beak are alike with the head being wide and rather more round than oval with a sharp rise from the wattle. The beaks should be stout and of equal thickness. The birds are of medium sized and have always attracted a good following.

- **Long-faced Muffed Tumbler.** The muffed tumbler is very much the same standard of bird but with the hocks and feet covered with feathers.

- **Jacobin.** The Jacobin is almost the 'prince among pigeons' being greatly admired at the shows because of its ornate silky feathering especially on the hooded head. The head covering is in four parts, the hood which should obscure all but forward vision, the chain, the main and the rose. There are many variations of colour but with the hood being accorded the greatest importance. The bird is quite slender and gives the impression of being much larger than it is.

- **Modena.** In terms of following the Modena is probably the most popular exhibition pigeon. Coming from Italy as its name implies, the Modena is found in a huge variety of colours and markings. There are two main divisions, the Gazzi - or pied and the Scietti - or self-coloured. It is a very ancient breed and as early as 1328 a statute prescribed rules for kit flying where Modenas were used to lure birds from other flocks to join them. Medium sized, they should be as short as possible with broad chest, wide back and generally 'cobby'. Carriage should be proud and erect with the plain head carried a little back and with the tail tilted upwards.

- **Nun.** The Nun is a very old breed. It is basically white with a coloured head and bib but with a broad and full white crest. The tail and primary flights should also be coloured. Nuns are active and easily managed birds.

- **Archangel.** The Archangel can only be described as a fairly conventional pigeon but with a wondrous bronze lustre-like colour extending from the head, to the neck, chest and underparts while the wings, back and tail are black. The iridescence of the colour is the main feature including a peak crest.

- **Antwerp.** The Antwerp is a strictly exhibition bird with homer body conformation. It is an erect and hard-feathered bird with a large, oval and massive head and face. The eye should be bright red and differentiates it from other 'homer' type breeds.

- **German Beauty Homer.** This attractive and strong pigeon is growing in popularity thanks to its attractive colours, pleasing appearance and ease of management. It is a product of the German racing homer and crosses with Antwerps and Show Homers although it carries the red eye of the former cross.

- **Show Homer.** The English breed has been derived from the imported Antwerps which were originally used for both racing and showing. The exhibition enthusiasts however wanted to enhance the head still further and the Scandaroon was used as an outcross. The result is the large Roman -nosed pigeon which has lost homing ability and is half as heavy again as the show racer. The head is the main point with most points for it. There is considerable length of face from the pearl coloured eye to the base of the thick beak.

- **Exhibition Homer.** This is another English breed allied to the homer and seems to be a cross between the show homer and other homer types to produce this upright pigeon so compact in appearance. The face is long and the beak strong and stout and the eye is pearl coloured.

- **Genuine Homer.** Another English pearl-eyed homer type, this bird possesses many of the features of the racing homer but it is in the head that the main difference will be seen. In profile the head should rise from the wattle to its highest point immediately in front of the eye.

- **Dragoon.** The Dragoon is another old English breed descended from a collection of breeds including the racing homer, the Horseman and the Carrier. It was formerly a flying breed used for message carrying. Of all the homer-related breeds, the dragoon seems the most natural having great bearing and plenty of vigour. The feathering is tight and the racing type is still plain to see especially as the eye is red coloured and the head not as accentuated as some of the previously mentioned breeds.

- **Show King.** The King is a table pigeon developed in the U.S.A. using various breeds including Mondains, Runts, Maltese and Homer strains. It is a short-bodied, thick-necked bird which can weight in at over thirty ounces. The King is a happy breed and appears in many attractive colours with the whites being the most often seen. It is becoming increasingly popular as an exhibition breed.

- **Runt.** This is the largest exhibition fancy pigeon and is a very old breed. It has a large head in a clean conventional shape, with a medium length but strong beak. The breast is wide and full and the flights and tail feathers should be long. Size is very important and it is said that they cannot be too large. They fly quite well and are known to act as deterrents to raptors because of their sheer size.

- **Old Dutch Capuchine.** At first appearance the capuchine could be taken as a smaller version of the Jacobin. It is not however and there is some doubt that any relationship exists between the two breeds. The capuchine is always monkmarked with the head being white and with the eyes clearly visible from the side with no impairment of vision. It is a most attractive pigeon with a dedicated band of followers.

The Short-faced Varieties

As stated, all short-faced breeds require feeders or foster parents to adequately rear their youngsters. Some will quite happily rear their young for a few days on soft food but when the food changes to grain they are often incapable of further feeding. However the short-faced breeds are quite capable of fostering youngsters of the long-faced breeds.

- **African Owl.** An attractive little pigeon originating from North Africa. It should be short and cobby with a good round head. The little face gives a nice expression with fine wattle and the eyes should appear to protrude slightly, It should carry a pronounced frill at the front of the neck. The legs are clean and present a carriage which is upright, active and bold. This owl is to be seen in a large variety of colours.

- **English Owl.** This bird is almost the same as the African Owl but in larger form making it a medium sized pigeon.

- **Chinese Owl.** This is a popular variety about the size of the African Owl. Frilling is the main feature and it is far more extensive than in other owls, with a large portion of the neck and breast feathers reversed. The underparts at the tops of the legs are also frilled and regarded as pantaloons. This is a delightful little breed with a good following.

- **Oriental Frill.** This is a most handsome Turkish breed with the characteristic breast frill and it also carried a pronounced peak crest and with grouse-legs. The Oriental Frill is a most beautiful pigeon admired by so many for its beautiful array of colour variations. Three main groups exist: Satinettes, Blondinettes and Turbiteens, each with wide colour variation.

- **Turbit.** Similar to the African Owl in size this attractive breed is a very old one. It possesses a delightful temperament and being clean legged is easier to manage. It bears a frill or gullet at the front of the neck, and the flattish head top extends to a peak. It is basically a white pigeon with coloured and barred wing coverings.

- **Short-faced Tumbler.** This breed is one of the oldest known fancy pigeons. It is a very small bird with wings carried beneath the tail with a carriage, which is jaunty, erect and dignified. The head should be broad, yet round and as short as possible from front to back, and carrying a beak which is short, straight and pointed. There are many colours with the almond being perhaps the most prized. Similar markings are to be found as in the Long-Faced Clean-Legged tumblers with balds, beards and mottles.

- **Barb.** The Barb always attracts attention because of it heavy wattles and ceres. In many ways the breed is fairly conventional with clean legs and no adornments except for the heavily wattled and cered face surrounds. The skull should be broad and quite square and the short beak should be strong. The wattles, both beak and jowl, should not conceal the beak although this is a problem with mature birds. The cere or eye wattle should be full and clearly defined forming clean-edged red circles around the eyes. The Barb is a border-line short-faced breed.

Concluding thoughts

The above descriptions provide little but a summary of what each breed represents. Each breed has its followers and devotees who seek to perpetuate each and every one for the future. Each also presents its own challenge and this is where I started by asserting that challenge is involved in every breed of pigeon but in some, especially the short-faced pigeons and the more ornate varieties; the demands on time and patience are even more daunting. Throughout the world fancy pigeons are kept and greatly valued. Every country possesses breeds which are almost unique, yet known by repute or by reporting in other parts of the world. Through the ages man has enjoyed the company and the pleasure of keeping pigeons and through the keen diligence of those who enjoy their own breed and who aim to improve on it, will thereby perpetuate the hobby.

Fancy pigeons are all most fascinating in their own way and offer bountiful rewards in personal satisfaction when good examples of the breed are produced, successfully exhibited and especially when they are appreciated and admired by fellow pigeon fanciers. This, after all is what the hobby is all about!

Chapter 22

The Flying Breeds

THE flying breeds are truly magnificent little pigeons. I have always greatly admired them and have always counted those fanciers who specialise in them as some of the most talented and knowledgeable. My enthusiasm for racers and show racers has curtailed my ability to be able to keep them as a specialised breed but over the years I have been fortunate enough to own, keep and breed quite a number. Indeed, if I had to advise a complete novice to pigeons as to an enjoyable breed I would strongly recommend the flying breeds as providing an ideal way to start.

These delightful pigeons offer just about everything that the fancier seeks in pigeons. They are hardy, easy to keep and breed, they rear their youngsters well, are full of vigour and energy, they fly and home well and of course in their huge array of colours are extremely beautiful. They adapt to almost any loft or structure using their natural intelligence and will feed on a wide variety of grains from the cheapest to the most expensive. They will 'stand their ground' with almost any other breed of pigeon so can be kept with other breeds.

In short, the flying breeds are the complete pigeon, an ideal bird for the novice and expert alike and each in its own way is close to being pigeon perfection. Readers will appreciate from my opening remarks that I am an enthusiast of the fliers both in their competition abilities and also in their exhibition mode.

I mentioned the ability of the enthusiasts who keep the flying breeds. Even the newest novice would have the capability to manage a little team of fliers effectively. The real experts are some of the most proficient fanciers I know especially those involved in competition flying. For instance to produce a team of high flying tipplers to fly continuously in a kit for periods in excess of 20hours can only be marvelled at. The training and the feeding expertise involved is an extraordinary feat of fanciership.

I have always felt that some of the best fanciers in pigeon racing, in the exhibition of show racers and other breeds, are those who have previously been involved in competition flying. For in being able to master the art of competing in flying competition, other facets have also been mastered especially that of being able to feed the right sort of food and in the manner and quantities demanded by such a demanding sport.

As for the exhibiting of the flying breeds at shows, the birds represent some of the best-presented pigeons to be seen anywhere. Their general condition coupled with their superb variety of bright colours makes them a most attractive spectacle and they are generally much admired by fanciers and non-fanciers alike.

It would be impossible to deal with every flying breed in the space of this chapter so I intend to attempt to describe those which are most popular by way of numbers and of enthusiasts.

West of England Flying Tumblers

The West of England is a breed of pigeon which was created for flying and tumbling. Along the way it has developed into a most beautiful bird with a wonderful selection of colours and markings, top class feather and body condition; making it a truly lovely dual-purpose pigeon for showing and flying. Its history is quite an interesting one especially for fanciers who seek to keep flying breeds at distance from showing standards. The origins seem to be the Bristol and surrounding area in the late 1800's and believed to have developed from the Cumulet and Muffed-Tumbler with flying tipplers and rollers also used.

The compiling of breed standards began in earnest towards the end of the nineteenth century and had the effect of most flying tumblers becoming purely show tumblers. In the Birmingham area the fanciers whose birds were usually heavily muffed allowed their flying tumblers to develop into the English Muffed Long Faced Tumblers. Elsewhere flying tumblers turned into clean-legged show tumblers with markings designated as long-faced, Balds, Beards, Whiteside, Mottle and Self. Fortunately a few fanciers in the Westcountry rejected the idea of breeding to a rigid standard. They wished to perpetuate their non-standard flying breed in the same manner as racing homers, flying tipplers, Birmingham Rollers and others. They argued that to adopt a standard resulted in a gradual conversion to an exhibition breed. The result was that the present beautiful West of England Flying Tumbler - a true dual-purpose pigeon - is with us today in its intended form.

There is only one type of West of England Flying Tumbler or 'West' as it is often referred to in its abbreviated title. It is a true dual-purpose pigeon intended and bred for two purposes, one to be shown and the other to fly with some birds excelling at both aspects. The breed is now 'grouse muffed' which means that the legs are feathered to a moderate degree. 'Wests' fly very high and for long periods. They turn or tumble from time to time and then regain their place in the flying kit.

'Wests' are beautiful and fascinating birds combining excellent flying ability with splendid feathering and condition. They are to be found in many colours with the most popular marking being that of the 'bald when it may be chequered, barred or a 'whole' colour in red, yellow, black, dun, blue, silver, cream, mealy, lavender, bronze and strawberry. Spangles and splashes may have the 'V' necked bald markings or badge markings on the head. There are also some saddles and bell necks but these are usually only seen in reds. Birds carrying coloured markings on the head with a body colour too solid for the spangle description are classed as 'badges'.

Prime importance in the show pen as with any flying breed is the condition of both feather and body to provide balance which is a top priority. The West of England is the only true dual-purpose flying tumbler native to the British Isles. It has a wide following and there are several societies catering for this delightful and attractive breed of pigeon.

Flying Tipplers

The flying tippler is another very English flier. The flying tippler is renowned for its flying ability which in competition flying in kits, are capable of great endurance. Times well in excess of twenty hours are on record with kits having to remain intact, in the air without food and water for such long periods. The birds fly high and are trained for duration flying and not for style. Indeed aerobatics are frowned upon and bred out of the breed as such activity is energy using and wasteful of the sheer effort required to remain air-borne for such long periods.

Old birds in kits have produced the top performances but kits of young birds have been known to fly in excess of seventeen hours. Training is very specialised with the fancier in absolute control over the birds. The pigeons should never come down except to their loft and then only at the command of the fancier. Dropping elsewhere than on the loft is a serious fault. Fanciers who specialise in competition flying are extremely proficient and are probably some of the very best to be found in any breed. They operate a regime which is strict and designed to have control over the birds at all times.

Feeding is likewise specific with birds trained to go without food and water for long periods of hours and fed a diet consistent with the high-energy needs of duration and endurance flying. There is no cruelty in this because the bird is a specialist, bred for long flying and is well able to handle strict training and regime. The birds seem to positively enjoy their flying and have a great love of this, of their lofts and of their owners. The great threat to the sport is the growing menace of the raptor population.

It is generally accepted that the flying tippler developed from the English flying tumblers with input from the high flying French Cumulet. The flying tippler was developed for its ability to fly for long periods with freedom from tumbling. It is felt that the title of 'tippler' derived because its white wings and tail feathers were often tipped with colour. The Macclesfield strain carries the grilling factor from the use of the Cumulet and Blue Tumbler crosses, whereas the Sheffield strain is mostly self or barred.

For exhibition purposes a slightly different and slightly larger bird has developed. In the early part of the twentieth century the flying tippler fanciers of the day began showing their better looking birds at the local shows with the obvious analogy between the racer and the show racer. Therefore whilst the flying tippler remained a flying breed, the slightly more showy became known as show pen flying tipplers for a while.

Over the years the Exhibition Flying Tippler has developed and is now a couple of ounces larger than the pure flying tippler. Various crosses have been used to 'improve' type including English Owls, English Long-Faced Tumblers, Genuine Homers and Show Racers. Nowadays the Exhibition Flying Tippler is held mainly as a show bird, but every importance is applied to the judging to ensure that it is judged as a flying breed. It follows therefore that condition and feather quality are often the deciding factors.

The Exhibition Flying Tippler is found with two distinct colour variations. Firstly there are the light prints and mottles. The print marked birds have dark printed flights and tails with dark peppering around the neck with a basic white body marking. Blacknecked prints are much darker while the mottles carry the mottling on the white wing shields. White primaries and tail feathers are penalised. The other colours carry a large variation with blue, silver, chequers, grizzles and self in dun, black and indigo. New colours are constantly being developed.

The Exhibition Flying Tippler should not be confused with the Show Tippler which is a purely exhibition breed resembling the Flying

Tippler but with more emphasis being placed on the roundness of head, eye colour and depth and arrangement of feather colour. The show tippler developed from the flying tippler following the formation of the Tippler Club in 1891 and a breed show standard being adopted. Several breeds were then used to develop the show version especially to improve colour and show type.

The Birmingham Roller

I can immediately declare an interest here in that I regard the little roller as being a really wonderful pigeon. It possesses just about everything a pigeon should have, good looks, lovely colour, flying and performing ability and great vigour and character. They are wonderful workers and feed youngsters in their care with great enthusiasm and success.

To see a large kit rolling and performing in the morning sunshine is one of the most stirring spectacles in pigeondom. With the rays of sunshine catching the brightly coloured feathers, they appear as glistening steaks of light as they roll and fly as though competing with one another to be the best performer. What pigeon fancier could resist such a sight and not be thrilled by it.

The Birmingham Roller as its name implies originated in the Midlands area of England, known as the Black Country, in and around the city of Birmingham. It is said to originate from the common tumbler when combined with European species to foster and improve aerobatics, thus proving the ace performer, as we know it today. The breed was briefly mentioned in Fulton in 1876[1] and was imported into the United States in the late 1870's.

As an aerial performer the Birmingham Roller has few equals. It performs backward somersaults in a continuous and unbroken sequence at speed and a second of roll or spin sees this little bird turn over five times and it will have descended about five feet (1.5m) while doing so but rolling can continue for several seconds.

The Roller is a neat pigeon with fairly tight feathering, carrying the wings neatly folded over its tail. They come in a large array of colours with red being the most numerical, but it is said that most colours are produced in the general mixture of colours involved in successive generations. The weight ranges from 7 to 10 ounces from the pure fliers to the more showy types used in the shows.

The showing of the Rollers has become extremely popular but

---

[1]*Book of Pigeons* by Robert Fulton

there are still many enthusiasts who fly the birds competitively with aerobatic excellence being the aim. The biggest threat to the competition aspect is of course the predation by raptors as an ever-growing threat and possibly explains the popularity of showing this lovely little breed.

In the shows the Birmingham Rollers are always most attractive and admired in their array of colours and showing excellence in condition. There is no written standard for the breed in the United Kingdom but there are some general expectations including the fact that the legs are clean and the head free from any adornment. The keel should be tapering to the vent and the flights should be strong with good feather quill reaching about half an inch (1cm) from the tail tip. As with all flying breeds the flying aspect is the first consideration with type and condition coming next. Good body with excellence of balance is very much a part of the judging.

It is an excellent breed for fanciers to start with offering great interest and satisfaction with no great amounts of work. They fit into almost any loft structure and live quite happily with other breeds. The bird is a true dual-purpose pigeon providing interest both as a spectacle outside the loft and as a near perfect inmate inside.

Other Fliers

There are numerous flying breeds to be found in the World and an excellent source is Levi's encyclopaedia of breeds[2] This great work lists many by description and colour photographs. I have detailed the native breeds to the United Kingdom and would conclude by mentioning some of the remaining best known examples of the fliers.

- **Cumulet.** The Cumulet is a high flier from France and gets its name from the Cumulus Clouds at the sort of heights to which these high fliers soar. The Cumulet was first noted in the United Kingdom in the 1870's. It is known as the all-white flier and has clean legs and is plain-headed. Indeed it is a plain yet beautiful pigeon with a very light eye set in a slender head with none of the dome head of the tumblers. It is bred for high flying and enjoys flying for periods up to ten hours in its flying form. It is said to be one of the ancestors of the present day racing pigeons.

  As with most forms of the flying breeds, a show Cumulet has developed for showing purposes and is a little larger being a couple of ounces heavier indicating that an outcross has been

---

[2] *Encyclopedia of Pigeon Breeds* by Wendell M.Levi.

used in its production. Although a white pigeon, the young-sters are often born with a red flecking in their necks feathers but this more often than not disappears during the first moult.

The Cumulet has been used in the production of other breeds besides the racer and is known to be one of the ancestors of the present Flying Tipplers. Its decline in popularity came about because of the growth in importance of pigeon racing. The Cumulet is an easy breed to keep and in keeping with the flying breeds provides ample rewards both in performance and in the loft.

- **Danzig High Flyer.** The history is a little uncertain but it was known to be common and popular in South Poland in the early twentieth century. Polish ex-servicemen are thought to have brought the breed to the U.K during and after the Second World War.

The Danzig is a solo flier at great height and not usually keep-ing to kits using a strong but slow wing beat. It also possesses excellent homing ability. The head is long-faced and narrow with a shell crest, short legs and a low squat body. The tail is low and broad containing up to eighteen feathers and carried in spread fashion rather like a garden fantail. There are a good variety of colours and the eye should be pearl. The Danzig is an attractive and ideal high flier.

- **Polish Orlik.** Originally from the Ukraine it was developed by Polish fanciers. It is a flying tumbler with an unusual flying ac-tion, often spreading its tail while in flight. It is a bird which prefers the gliding action using thermals to soar at height and its beauty is seen when it spreads its primaries, secondaries and tail to form a half-circle

- **Oriental Roller** is the oldest known performing pigeon though its performance is less obvious than in some of the other bet-ter-known breeds. It kits with other rollers but tends to fly at higher altitude before rolling down to the main group. It comes in a variety of colours and is plain-headed and clean-legged. The tail which contains an average of sixteen retrices is carried a little high with the wing tips carried below the tail. A notable difference with this breed is that it carries no oil gland and tends to be rather loose-feathered compared to other rollers. Young-sters are born with little or no down on their bodies. This is a breed for the specialist who enjoys keeping a rather unusual breed with good but unspectacular flying ability but with a wonderful variation of colour.

- **Budapester Tumbler.** As its name applied it hails from Hungary's Budapest and appears to have arrived in the U.K after the Second World War brought in by settlers from that country. It was bred as a performing pigeon but is now used mainly for exhibition.

  It is a small white pigeon which is well proportioned, carrying a small plain head which appears quite square; and is clean-legged. The eye is pearl coloured and is set in a prominent dark cere. The beak is black. It tends to give the impression being nervous and twitchy due perhaps to the rather bulging eye appearance. Although generally white, the outside six or seven flight tips may be tipped with grey/black markings and the tail may likewise carry a striping of the same colour.

- **Komorner Tumbler.** It is little wonder that the Komorner enjoys such a loyal and dedicated following because it is a superbly interesting little pigeon, about the size of a Birmingham Roller. It is a flying breed with ability to execute somersaults at height, although it has now been developed as a show breed also. It is clean-legged and has a shell crest terminating on each side of the head in little rosette formations. It comes in a large array of colour and this adds to the attraction of this attractive little dual-purpose pigeon.

The flying breeds are exciting little pigeons with the ability to provide immense pleasure and ample reward for the work and time invested in them. They are easy to keep, are good breeders and feeders and being of a working strain can be kept on the most basic of ration. They are excellent at providing new fanciers with experience at pigeon management but once kept, they will never be forgotten or put to one side for they are indeed perfect little pigeons.

Chapter 23

The Show Racer

THE show racer is a pigeon of beauty, dignity and grace. Pre sented in the show pen in peak condition it is a joy to see and it is little wonder that its popularity is ever growing. This is how I began my first book in 1976[1] and nearly a quarter of a century on; I still believe this passionately having been a devotee of the breed for most of my life. In all this time my love affair with the show racer has flourished so I intend this chapter to describe the prince of pigeons and to look back, and to take a look forward into the future of the breed.

What is a Show Racer?

The show racer is a racing pigeon with looks. This is the simple description but the one on which we can build the overall picture. In the United Kingdom the aim has always been to keep the show racer as a dual-purpose breed under the control of the governing body of the pigeon racing sport. It follows that any suggestion of producing a standard for the 'breed' has fortunately been resisted and as a result the show racer has been able to adjust over the years in answer to the demands of the day. In other words, had there been a written standard, flexibility would not have been possible in this way.

So, when we think of the show racer, we think of the racing pigeon in its many colours and types. The show racer is simply the show version of it. The best analogy would be that of a racing greyhound compared to a show greyhound. To the uninitiated they look the same, but to the enthusiast there is a world of difference.

The show racer is easy to acquire, simple to keep and reasonably straightforward to produce for the shows. It can fly out and can even be used for racing purposes and seems to provide a good link between showing and racing, especially with so many racing enthusiasts being deterred by the ravages world-wide of the growing raptor populations.

---

[1] *The Show Racer - How to Show Racing Pigeons* by Douglas McClary.

Colours

Just about every coloration is allowable in the show racer. The most popular are the solid colours, the chequers, dark, blue, and grey, the red chequers with just a few of the solid reds available, the blues, and the mealies. The opal mosaics (a very British term for what is an Opal Chequer) are now extremely popular and growing in favour are the dilutes and the less known colours of yellows, creams, lavenders, silver chequers silver blues, grizzles, and even whites and blacks.

There are far more colours to be seen nowadays and when the pieds and white-flights are added to these, the contents of any great class of mixed show racers can contain quite a large variety. In the United Kingdom the quality of the colour is probably more important than in some other countries. Therefore chequers need to be of good and consistent covering of colour and it seems accepted that blue bars and mealies should carry a good width of barring. The better the colouring the better the chances of success although some racing enthusiast judges seem quite willing to put type and condition before colour considerations. Colour classification in the U.K. is still quite uncommon while in the United States most shows are classified into a series of colour divisions.

There are some anomalies in the way show racers are faulted for colour. Take the blue bar and the mealy (silver in the U.S.A.) The birds are quite similar, yet a blue is far more likely to be faulted for lack of width in the bar than the mealy. Likewise a lighter beak in a mealy is likely to be excused but rarely so in a blue bar. Blue and dark chequers are far more likely to be downgraded for lacking uniformity of chequering than a red chequer and in opal mosaics (chequers) there is a wide divergence of opinion as to what exactly it should be. There are grey based ones and red based ones but the true opal should be a good chequer with each of the cover feathers being edged with a lighter colour which appears to show the true opal coloration.

Size

The ideal size is that of a good racing pigeon, not too small as some of the distance pigeons would be, but neither should it be too large as is seen in some of the 'sprint' families. It should fit quite easily into the hands with good balance. The acceptable weight seems to be about 16ozs, (0.453Kg) in normal showing condition. Anything in excess of this weight would probably indicate fatness and unfitness.

The body weight should be commensurate with the build of the bird in order to provide balance both in the hand and when viewed from outside the show pen.

Obviously there are variations within this weight structure for without a written standard the variations are as dictated or accepted by the judges. Smaller show racers with shallow keel structures are liked by many because they are easier to condition and seem to carry 'body' because of their shallow nature. Larger birds with a keel structure which is more defined need to have more body to support the larger bones but when in perfect condition are balanced and to the liking of many judges. The main object seems to be the production of pigeons which are naturally balanced and which are pleasing to handle, with the actual size being subsequent to this.

Type

This has been mainly covered in the preceding paragraph. To do well in the show pen, the show racer needs to be balanced so that it looks this both when standing in the pen and when handled by the judge. My guess has always been that many of the judging decisions are made in the hand as the bird is taken from the pen. In other words a bird which is too deep in the keel, too shallow and small, out of condition or too long or too short will rarely find favour.

Type is a most inclusive state of most of the features of the show racer, demanding correct size, good station or posture, good colour, alertness, calmness and excellent condition which will be revealed in the brightness of the eye, the whiteness of the wattles and the quality of the feathering. All these added together in a bird of correct size seem to produce that description we all use and know, yet find it difficult to explain, type.

Condition

For showing, the condition required is quite different from that required for the true racing pigeon while racing. The show racer requires to be well bodied and muscled without being overweight, fat and apparently heavy in a leaden sort of way. Good 'body' without the weight seems to be the aim. Any bird which is grossly overweight should not get consideration especially by judges who are supposed to be experts. Birds which have to gasp or breathe heavily even when handled are clearly overweight and need to be better prepared. Likewise birds which are too light, too deficient of body are unlikely ever to be considered. Of course some racing enthusiast judges prefer their chosen card winners to be lighter in body as required for racing purposes, but in average show conditions, the judges generally prefer birds which carry a good 'corky' feel body weight.

As for the rest, condition means the conditions of health and exuberance that will be found in fit pigeons. The fitness stands out, with feathering which is gleaming and well defined, with clarity of eye and whiteness of wattles. When seen, true top condition is recognised as such and can hardly be ignored by any judge. Any judge who cannot recognise true condition needs to find an alternative occupation.

For success

- Good stance or station, preferably with the head held high and the tip of the tail almost reaching the ground
- The peak of condition
- Good colour with consistency of chequering and other markings.
- Calmness in the show pen and when handled
- The 'type' of the day, birds which conform to current expectations or desires.

Against success

- Wildness
- Dirty feathers
- Lack of condition
- Lack of 'type' or balance
- Birds carrying insect life
- Birds with 'broken' or bull-eyes
- Birds with obvious defects i.e. broken flights, missing claws, cross-beaks.
- Colour deficiencies such as lack of barring or gaps in bars, poor chequering or other disadvantaging colour faults.
- Damaged vent bones or keels.
- Guttering or frills in the neck.
- Fret-marked feathers

Desirable Points

Head The head should be broad and shaped sufficiently to avoid any form of flatness. The highest point of the head should be directly above the eye and should descend to the beak in a straight line or with a curvature upwards. There should be no dip behind the wattle. In cocks the head should be strong and masculine but in hens whilst strength is desirable, there should be a feminine look so that there is no doubt as to the sex of the bird.

Beak. This should be strong and straight. In colour it should normally be dark in colour although in reds, mealies, yellow chequers, cream bars and silvers, it can be lighter and more 'horn' colour. Whiter beaks can be tolerated in gay pieds.

Wattles. The wattles should be snow white and small with no coarseness. In cocks the wattles should complement the head and face and one should expect a little more coarseness as the years pass. Excessive coarseness however is not good for showing success.

Neck. The neck should be medium length and suitable to the build of the bird. The feathering should be tight with good colour with no gullets or frills. The neck and its covering of feathers should taper uniformly into the shoulder, breast and back areas.

Breast. The breast should be broad to provide the bird with a 'substantial' look. It should taper into the lower body and should not appear to be distended even after the bird has taken food and drink.

Keel. The keel should be straight and free from waving; normally a fault in rearing. Medium to shallow is preferred and well covered with flesh and quality feathering. Slight dents are regarded as a fault by most judges but I have always been prepared to make allowance for minor ones providing that all else is satisfactory.

Legs. The legs should be substantial and suitable to the size of the bird. They should not be too long to make the bird look high while in the pen and shorter to medium length legs are preferred. Feathered covered feet are not ideal and will be faulted by some judges.

Eye. I have always believed that the eye should complement the head and face so that colour is incidental. Light eyes are not desirable, especially pearls and there should be no broken or bulling to the eye. In most birds dark eyes are preferred, ranging from dark red to nut brown and even those which appear as violet with a slaty dark appearance. The eye should be bright and clear as a confirmation of good health.

192

Ceres. These should be as inconspicuous as possible, therefore neatness is essential and ceres free from coarseness. In cocks a certain allowance can be made providing that the cere complements the expression.

Back and rump. Should be broad and strong. Weakness will cause the tail to raise when the bird is handled, thus destroying balance. In the best birds the back is well covered with feathering and there should be no light coloured 'saddle' in the area behind the neck.

Wing. The wing should be well proportioned so as not to provide either too much cover, or insufficient. The wing butts should be thick and these can either blend in to the body or in some cases may rest in a slightly 'proud' manner. The ten primary flights should be wide and strong and free from frets or blemishes and from any insect life. Additional flights are generally regarded as faults despite the fact that there is nothing written to dictate this.

Tail. The twelve tail feathers should be strong and broad but should fold to appear as one. Tail flights which are too long upset balance and it is usual for there to be about an inch between the end of the primaries and the end of the tail.

The above notes are for guidance only and must not be regarded as being any sort of standard. In the U.K. there has never been a standard and I sincerely hope that there never will. The show racer is a show version of the racing pigeon and any developments or changes should be in line with those of the parent sport, gradual and at the wish of the participants.

The Intervening Years

I started this chapter with the opening words used in 1976 in my first book on the show racer.[2] I thought that I would like to discuss what has happened within my chosen sport in the intervening quarter of a century. I have the situation in the United Kingdom mainly in mind when I do this although I have had the privilege of much contact with shows and showing in the United States and so can cast my mind to the situation there also. I have enjoyed some judging appointments in that country and have always been impressed by the friendliness of the exhibitors and their enthusiasm in their promotion of their sport.

The most notable change has been in the methods of showing. The use of the railway system has just about disappeared so that all entrants travel to the shows by road. Gone are the days of taking

---

[2] *The Show Racer, How to Show Racing Pigeons* by Douglas McClary 1976

the birds to the local railway station for them to be delivered to the show and then returned afterwards. Additional expense is caused through this especially at the two-day events where exhibitors have to find accommodation as well as their transportation costs. On the upside, the attendance of more exhibitors has resulted in a better social enjoyment.

Changes in colour are one of the biggest changes. When I wrote my book, the solid colours dominated the shows and hardly any fanciers other than a few specialists bothered to carry the less common colours such as the opal mosaics, (chequers) yellows, creams, lavenders, silvers and so on. The few who cultivated the colours were aware that their chances of winning were very restricted but they persisted for the sheer joy of producing something different. Also, the few coloured birds which existed were often lacking in good head properties and good eye colour.

In those days I opined that the opal mosaics (Opal Chequers) were about the only unusual colour to win thanks to the excellence of one or two of the lofts carrying that colour until the Old Comrades show was won with an opal mosaic cock for two years. Suddenly the opal mosaic colour (Opal Chequer) became very popular with fanciers chasing success built upon the superb type of that one opal mosaic cock. The result was that nowadays the opal mosaic (Opal Chequer) colour is to be found in most U.K. show teams and is in effect no longer an unusual colour. Indeed some classifications insist that it be placed in the chequer classes. As a 'spin-off' those who sought to produce their own opal chequers, produced some of the other rarer colours, firstly by chance and then by intent.

Now many more fanciers are investing in a few of the more unusual colorations with the silver blues and chequers being most popular followed by the yellows and creams, but with the occasional lavender winning quite well. I believe that most fanciers who keep the 'colours' simply enjoy having something different in their lofts and enjoy breeding from them, never quite knowing what is likely to emerge from the unusual pairings.

Over the quarter of a century in question, there have been cyclical changes in fads of colour for winning. The blue bars dominated for some while until the mealies reigned supreme followed by the red chequers a few years later. Then the opal chequers (opal mosaics) seemed to have its turn although it has never dominated the show scene as some of the other fads have. For instance when the mealies were at their most popular, it would be likely that at the top shows most, or well over half the winners were of that colour.

194

I think it fair to say that many fanciers try to follow the success of the successful. In other words they try to copy what is winning either by buying into the colour for success, or by attempting to breed their own. It is remarkable however how the fads do occur and persist for a few years until birds of another colour suddenly do well at a top show and interest transfers to them.

One of the main features in the U.K. has been the success of the Show Racer Societies under the umbrella of the British Show racer Federation. Although never consulted on showing matters, these organisations have allowed enthusiasts to get together and to produce the sport as they wish to have it staged and organised. With so many smaller shows closing down the Societies have provided an alternative venue for the show racer and the result has been high expertise and some degree of uniformity. As a result attitudes to the showing side of pigeon racing have improved with less friction than existed in days gone by.

I would love to be able to claim that interest was growing year by year but the reality is that there is a decline. One needs only to look at the size of the classes at the early shows of the thirties, forties and fifties to note classes of up to two hundred entries at the main classic shows. Whilst showing is still strong it is having to compete with all other forms of leisure, which aided by better and improving communication allow participation in just about anything desired.

What of the standard of entries and the type of the show racer? At one time in the fifties there was a danger of the show racer becoming too far removed from the racing pigeon. It was getting larger and more loose-feathered with a commensurate lack of appealing and intelligent expression. Then, some enthusiasts responded to the criticism which was being voiced by producing birds more allied to the racer, making them slightly smaller, more attractive and tighter in feather. All round these birds possessed better type to suit both the racing enthusiast and of course the show racer exhibitor. Ties with the pigeon racing sport has brought this about with top quality racing men judging and seeking birds which provided them with their vision of the show racer being a good looking form of the racing pigeon.

Those are the changes as I have seen them and I firmly believe that providing nothing untoward happens, there is an excellent future for the show racer as long as it remains as part of the pigeon racing sport. The changes have been gradual, not entirely pain-free but with no lasting disadvantages to harm entry into a bright and interesting future.

Colour determination and Sex Inheritance in the Show Racer

For many years I felt able to predict the colour of the youngsters from pairings and in many cases to be able to determine their sex. without really knowing why. Over the years I have grappled with the writings of genetic experts and tried to understand the subject but in almost every case I foundered at the attempt by being unable to understand the terms and descriptions used.

Yet, to the average showman it is a most interesting subject and one which provides endless pleasures during the breeding process. In my book, 'The Show Racer'[1] - I produced a simple table which has helped many to understand the situation of sex and colour inheritance. I would now like to move on somewhat to embrace some of the colours which were rare in those days but which now form a large part of the entries at the shows of the U.K.

I am indebted to friends who have provided me with information and who have checked my work against glaring inaccuracies.

Basic Colours

There are three BASIC colours in the show racer and are, in order of dominance:

- Ash red — Red chequer and mealy

- Blue — Dark Chequer, Chequer and Blue Bar

- Brown — Brown chequer, Chequer and Bar. (The brown colour can almost be discounted as it has become very rare and is hardly ever seen. Brown birds carry light eyes.}

These basic colours are carried in the 'X' chromosome and are termed as 'sex linked'. A cock carries two 'X' chromosomes which can be two different colours with the most dominant colour being expressed - e.g. a mealy cock carrying black flecking is usually carrying blue so is termed as 'Ash Red/Blue'. This is termed as Heterozygous (Impure). Of course the mealy· cock can be Homozygous (Pure) for colour if the same colour if the same colour is carried on both 'X' chromosomes (Ash Red/ Ash Red).

A hen possesses only one 'X' chromosome is always pure for colour. Her 'Y' chromosome is non-viable for colour so that if a hen is a blue - that is all she can be - blue.

---

[1] *The Show Racer - How to Show Racing Pigeons* by Douglas McClary.

Pattern

There are four pattern genes in the show racer. These are in order of dominance:

- ■ T-pattern   – Dark Chequers
- ■ Chequer   – Other Chequers, blue, grey, light.
- ■ Barred   – Blue Bar, Mealy
- ■ Barless   – Rarely, if ever seen in the show racer.

These pattern genes are termed 'Autosomal'; i.e. carried on a chromosome other than the 'X' chromosome. Therefore, both cocks and hens can carry two different Pattern Genes with the most dominant being expressed in the order given i.e. 'T' Pattern, Chequer, Barred and Barless. This is why two chequered pigeons can breed barred youngsters, but why two barred birds are unable to breed birds with chequering.

Colour Altering Genes

This is where the plot thickens and why so many find genetics so confusing. The three Basic Colours can be changed or altered by the introduction of certain other genes with the most common being:

- ■ DILUTE. This is a recessive, sex-linked mutation that 'dilutes' the strength of colour. This is the gene responsible for altering an Ash Red to Ash Yellow (Red/Mealy to Yellow/Cream), Blue to Silver and Brown to Khaki. Thus, if two blue bars are paired and produce a Silver, you know that the Sire in Heterozygous (Impure) for Dilute (Blue/Dilute Silver), as the hen can only be Homozygous (Pure) for colour. It is also certain that the young Silver is a hen.

  Any Dilute youngster produced from two intense coloured parents will be a hen.

- ■ POWDER. This is a recessive autosomal mutation responsible for lightening the basic colour of a pigeon resulting in 'powder blues' and 'light or powder mealies'.

- ■ RECESSIVE OPALS. This is another recessive autosomal mutation. It has the effect of diminishing the black bars of a Blue, the black chequering of a Chequer to a Rust/Red. It also has a lightening effect on the body, flights and tail bar. We see the result as:

- ■ Recessive Opal with Chequer Pattern   - Opal Mosaic (Opal Chequer)

- Recessive Opal with Barred Pattern - Lavender
- Recessive Opal paired to Recessive Opal will produce only Recessive Opal youngsters

If two Blue Barred pigeons are paired and produce a Lavender, it is known that both parents are carrying Recessive Opal

Grizzles

A grizzle is a Dominant Autosomal factor making it Dominant to any non-grizzle whatever colour or pattern. If Grizzle is present it must be expressed. As an Autosomal factor it is not sex-linked.

Sex Linked Pairings

In this context think only Colour, and put to the back of the mind, Pattern. This is very important. The classic Sex-Linked pairing is ANY Recessive Coloured Cock to a Dominant Coloured hen. Again, I state, forget pattern, think only Colour.

Examples:

Cock	Hen	Progeny
Blue	Ash Red	Ash Red cocks and Blue hens
Silver	Blue	Blue cocks and Silver hens
Silver	Ash Yellow	Ash Yellow cocks and Silver hens
Ash Yellow	Ash Red	Ash Red cocks and Ash Yellow hens

It will be noted that in a sex-linked pairing, a criss-cross inheritance takes place in that all young cocks will take the colour of the dam and all the hens will resemble the sire.

The most difficult part to accept is that there are only THREE BASIC COLOURS. However, from the TWO BASIC COLOURS most widely seen and known, there are eleven variations by simple use of the Pattern genes and the introduction of the Dilute and Recessive factors, even more if the powder factor is included. These are tabled as follows

Colour	Pattern and Factor	Pigeon
Ash Red	Barred Pattern	Mealy
Ash Red	Chequer Pattern	Red Chequer
Ash Red	Barred and Dilute	Cream Bar
Ash Red	Chequer and Dilute	Yellow Chequer
Blue	Barred Pattern	Blue Bar
Blue	Chequer Pattern	Blue Chequer
Blue	'T' Pattern	Dark Chequer
Blue	Bar Pattern and Dilute	Silver
Blue	Chequer and Dilute	Silver Chequer
Blue	Bar Pattern & Recessive Opal	Lavender
Blue	Chequer & Recessive Opal	Opal Mosaic (Opal Chequer)

Colour inheritance from cocks which are homozygous for colour

N.B. Reference is to colour only - disregard pattern.

PAIR			PROGENY
1.	Sire:	Blue	All blues, cocks and hens
	Dam:	Blue	
2.	Sire:	Blue	All blue, cocks and hens
	Dam:	Silver	
3.	Sire:	Silver	Blue cocks, silver hens ***
	Dam:	Blue	
4.	Sire:	Silver	Silver cocks and hens
	Dam:	Silver	
5.	Sire:	Blue	Ash red cocks and blue hens ***
	Dam:	Ash Red	
6.	Sire:	Blue	Ash red cocks and blue hens ***
	Dam:	Ash Yellow	
7.	Sire:	Ash Red	Ash red cocks and hens
	Dam:	Blue	
8.	Sire:	Ash Red	Ash red cocks and hens
	Dam:	Ash Red	
9.	Sire:	Ash Red	Ash Red cocks and hens
	Dam:	Ash Yellow	
10.	Sire:	Ash Yellow	Ash Red cocks and Ash Yellow hens ***
	Dam:	Ash Red	
11.	Sire:	Ash Yellow	Ash Yellow cocks and hens
	Dam:	Ash Yellow	
12.	Sire:	Ash Yellow	Ash Yellow cocks and hens
	Dam:	Silver	
13.	Sire:	Silver	Ash Yellow cocks and Silver hens ***
	Dam:	Ash Yellow	

It will be noticed that Pairs 3, 5, 6, 10 and 13 are sex-linked pairings with a recessive coloured cock paired to a dominant coloured hen. Therefore a criss-cross takes place so that all young cocks resemble the dam and all young hens resemble the cock. In pair 7 all the young birds produced are ash red. The young cocks will be known as soon as they feather which will show the black flecking on their flights and tail feathers.

Recessive Opal (opal chequers and lavenders) colour derivations, colours which can be expected from pairings using Recessive Opal.

PAIR			PROGENY
1.	Sire:	Blue	All Blue cock and hens
	Dam:	Recessive Opal	
2.	Sire:	Recessive Opal	All Blue cocks and hens
	Dam:	Blue	
3.	Sire:	Recessive Opal	All Recessive Opal cocks and hens
	Dam:	Recessive Opal	
4.	Sire:	Blue carrying Rec. Opal	Blue cocks and hens
	Dam:	Blue carrying Rec. Opal	Recessive Opal cocks and hens
5.	Sire:	Blue, carrying Rec. Opal	Blue cocks and hens
	Dam:	Recessive Opal	Recessive Opal cocks and hens
6.	Sire:	Recessive Opal	All Blue cocks and hens
	Dam:	Silver	
7.	Sire:	Silver	All Blue cocks and hens
	Dam:	Recessive Opal	
8.	Sire:	Ash Red	All Ash Red, cocks and hens
	Dam:	Recessive Opal	
9.	Sire:	Recessive Opal	Ash red cocks
	Dam:	Ash Red	Blue hens
10.	Sire:	Ash Red carrying Recessive Blue & Opal	Ash Red cocks and hens Blue cocks and hens
	Dam:	Blue carrying Rec. Opal	Recessive Opal cocks and hens

I am rounding off this section of the Show Racer chapter by providing a list of typical colour pairings which might be found in any loft. Obviously it cannot be entirely comprehensive but the reader should find almost any colour combination as an ongoing guide.

PAIR		PROGENY
1.	Sire: Blue Bar	Blue Bar cocks and hens
	Dam: Blue Bar	
2.	Sire: Blue Bar	Blue Chequer and Blue Bar cocks and hens
	Dam: Blue Chequer	
3.	Sire: Blue Chequer	Blue Chequer and Blue Bar cocks and hens
	Dam: Blue Bar	
4.	Sire: Blue Bar carrying Dilute	Blue Bar cocks, Blue Bar and Silver hens
	Dam: Blue Bar	

PAIR	PROGENY
5. Sire: Blue Bar carrying Dilute	Blue Bar cocks and hens, Blue Chequer cocks
Dam: Blue Chequer	and hens, Silver Chequer and Silver Bar hens
6. Sire: Blue Cheq. carrying Dilute	Blue chequer cocks & hens, Blue Bar
Dam: Blue Bar	cocks & hens, Silver Cheq. and Silver Blue cocks and Hens
7. Sire: Blue Bar	Blue Bar cocks and hens
Dam: Silver bar	
8. Sire: Blue Chequer	Blue Chequer and Blue Bar cocks & hens
Dam: Silver Bar	
9. Sire: Blue Bar	Blue Chequer & Blue Bar cocks and hens
Dam: Silver Chequer	
10. Sire: Blue Bar carrying Dilute	Blue Bar cocks and hens
Dam: Silver Bar	Silver Bar cocks and hens
11. Sire: Blue Bar carrying Dilute	Blue Chequer and Blue Bar cocks & hens
Dam: Silver Chequer	Silver Chequer and Silver Bar cocks & hens
12. Sire: Blue Chequer carrying Dilute	Blue Chequer & Blue Bar cocks & hens
Dam: Silver Bar	Silver Chequer and Silver Blue cocks & hens
13. Sire: Silver Bar	Blue Bar cocks and Silver Bar hens
Dam: Blue Bar	
14. Sire: Silver Chequer	Blue Chequer and Blue Bar cocks
Dam: Blue Bar	Silver Chequer & Silver Bar hens
15. Sire: Silver Chequer	Blue Chequer cocks, Silver Chequer hens
Dam: Blue Chequer	Blue Bar cocks & Silver Bar hens
16. Sire: Blue Bar	Mealy cocks and Blue Bar hens
Dam: Mealy hens	
17. Sire: Blue Chequer	Red Chequer and Mealy cocks
Dam: Mealy	Blue Chequer and Blue Bar hens
18. Sire: Blue Bar	Red Chequer and Mealy cocks
Dam: Red Chequer	Blue Chequer and Blue Bar hens
19. Sire: Blue Bar	Red Chequer and Mealy cocks
Dam: Yellow Chequer	Blue Chequer and Blue Bar hens
20. Sire: Blue Bar	Mealy cocks and Blue Bar hens
Dam: Cream Bar	
21. Sire: Blue Chequer	Red Chequer and Mealy cocks, Blue
Dam: Cream Bar	Chequer & Blue Bar hens

PAIR	PROGENY
22. Sire: Blue Bar carrying Dilute Dam: Red Chequer	Red Chequer and Mealy cocks, Blue Chequer and Bar Bar hens, Silver Chequer and Silver Bar Hens
23. Sire: Blue Chequer carrying Dilute Dam: Red Chequer	Red Chequer cocks, Blue Chequer and Silver Chequer hens
24. Sire: Blue Chequer carrying Dilute Dam: Mealy	Red Chequer and Mealy cocks, Blue Chequerand Blue Bar hens, Silver Chequer and Silver Bar hens.
25. Sire: Blue Bar carrying Dilute Dam: Yellow Chequer	Red Chequer, mealy, yellow chequer and cream bar cocks, Blue Chequer, Blue Bar, Silver Cheq and Silver Bar hens.
26. Sire: Blue Chequer carrying Dilute Dam: Cream Bar	As above in 25.
27. Sire: Blue Bar carrying Dilute Dam: Cream Bar	Mealy and Cream Bar cocks Blue Bar and Silver Bar hens
28. Sire: Blue Chequer Dam: Blue Chequer	Blue chequer cocks and hens, Blue Bar cocksand hens. N.B. If both parents are carrying Recessive opal, Opal Chequer cocks hens may be produced
29. Sire: Red Chequer Dam: Red Chequer	Red Chequer and Mealy cocks and hens
30. Sire: Red Chequer carrying blue Dam: Red Chequer	Red Chequer and Mealy cocks and hens Blue Chequer and Blue Bar hens
31. Sire: Mealy Dam: Mealy	Mealy cocks and hens
32. Sire: Mealy carrying Blue Dam: Mealy	Mealy cocks and hens, Blue Bar hens
33. Sire: Red Chequer Dam: Mealy	Red Chequer and Mealy cocks and hens
34. Sire: Mealy carrying Blue Dam: Red Chequer	Red Chequer and Mealy cocks & hens Blue Chequer and Blue Bar hens
35: Sire: Red Chequer Dam: Blue Chequer	Red Chequer & Mealy cocks and hens,
36: Sire: Red Chequer Dam Blue Bar.	Red Chequer and Mealy cocks and hens
37. Sire: Red Chequer carrying Blue Dam: Blue Bar	Red Chequer, Mealy, Blue Chequer and Blue Bar cocks and hens
38. Sire: Red Chequer carrying Blue Dam: Blue Chequer	Red Chequer, Mealy, Blue Chequer and Blue Bar cocks and hens

PAIR	PROGENY
39: Sire: Mealy Dam: Blue Bar	Mealy cocks and hens
40. Sire: Mealy carrying Blue Dam: Blue Bar	Mealy cocks and hens Blue Bar cocks & hens
41: Sire: Mealy carrying Blue Dam: Blue Chequer	Red Chequer, Mealy, Blue Chequer and Blue Bars cocks and hens
42. Sire: Red Chequer carrying Blue Dam: Silver Bar	Red Chequer, Mealy. Blue Chequer and BlueBar cocks and hens
43. Sire: Red Chequer carrying Blue Dam: Silver Chequer	As above in 42
44. Sire: Mealy carrying Blue Dam: Silver Chequer	As above in 42
45. Sire: Red Chequer carrying Dilute Dam: Silver Bar	Red Chequer, Mealy, Yellow Chequer & Cream Bar cocks and hens
46. Sire: Mealy carrying Dilute Dam: Silver Chequer	As above in 45
47. Sire: Mealy carrying Dilute Dam: Red Chequer	Red Chequer and Mealy cocks and hens, Yellow Chequer and Cream Bar hens
48. Sire: Red Chequer carrying Dilute Dam: Silver Chequer	Red Chequer and Yellow Chequer cocks and hens
49. Sire: Red Chequer Dam: Silver Bar	Red Chequer and Mealy cocks and hens
50. Sire: Mealy Dam: Silver Bar	Mealy cocks and hens
51. Sire: Red Chequer Dam: Silver Chequer	Red Chequer and Mealy cocks and hens
52. Sire: Red Chequer Dam: Yellow Chequer	As above 51
53. Sire: Mealy Dam: Yellow Chequer	As above 51
54. Sire: Red Chequer Dam: Cream Bar	Red Chequer and Mealy cocks and hens
55. Sire: Yellow Chequer Dam: Silver Bar	Yellow Chequer and Cream Bar cocks and hens. N.B. If the sire is carrying silver, Silver chequer and Silver Bar cocks & hens will be produced.
56. Sire: Cream Bar Dam: Silver Chequer	As in 55 above
57. Sire: Yellow Chequer Dam: Silver Chequer	As in 55 above

PAIR	PROGENY
58. Sire: Red Chequer carrying Dilute Dam: Red Chequer	Red Chequer and Mealy cocks. Red Chequer, Yellow chequer & Cream Bar hens
59. Sire: Red Chequer carrying Dilute Dam: Mealy	As in 58 above
60. Sire: Silver Chequer Dam: Yellow Chequer	Yellow Chequer & Cream Bar cocks Silver Chequer & Silver Bar hens
61. Sire: Silver Bar Dam: Cream Bar	Cream Bar cocks Silver Bar hens
62. Sire: Silver Bar Dam: Yellow Chequer	Yellow Chequer and Cream Bar cocks Silver Chequer and Silver Bar hens
63. Sire: Red Chequer carrying Dilute Dam. Blue Chequer	Red Chequer and Mealy cocks, Red, Mealy and Yellow Chequer and Cream Bar hens
64. Sire: Mealy carrying Dilute Dam: Blue Bar	Mealy cocks, Mealy and Cream Bar hens
65. Sire: Red Chequer carrying Dilute Dam: Blue Bar	Red Chequer and Mealy cocks. Red Chequer Mealy, Yellow Chequer and Cream hens
66. Sire: Red Chequer carrying Dilute Dam: Silver Chequer	Red and Yellow Chequer cocks and hens
67. Sire: Mealy carrying Dilute Dam: Silver Bar	Mealy and Cream Bar cocks and hens
68. Sire: Red Chequer carrying Dilute Dam: Silver Bar	Red and Yellow Chequer, Mealy and Cream Bar cocks and hens
69. Sire: Red Chequer carrying Dilute Dam: Yellow Chequer	Red Chequer and Yellow Chequer cocks and hens.
70. Sire: Mealy carrying Dilute Dam: Yellow Chequer	Red Chequer, Yellow Chequer, Mealy and Cream Bar cocks and hens.
71. Sire: Red Chequer carrying Dilute Dam: Cream Bar	As 70 above
72. Sire: Yellow Chequer Dam: Red Chequer	Red Chequer cocks and Yellow Chequer hens
73. Sire: Cream Bar Dam: Red Chequer	Red Chequer and Mealy cocks. Yellow Chequer and Cream Bar hens

PAIR			PROGENY
74.	Sire:	Yellow Chequer	As 73
	Dam:	Mealy	
75.	Sire:	Blue Bar	Blue Chequer and Blue Bar cocks & hens
	Dam:	Opal Chequer	
76.	Sire:	Blue Chequer	Blue Chequer &Blue Bar cocks and hens
	Dam:	Lavender	
77.	Sire:	Opal Chequer	Blue Chequer and Blue Bar cocks and hens
	Dam:	Blue Bar	
78:	Sire:	Opal Chequer	As 77 above
	Dam:	Blue Chequer	
79:	Sire:	Lavender	Blue Bar cocks and hens
	Dam:	Blue Bar	
80.	Sire:	Opal Chequer	Opal Chequer and Lavender cocks and hens
	Dam	Opal Chequer	
81.	Sire:	Opal Chequer	Opal Chequer and Lavender cocks and hens
	Dam:	Lavender	
82.	Sire:	Lavender	Lavender cocks and hens
	Dam	Lavender	
83.	Sire:	Silver Chequer	Blue Chequer and Lavender cocks and hens
	Dam:	Opal Chequer	
84.	Sire:	Silver Bar	Blue Bar cocks and hens
	Dam:	Lavender	
85.	Sire:	Silver Chequer	Blue Chequer and Blue Bar cocks and hens
	Dam:	Lavender	
86.	Sire:	Opal Chequer	Blue Chequer and Blue Bar cocks and hens
	Dam:	Silver Bar	
87.	Sire:	Lavender	Blue Bar cocks and hens
	Dam:	Silver Bar	
88.	Sire:	Opal Chequer	Blue Chequer and Blue Bar cocks and hens
	Dam:	Silver Chequer	
89.	Sire:	Blue Bar carrying Rec. Opal	Blue Bar cocks and hens
	Dam:	Blue Bar	
90.	Sire:	Blue Bar carrying Rec. Opal	Blue Chequer and Blue Bar cocks and hens
	Dam:	Blue Chequer	
91.	Sire:	Blue Chequer/ Recessive Opal	As above 90
	Dam:	Blue Bar	
92.	Sire:	Blue Bar carrying Rec. Opal	Blue Bar and Lavender cocks and hens
	Dam:	Blue Bar carrying Rec. Opal	

PAIR			PROGENY
93.	Sire:	Blue Cheq. carrying Rec.Opal	Blue Chequer, Blue Bar, Opal Chequer
	Dam:	Blue Bar carrying Rec. Opal	and Lavender cocks and hens.
94.	Sire:	Blue Cheq. carrying Rec.Opal	Blue Chequer, Opal Chequer, Blue Bar and
	Dam:	Blue Cheq.carrying Rec.Opal	Lavender cocks and hens
95.	Sire:	Red Chequer	Red Chequer cocks and hens
	Dam:	Opal Chequer	
96.	Sire:	Mealy	Mealy cocks and hens
	Dam:	Lavender	
97.	Sire:	Red Chequer	Red Chequer and Mealy cocks and hens
	Dam:	Lavender	
98.	Sire:	Opal Chequer	Red Chequer and Mealy cocks, Blue Chequer
	Dam:	Red Chequer	and Blue Bar hens
99.	Sire:	Lavender	Mealy cocks and Blue Bar hens
	Dam:	Mealy	
100.	Sire:	Lavender	Red Chequer and Mealy cocks, Blue Chequer
	Dam:	Red Chequer	and Blue Bar hens
101.	Sire:	Red Chequer carrying Blue and Recessive Opal	RedChequer, Blue Chequer, Mealy, Blue Bar Opal Chequer and Lavender cocks and hens
	Dam:	Blue Bar carrying Rec.Opal	
102.	Sire:	Mealy carrying Blue and Recessive Opal	Mealy, Blue Bar and Lavender cocks and hens
	Dam:	Blue Bar carrying Rec. Opal	
103.	Sire:	Red Chequer carrying Blue and Opal Recessive	Red Chequer, Opal Chequer, Blue Chequer Lavender and Blue Bar cocks and hens
	Dam:	Blue Chequer carrying Opal Recessive	
104.	Sire:	Mealy carrying Blue, Opal Recessive and Dilute	Red Chequer, Mealy, Blue Chequer,Blue Bar, Lavender, Opal Chequer cocks and hens
	Dam:	Blue Chequer carrying Recessive Opal	Silver Chequer, Yellow Chequer, Silver Bar and Cream Bar hens
105	Sire:	Blue Grizzle	Mealy cocks, Mealy Grizzle cocks
	Dam:	Mealy	Blue Bar and Blue Grizzle hens

206

PAIR			PROGENY
106	Sire:	Blue Bar	Blue Bar and Blue Grizzle cocks & hens
	Dam	Blue Grizzle	
107	Sire:	Blue Grizzle	Red Chequer, Mealy, Red Grizzle and
	Dam:	Red Grizzle	Homozygous Red Grizzle cocks.Blue
			Chequer, Blue Bar, Blue Grizzle,
			Homozygous Blue Grizzle hens
108	Sire:	Red Chequer	Red Chequer, Mealy, Red and Mealy
			Grizzle cocks and hens
	Dam:	Red Grizzle	
109	Sire:	Mealy	As pair 108
	Dam:	Red Grizzle	
110	Sire:	Blue Chequer	Red Chequer, Mealy, Red & Mealy Grizzle
	Dam:	Red Grizzle	cocks, Blue Chequer, Blue Bar and Blue
			Grizzle hens

The above table is fairly comprehensive but is not a complete list of pairings possible in the modern show racer loft. Reference to the more general tables and the text will allow the reader to determine colour expectations from almost any pairing and in many cases a sex-linkage also. The variations are truly staggering and represents one of the greatest changes to be seen in the show racer loft thanks to the growing interest in the more unusual colours.

Some of the basics which can help the reader to grasp the subject relating to colour and to some extent to sex determination in the show racer are as follows:

■ Ash Red is Dominant to Blue and Brown

■ Sex linkage can be determined in any pairing of a Recessive Coloured cock to a Dominant Coloured hen. All young cocks from the pairing will take the colour of the dam and all young hens take their colour from the sire in a colour exchange..

■ Cocks carry their colour on two 'X' chromosomes which can be the same making them pure for colour and are Homozygous, or can be two colours, impure for colour and are Heterozygous.

■ Hens carry only one 'X' chromosome so are always pure for colour.

■ Any Dilute youngster produced from two intense coloured parents will always be a hen.

- If two Blue Barred pigeons are paired together and produce a Lavender, it is known that both parents are carrying Recessive Opal.

- Two Opal Chequers paired together will produce only Opal Chequers or Lavenders.

- A Heterozygous cock of the Red or Yellow Chequer, Mealy or Cream Bar colour will usually be identified by black flecking in the wing feathers.

Concluding thoughts

The show racer represents a real challenge. In terms of numbers it is probably the most popular pigeon kept for showing purposes. The reasons are obvious in that it is easy to keep and to breed yet offers great challenge to those who continually strive to produce something 'just that little bit better'. The show racer is a variant of the true racing pigeon and enthusiasts should never lose sight of this, aiming to keep the show racer as just that, a better looking version of the racer.

The moment we start thinking of standards, the ideal will veer away from a bird which looks and feels like a real pigeon, into some of the birds which have been produced in the name of a standard in the past. Whenever there is a standard, someone always wants to 'improve' on it, to further exaggerate points, to stress certain aspects, with the resulting loss of practical type. Hopefully the mistakes of the past will not be repeated and the show racer can remain as a beautiful form of the racer, firm in body, tight in feather and with an obvious intelligence and grace.

Chapter 24

A Review of Pigeon Books for Reference and Enjoyment

AS a lifelong pigeon fancier, I can safely claim that my enjoyment has always been heightened through my collection of pigeon books. In my view books on pigeon provide not only enjoyment but also act as a source of knowledge and reference using the experience of the experts past and present. It is not often that one would sit down to read a pigeon book from cover to cover but more to use it as a source of knowledge and information whenever it is required.

I consider that I have been fortunate in building a little collection, mostly through purchases but sometimes by gifts from family and friends. Some books have been with me throughout my time in pigeons while others have been added in more recent times. I have always found them fascinating and enjoyable but refer to them whenever a need for information arises.

It is not necessary to own a collection of books in order to be a pigeon fancier especially as most libraries will obtain books to order. However, there is nothing like having a book or two on the shelf for more immediate reference for sometimes problems cannot wait for too long and need more urgent attention. Older books no longer in print can be obtained from book sales, clearance advertisements in the fancy press papers and through sellers of new and second-hand books specialising in pigeons and other small livestock. I have simply selected those books which I have found most useful and enjoyable over the years with a view to sharing my appreciation of them to readers of this book.

- **Barker's Pigeon Racing - a practical guide to the sport by Dr.W.E.Barker. Published in 1950.**

  This was the first ever pigeon book I bought so it has been my companion for many years. It is a most wide-ranging and learned work and is a most comprehensive guide to the management of pigeons. Despite being written for the sport of pigeon racing it has much to interest the exhibition fancier whether of racing pigeons, show racers or fancy and flying breeds; indeed the chapter on pigeon showing is still extremely relevant.

Changes within the sport are always taking place and the majority of fanciers seem to heed only the latest offerings, ignoring the wisdom and experience of authors of the calibre of Dr Barker. Owing to some much-appreciated advice, I have recently increased the amount of natural sunlight into my lofts. The idea was that the natural sunlight could not be bettered for health and also for inducing the circulation of air for ventilation and for ensuring dryness. The aim is to allow sunlight and its warming rays in to reach the floor area to induce these effects. Imagine my chagrin when I noted that the Doctor had been advocating this in the fifties, when in his chapter on loft design he made particular mention of skylights for allowing sunlight in.

This is but one example of the knowledge to be found in this volume. As well as the opening chapter on lofts, I particularly like those on food and feeding, the management of the breeding pairs, the moult and on ailments and their treatment. I strongly recommend this book as a great reservoir of pigeon knowledge with as much relevance to the exhibition enthusiast as to the racing fancier. Good copies can be obtained at quite reasonable prices, representing excellent value.

■ The Pigeon by Wendell M. Levi

This is a short title but a mammoth production. In short it is the complete book on pigeons, a definitive source or information and knowledge; indeed the pigeon fancier's bible. Weighing in at 5 ° lb. (2.5 kg) this large volume of over 600 pages is packed from hard cover to hardcover with pigeon material. The author must rate as one of the foremost pigeon fanciers of his time who left behind him a huge amount of information on pigeons through his writing.

If I could keep but only one book on pigeons, this would be it. It is as complete as any book is ever likely to be for the publication costs must have been huge. Despite being first published in 1941 and subsequently revised on a number of occasions, most of the material is fresh and valuable. Much of the photography is in black and white, but simply stunning is a page of twenty-eight colour reproductions of colour types in pigeons contained in the chapter on Genetics - Variation and Inheritance. Just about every subject in the pigeon world is covered in a most learned and knowledgeable manner with each section being almost encyclopaedic in scope.

This is a book for any serious pigeon fancier for most problems can be solved through reference to its pages. The book is not aimed in the direction of the pigeon-racing fancier, yet there is much information which is useful to the enthusiasts of the sport. For the show and flying fanciers however the book is a veritable feast of information especially in the large section of over 200 pages describing pigeon breeds. Other sections include anatomy, physiology, behaviour food and feeding and much more. Whether you want to know about pigeon photography, pigeon bells and flutes, squab production, extinct breeds, sleep, pellet feeds and a myriad of other subjects, the information will be found in the pages of this wonderful book. It is one of the finest investments that any serious pigeon fancier can make.

■ **Encyclopedia of Pigeon Breeds by Wendell M.Levi.**

This wonderful reference book was first published in 1965 and is indeed what its title claims to be. It commences with sixteen short chapters on pigeon management in which the beginner can find out what he needs to know. Never before had there been a book of this detail. Its photography is in living colour which took five years to research and prepare using the lifetime experience of the author with the help of fanciers from 27 pigeon-keeping nations.

There are 768 original colour photographs of pigeon specimens, none of which has been re-touched in any way. Each breed is given information including country of origin and any names given to it in their respective countries. Descriptions reinforce the photographs and include reference to each breed's size, ornaments and colours and the author comments on each and every breed.

This is a truly wonderful work and no fancy pigeon enthusiast should be without it. It is a genuine world-class publication.

■ **Fancy Pigeon Standards - Published by the National Pigeon Association and edited by Mr. D.F.Ison.** Supersedes the 1969 edition edited by Bert Shrives.

This is the British equivalent of Levi's 'Enclyclopedia of Pigeon Breeds' and is the 'bible' of all N.P.A. members in the United Kingdom. It is a complete and comprehensive record of over 200 breeds in over 400 pages. The standard of each breed is detailed and is one of the most complete books of pigeon standards in the English language.

Many of the standards were translated from other languages so the resulting reference of breed standards is a considerable achievement. This book is a 'must have' for all judges of fancy breeds.

■ **The Illustrated Book of Pigeons by Robert Fulton 1879**

This is a nineteenth century classic and one of my most treasured books. 'Fulton' is known the world over and is keenly sought by pigeon enthusiasts. In its day it must have presented a huge challenge in production with 50 colour plates of ideal pigeons, over 50 wood-block illustrations and nearly 400 pages it is nearly the size of Levi's encyclopedia above. The colour plates are wonderfully reproduced from paintings by J.W.Ludlow and are sought simply for framing and display.

Twenty-four chapters are devoted to individual breeds and these follow a learned introduction to the pigeon fancy and explore the poetry of pigeons with reference to the early writers on pigeon breeds. These two offerings are worth reading time and time again as a delightful trip back into history. There are also chapters on basic management, which provide interest bearing in mind the times in which written.

Fanciers who possess a 'Fulton' are indeed fortunate, as this large volume is indeed a magnificent pigeon book, full of interest and knowledge. It is indeed one of the historical standard bearers of the pigeon fancy.

■ **Pigeons: their Structure, Varieties, Habits and Management by W.B.Tegetmeier, F.Z.S., first published 1868.**

This work was originally issued in eight monthly parts each containing two coloured plates and woodcuts before being published in book form of 190 pages. The author was a naturalist of repute and a Fellow of the Zoological Society and an authority on pigeons, poultry and pheasants. The author produced a most scholarly work in line with his aims which he described as follows: . . . the Editor has endeavoured to produce a Treatise that should not only furnish the amateur of pigeons with a greater amount of practical information on the different varieties than is to be found in any previous volume, but also to treat the whole subject in a more scientific manner than has hitherto been attempted'.

This is a famous book presented in half leather binding with raised bands and gilt lettering. It is a famous book and fortunate are those who own a good copy.

■ **Racing Pigeons by Joe Rotondo 1980.**

This is a large book by a plain speaking New Yorker who won out of turn at all levels of competition. Joe Rotondo in his unique fashion outlines in great detail every phase of the sport of pigeon racing from selecting breeding stock, loft management, feeding, health programmes, preventive maintenance and how to live with success!

This book is a most useful reference and guide to the sport of pigeon racing but the good common sense has relevance to all pigeon fanciers. The style of presentation is very individual and straightforward and above all is a book of instruction based on methods which worked for the author as a most successful pigeon fancier.

■**The Secret of Speed by E. J. Sains 1984.**

I believe this to be one of the best and most knowledgeable racing pigeon books. Mr. Sains has the ability to deliver his message in an unambiguous manner using a minimum of words to do so. It is an accurate account of modern racing Belgian racing methods. There is advice on the building of a widowhood loft, the most useful starting point to a successful racing career.

There is good advice on acquiring and recognising good pigeons, on breeding successful pigeons, on selling them and on how to keep and maintain a productive stock loft. Fitness and form as are winning methods for widowhood flying and for young bird racing. There are numerous hints and tips normally known only to long-established and successful fanciers. The chapter, 'Widowhood - the fastest method on earth' is one of the best instructional ones I have ever known and the section 'A winning method' is excellent and makes any cost in acquiring this superb little book, well worth while.

■ **The General Management of Pigeons by 'Violette' (Mons. Somville) authorised English translation by Col. A. Hopas 1933.**

This is an important Belgian work written by Mons. Somville who wrote for the 'Mesager Columbophile' for many years under

213

the pen name of 'Violette'. Although dated in some of the racing content, it is none the less a remarkable source of knowledge on pigeon management in general and will therefore have relevance to all pigeon keepers.

The author has provided a record of his great knowledge on pigeon matters including the housing and feeding which is covered in depth and also a wide-ranging exposition on breeding methods which will reward careful study.

■ **The Book of the Pigeon by Carl A Naether 1939.**

Written by a university professor, this book is a fairly lighthearted examination of pigeons and pigeon methods based upon a lifetime interest and enjoyment. It is a very individual approach to the pigeon and exudes an obvious love between the author and his pigeons. There is a large selection of black and white photographs of an almost historical nature of lofts and equipment.

The large section on fancy pigeons is a most useful one without any aim to catalogue all known breeds, but to describe them in words and occasionally pictorially, in a manner which appeals to the ordinary man. The style is practical explaining both the advantages and drawbacks of the various breeds selected yet avoiding using the written standards of the day because of their ever-changing nature.

The book has proved to be one of the most useful in my library and I rarely refer to it without coming away with some new information, but above all with pleasure at the author's very readable style of presentation. The photographs alone make the seeking out of this book well worth while. There is an additional chapter on foreign doves and is one of the few references in pigeon books of these very interesting little birds. It is an unpretentious work yet is full of interesting and useful pigeon information.

■ **The Homing Pigeon by Edgar Chamberlain 1907.**

This is a most scholarly work on pigeons in general. The opening chapters on the Columba Livia following Darwin's assertion that all pigeons are descended from the Blue Rock Dove is truly masterful. The same applies to his chapter on the

214

history of the pigeon from pre-Christian times is one of the best and most comprehensive I have ever read.

The closely printed book is full of information with each subject examined in depth; albeit in a rather prosaic use of English. The result is that the book is a source of reference based upon the experience of a fancier who was obviously a deep thinker who set out to inform and teach. Despite that some of the book is aimed at the racing fancier, the general content is bound to be of interest to all pigeon fanciers. The final chapter of miscellaneous information is extremely interesting and valuable especially to the novice. I came across this book by accident and now consider it one of my most valued.

■ **The Widowhood Year by Dave Allen 1987.**

This is one of the most colourful pigeon books on the market. It is an ideal publication for the racing enthusiast who wants to be instructed on how to race pigeons on the widowhood system of racing. It is a step by step account of ways of finding success by a fancier who has found success himself both at pigeon racing and in other fields.

Some of the colour photography is stunning while the advice provided is in good bold type with a minimum of fuss. Every fancier, whether novice or expert can learn much from the presentation and style of the Dave Allen methods. Each subject is described in explicit detail so that any fancier can follow it and be able to anticipate success of the sort enjoyed by the author. There are few books which provide such down to earth and comprehensive knowledge as this one. Even for the show enthusiast there is plenty of interest especially on the feeding methods and on the use of specifics.

■ **Treatise on Domestic Pigeons - anonymous author, dated 1765.**

Now in re-printed form in a quaint form of the English language it contains thirteen plates depicting pigeons of the day together with a frontispiece picture. The reprinted edition also carried four black and white photographs. This is an excellent historical pigeon book containing a great deal of management information.

■ **Fancy Pigeons by J. C. Lyell 1880.**

330 pages with woodcuts and 30 plates. The second edition is in 348 pages and the third edition contains eighteen coloured

plates (1885-6) and as a result is generally the most sought. This book was first issued in eleven monthly parts in coloured paper wrapper. In its day it was described as 'one of the most useful books to the student either of ancient pigeon lore or modern pigeon culture'.

This is a very neat little book and one to be valued by any serious pigeon fancier.

■ **Bilco's Pigeon Gas by W. C. A. Cowell 1992.**

In my introduction I mentioned that not many pigeon books would be read from cover to cover but this is an exception. In concluding this chapter I have selected this one as something different providing not only sound advice but also an entertaining story section. Bill Cowell (Bilco) is noted for his enthusiasm for the sport and the philosophy behind it; and also as a writer of short stories - many about pigeons. One part deals with management aspects including methods of selection, while the second part consists of a series of short stories. It is a lively, energetic book suitable for all members of the family. From the opening assertion 'that if you don't like someone, you should give them a pair of pigeons' right through to the story about the black cocks of Foulmire, the author's individualism shines through with the resulting 'good read'.

*   *   *   *   *

The books chosen in this chapter have been taken at random but also on the basis of personal enjoyment and by way of the value I obtain from them. A good book can be used at any time and there-fore a good selection is a 'must' for me and for many fanciers who take the hobby and sport involved in keeping pigeons, seriously. Always be watchful for good quality pigeon books and never turn down the chance of adding to a collection.

A pigeon book is also in many ways a reflection on the social structure of their time. Many of the older and better-known books are marvels of production and presentation especially bearing in mind the lack of technical support which existed when they were written. A good older book is something to be looked at, to be handled and to be enjoyed while some of the more modern volumes are full of infor-mation and guidance on how to succeed with pigeons. A good book, just like the keeping of pigeons, is to be enjoyed, to be cherished and to be kept well and safely.

Chapter 25

Pigeons in the Service of their Country

SURP 41 L3089 White Vision.

*This pigeon was carried in a Catalina flying boat
Which owing to engine failure had to ditch in rough seas
In Northern waters at approx.0820hrs on the 11th October 1943.
Owing to a radio failure no SOS was received from the aircraft
and no fix obtained. As the aircraft was overdue and suspected
to be in difficulties rescue searches were made but were limited
owing to severe weather conditions. No aircraft were permitted
to take off.
At 1700hrs 'White Vision' arrived with a message giving the
Position and other information about the aircraft and crew.
Time of origin of this message of this message was 0820hrs. As a
Result a sea search was continued in the direction indicated by
H.S.L. and the crew rescued. The aircraft had to be abandoned
and sank. Weather conditions: Visibility at place of release of
pigeon 100 yards. Visibility at Base when pigeon arrived 300 yards.
Head wind for pigeon 25 miles per hour. Heavy sea running, very low
Cloud 10/10ths, distance about 60 miles. Number of lives saved 11.
Bred by Messrs Fleming Brothers, Motherwell, Scotland. Trained
By R.A.F.Sollum Voe, Shetlands.*

'White Vision' was awarded the Dickin Medal.

Who could read such an account without having a great admiration for 'White Vision' and for all the other valiant pigeons which performed such brave flights during periods of conflict throughout the world. One can but marvel at the fantastic performances put up by birds which very often operated through the most extreme of conditions of weather, ill-handling and by enemy fire. Birds were liberated at all times of day or night, in all weather conditions and in areas where they were shot at on sight, yet many of these gallant winged messengers managed to get through. The importance of their role to war efforts can never be fully appreciated.

R.A.F. crew saved by 'White Vision'. Left to right: Back row, Jack Southern. 'Tiny' Merrick, Cliff Ludgate. Ron Vaughan (Captain), Geoff Gibbons. Front row: Ralph Graham, Tom Carter, Ken (Benny) Bennett and John Peberdy. Below: 'White Vision'

The extreme service in war times of course is but a part of the general service to mankind performed by our pigeons. Message carrying in times of war resulting in the saving of human life is the most tangible evidence of service. But in the development of mankind, the humble pigeon has played a vital role by way regard, interest, company, in literature and poetry, genetic study and of course the more utilitarian supply of food. Levi asserts that *'Wherever civilisation has flourished, there the pigeon has thrived; and the higher the civilisation, usually the higher the regard for the pigeon'.*[1] Archaeological inscriptions of the pigeon or dove have been discovered which pre-date any documentary evidence which seem to prove that pigeons and doves were not only tended with care but held in great reverence and esteem. Pigeons in War.

It is well known that military strategists have appreciated the value of pigeons as messengers as a means of liaison and communication. Yet proof of this in pre-historical times is not available so much is conjecture though it is thought that King Solomon (about 1000 BC) is thought to have used pigeons for communication purposes. Persians, Assyrians, Egyptians, Lydians, Phoencians and other civilised races recognised the homing ability of the pigeon and used it to further their war efforts. Chamberlain states: 'these earlier civilised races must have been dependant in some degree on the homing pigeon's in prosecuting their military and naval campaign. . . people so intellectual and so utilitarian could not and would not miss the opportunity of establishing an animate postal service to assist them. . . .'[2]

Documentary evidence exists to state that the Romans used pigeons two thousand years ago and that Julius Caesar used pigeons as messengers in the conquest of Gaul. There is also a statement that in the siege of Mutina (Modena) in 43 BC that Hirtius and Brutus communicated with one another using pigeons.

In the Middle Ages the Saracens used pigeons during the Crusades and there have been many examples of pigeons being used during battles and sieges. It was at the siege of Paris in 1870/ 71 that the modern day homer came to international recognition. Balloons were released from the besieged city containing among other things, Parisian pigeons that were taken to various places including London and Tours and subsequently released with messages for the Parisians. By the aid of microphotography process, messages were copied upon thin films of collodian, each of which

---

[1] *The Pigeon* by Wendell M.Levi. [2] *The Homing Pigeon* by Edgar Chamberlain 1907

French mobile pigeon loft used during World War 1

could contain up to 2500 communications. As many as twelve of these films could be carried by a single pigeon by the use of goose quills which were bound to strong tail feathers using waxed silk thread.

During the four months of the siege it is thought that 150,000 official messages and up to a million private communications were carried into Paris in this manner. The popularity of the homing pigeon increased greatly and in 1875 John Van Opstal wrote that: 'flying pigeons could be of the greatest service, as has been proved in the late Franco-German war. The Russian, German and Italian Governments have established already columbaries within their fortifications, and the French Government is now buying in Belgium two thousand pair of Antwerp flying birds for the same purpose'.

Germany saw the possible value of the use of pigeons and was one of the first to establish military pigeon lofts and in 1887 each was said to contain about 400 trained pigeons.

World War 1

At the outbreak of war in 1914, it was felt by many that the modern communication inventions would render the pigeon redundant as a mode of communication. Such was not the case and the Belgians, the French and the Germans from the start appreciated the value of pigeons as messengers. As soon as they occupied Belgian of French territory, the Germans ordered the destruction of all resident pigeons, severely punishing anyone unfortunate enough to be discovered owning or selling them. It has been estimated that the Germans took at least a million Belgian birds.

In Great Britain it is generally admitted that the authorities failed to realise the potential value of pigeons in their war effort and for a time ordered the destruction or internment of all pigeons in the coastal areas. Crews of minesweepers were the first to recognise the value of pigeons and the Carrier Pigeon Service was established under Captain, later to be Lt.Colonel, A.H. Osman. Even so it was not until March 1916 that pigeons were sent to the war front where they performed great service in regular communication.

British Forces dropped pigeons in baskets from aeroplanes into friendly areas so that messages could be sent back. The Germans were aware of this and ordered severe punishment against anyone found opening one of the baskets without reporting it to the authorities and also ordered huge fines against any town in which such a pigeon should be discovered. British air force records show that pigeons delivered 717 messages from planes crashing on to the sea.

In praising the military value of the homer, Major General Fowler, Chief of the Department of Signals and Communication in the British Army is reported as saying: *'If it became necessary immediately to discard every line and method of communication used on the front, except one, and it were left to me to select one method, I should unhesitatingly choose the pigeons. It is the pigeons on which we must and do depend when every other method fails. During the quiet periods we can rely on telephone, telegraph; flag signals, our dogs, and various other ways in use on the front with the British Armies. But when the battle rages and everything gives way to barrage and machine gun fire, to say nothing of the gas attacks and bombing, it is to the pigeon that we go for succour. When troops are lost, or surrounded in the mazes on the front, or are advancing and yet beyond the known localities, then we depend absolutely on the pigeon for our communications. Regular methods in such cases are worthless and it is at just such times that we need most, messengers that we can rely on. In the pigeons we have them. I am glad to say they have never failed us'.*

That more or less sums up the faith the Forces had in the pigeons and the important job of work they were doing. Before proceeding from World War 1, perhaps more examples will even better describe that value.[3]

■ NURP17F3037 mealy hen. Liberated with message from seaplane down with engine trouble 30 miles from base. Pilot and observer stated that the information conveyed by the pigeon was the means of their being rescued. * NURP17F3534 red chequer cock. Seaplane failed to return. The first news came from the message carried by this pigeon from 100miles out at sea, with the result that the crew of six was saved after being on the water three days.

■ NURP18F15744 Blue Chequer cock. Following message brought in by this pigeon: 'Down, send assistance at once'. This was the first intimation received, and was the means of saving the crew and the machine. On several other occasions this pigeon has brought back valuable information.

■ HP16M492 Red chequer cock. Has completed 172 Active Service Patrols.

■ NU17GPS104 Blue chequer cock. Liberated from seaplane in difficulties, the message carried being the means of saving the

---

[3] Taken from *'Pigeons in the Great War'* by Lt.Col.A.H. Osman O.B.E.

lives of the pilot and observer. This bird has repeatedly done good work.

- ■ * NURP17F483 Blue chequer cock. Liberated 160 miles from land at 6.30pm in darkness and fog, and reached the station in good time.

The Second World War

Lessons from the Great War had been learned so that when the Second World War began in 1939 the British were not only aware of the value of pigeon-communication but were well prepared. The National Pigeon Service had been established in 1938 as a volunteer civilian organisation. Major W.H. Osman who, in the Great War had held three commissions in connection with pigeons had formed it following representations to the Committee of Imperial Defence and the British Government. . Major Osman took a leading role in the formation of the N.P.S. as his father, Lt.Col. A.H.Osman had in connection with the Army Pigeon Service in the previous conflict.

Never in recorded history was so much use made of pigeons They were used by all ground, air and naval forces, as well as by civilian establishments to overcome broken or damaged means of communication.

During the War over 200,000 young pigeons were provided free of charge by British fanciers to the National Pigeon Service. These birds were used by the Royal Air Force as standard equipment on all bomber and reconnaissance planes, and by the Army and the Intelligence Services.

Special Section

In a period of three and a half years the Special Section of the Army Pigeon Service parachuted 16,554 pigeons on to the Continent. There were 1842 returns, some of which were of immense value.

Table of returns	Despatched	Returned	Per cent
Up to September 1941	616	139	22.5
October 1941 to March 1942	74	14	19
April 1942 to September 1942	1342	267	20
October 1942 to March 1943	1664	113	7
April 1943 to September 1943	3793	528	14
October 1943 to March 1944	2819	161	5.75
April 1944 to September 1944	6246	620	10
Total for period of service	16,554	1842	11

Mr H C Woodman, Chief Pigeon Officer of the National Pigeon Service, with typical wartime pigeon equipment mentioned in this chapter

Pigeon Memorial Garden at Worthing, Sussex

The birds were collected from loft owners on the day prior to despatch and taken to an airfield where they were fitted with green message containers and packed into round single-bird cartons with parachutes attached, together with bags of food to last 10 days, instructions, questionnaires etc. With luck after being parachuted into enemy held territory, they might be found by a local resident who was brave enough to pick it up and to take it home - probably hidden from view.

When examined the contents of the container would reveal the pigeon and the corn together with instructions. These advised the finder of the great risk and cautioned that the parachute and all damning evidence should be disposed of immediately. The finder was asked to care for the bird, allowing it freedom of movement and to feed and water it. The finder was asked not to liberate the bird at dusk, in rain or in fog. There was a list of questions on local information and intelligence, instructions on how to place material in the message carrier, and in many cases some newspaper reports on the state of the war.

The Germans were fully aware of the dangers of such information being carried to England and offered large rewards for pigeons to be handed to them. They then used allied pigeons or birds rung with allied rings in order to plant them and to establish the identities of local people who were willing to pass on information. Such brave people were dealt with very harshly - often by being put to death.

Messages covering the widest range of fact were received through the service including intelligence on the V1 rocket sites and it is almost beyond belief that in the message container a pigeon brought back a message of 5,000 words with fifteen sketch maps giving a wealth of information.

Life Savers

Numerous lives were saved through the bravery of the winged messengers both in cases where individuals or groups were in peril, but also through the intelligence the birds brought in from enemy held territory. Great Britain owes a debt of gratitude to the humble pigeon described by J.L.Carney in 1935 when describing the military value of the homer as . . .' Into the Breach went the little racing pigeon, the most gallant little bird the world knows. . . .' It could not have been known then, just how soon the pigeons would be back in the service of their countries.

The National Pigeon Service provided the American Signal Corps with 46,532 pigeons. The United States Pigeon Corps at one time contained over three thousand enlisted men, one hundred and fifty officers and fifty four thousand pigeons. Wendell M Levi in his book 'The Pigeon' carefully explores the scale of the American use of pigeons.

The tails of pigeon heroes are legendary and perhaps the best way of detailing some of them is to include a list of Dickin medal winners - the 'Animals V.C.'

The Dickin Medal

Mrs M.E. Dickin, CBE founded the People's Dispensary for Sick Animals (P.D.S.A.), a charitable organisation encouraging the keeping of pets and the guarding of the health of speechless creatures. The Allied Forces Mascot Club, a subordinate body of the P.D.S.A. Inaugurated the Dickin Medal in 1943. The majority of Dickin Medals were awarded to pigeons in the Second World War, all of which were British birds except one, which was awarded to an American pigeon. The list of pigeon winners of the Dickin medal is reproduced herewith as the finest recognition of the role of the pigeon in the War.

- * 'Winkie' NEHU40NS1 Blue chequer hen, bred by A.R.Colley of Sunderland, trained by Ross and Norrie of Scotland. On the 23rd February 1942 escaped from its container in a crashed aircraft in the North Sea 120miles from the Scottish coast. The bird left the scene with ninety minutes of daylight left and reached its loft 129miles away just after dawn the next morning. It was exhausted, wet and oily - having fallen into the oil covered seas when it struggled from its container. An air search until then had been unsuccessful but Sergeant Davidson of the RAF Pigeon Service deduced from the arrival of the pigeon that the area of the search was incorrect. As a result a new search was commenced in accordance with his advice and within fifteen minutes the crew were found and ultimately rescued. This was the first rescue during the 1939-45 war attributable to a pigeon.

- 'George' MEPS43.1263. Red Chequer cock, bred at Maadi, H.Q. of the Middle-East Pigeon Service. On the 22nd June 1943 'George' was carried in a plane which crashed in the Mediterranean a hundred miles from base. In a visibility of two miles, a search for a dinghy had failed. The pigeon was released with information as to location and despite twice being dropped into the sea, it homed successfully and the crew of four from the aircraft was saved.

- 'White Vision' SURP41L3089, white hen - see commencement of this chapter and the photos of 'White Vision' and the crew saved as a result of his flight.

- 'Beachcomber' NPS41NS4230, bred by W.Lane of Ipswich, owned by W.H.Tompkins, Wolverton and trained by the Army Pigeon Service. Carried on a Commando raid on Dieppe in 1942 and delivered an important message back to Britain. One of a pair released but its companion was killed by enemy gunfire.

- 'Gustav' NPS4231066 Grizzle cock, bred by N.P.S. member Mr F.E.Jackson, Cosham, Trained by R.A.F. Thorney Island. This pigeon was the first to arrive from the Normandy Landings on D.Day carrying a message from Reuters' correspondent dispatched from landing-craft standing off the beach during the first landings. The weather was adverse and Gustav's time was 5hrs 16minutes. During two years of RAF service this pigeon had built a reputation for reliability.

- 'Paddy' NPS43.9451 Dark Chequer gay pied cock, bred by N.P.S. member A.S.Hughes of Northern Ireland trained at RAF Station Hurn. Of the several hundred pigeons used in the Normandy invasion, 'Paddy' recorded the fastest time with a message, namely 4hrs 50minutes, Originally in service in Northern Ireland, this cock was transferred to Hurn for re-settlement and re-training.

- 'Kenley Lass' NURP36JH190 Dark chequer hen, she was bred by W.H.Torkington, Poynton, and trained by N.P.S. member R.W.Beard, Kenley. She was the first to be used for secret communication from enemy-occupied France. She was parachuted with an agent who then had to walk nine miles with the hen secreted on him. The bird was then detained for eleven days in concealment. She was released with her most important information at 0820hrs on 20th October 1940, arriving at Kenley at 1500hrs that day having covered over 300 miles. The following February she was sent back and after detention for four days arrived back with the information the same day.

- 'Commando' NURP38 EGU242, Red Chequer cock, bred and trained by S.A.Moon, Haywards Heath. On three occasions in 1942 was sent into France with agents and on trip she returned home on the day of release with valuable information. On two occasions the weather conditions were exceptionally adverse.

- 'Flying Dutchman' NPS42NS44802 Dark chequer cock., bred by E.G.Forster, Walthamstow Trained by RAF Station Felixstowe. In addition to many flights from light naval craft in the North Sea, on three occasions in 1944 was dropped with an agent at various points on the Continent between 150 and 250 miles. On each occasion delivered valuable information.

- 'Royal Blue'NURP40GVIS453, Blue cock, bred and trained at the Royal Lofts, Sandringham. 'Royal Blue' was the first pigeon during the war to bring a message from a forced-landed aircrew on the Continent. On the 10th October 1940 this young cock was released in Holland 120 miles from base arriving at Sandringham at 1130hrs the same day with details of the situation of the crew.

- 'Dutch Coast' NURP41A2164. bred and trained by N.P.S. member J.Flowers, Ratcliffe on Trent, and operated from RAF Station Syerston. On The 13th April 1942 a ditched aircrew off the coast of Holland released this pigeon at 0620hrs providing their position. The bird delivered the message covering 288 miles in 7° hours in conditions, which were far from favourable.

- 'Navy Blue' NPS41NS2862 Blue cock bred by RAF St Eval. This bird had an excellent record in the RAF Air/Sea Rescue Service and was then sent on a special reconnaissance mission on the West Coast of France some 200 miles from Plymouth on the night of 17th/18th June 1944 with no time of release stated. Despite being injured the bird managed to reach Plymouth with her message which was described as being of immense value.

- 'William of Orange' NPS42NS15125 Mealy cock bred and owned by W.Proctor Smith, Knutsford, Trained by the Army Pigeon Service. On service with the Airborne troops at Arnhem was liberated at 1030hrs on the 19th September 1944 and returned home in 4 hours 25 minutes, a distance of 260 miles of which 135 miles were over open seas.

- 'Ruhr Express' NPS43.29018 Dark Chequer cock bred and trained by RAF Station, Detling. This bird was dropped by parachute within enemy lines, 300miles from base on 13th April 1945 and returned with very valuable information in what was said to be the best time in such operations.

- 'Scotch Lass' NPS42.21610 Blue chequer hen bred by Collins and Son, Mussleburgh, trained by the R.A.F Station Felixstowe. In the course of her service at RAF Wick and then at the Felixstowe base, she was sent on 43 flights from small naval craft in the North Sea. She was dropped with an agent in Holland in September 1944, and although injured by hitting telegraph wires when liberated in the dawn semi-darkness, successfully delivered her message and photo films on the same day at a distance of 260 miles.

- 'Billy' NU41HQ4373 Blue cock, bred and trained by J.Greenwood, Lincoln, RAF Waddington. Released with a message from a force-landed bomber crew in the Netherlands at 1000hrs on the 21st February 1942, he delivered his message the following day at 1340hrs in a state of complete collapse. The weather conditions were appalling with gale-driven snow. 'Billy' was eleven months old at the time when he flew this 250 miles.

- 'Cologne' NURP39NRS144 Red cock, bred and trained by N.P.S. member W.H.Payne, Nottingham. And from R.A.F.Bottesford. He flew on over a hundred bomber sorties and homed from diverted or force-landed aircraft from widely separated positions in Britain at various times. On 29th June 1943, its aircraft was lost over Cologne. On the 16th July the cock homed with severe injuries including a broken breastbone which was estimated to have occurred two weeks previously.

- 'Maquis' NPS42.36392 Blue chequer cock owned by P.Cope, Duxford and bred by Brown Brothers, Bedford and trained by the Army Pigeon Service. April 1943 returned to England with operational message in four days. May 1943 Returned from Amiens with operational message. February 1944 on service with Combined Operations, returned on day of liberation in good time. June 1944 returned with message from France, taking a month.

- NPS42NS2780 bred by B.Powell, Hereford owned by Sir Ernest Debenham, Dorchester. Three drops and returns from behind enemy lines

- NPS42NS7524 bred by C.Dyson of Barnsley and owned by Lady Mary Manningham-Buller this pigeon also had three drops behind enemy lines and returned each time.

- 'Broad Arrow' 41.2793 three drops behind enemy lines and returned each time

- 'All Alone' NURP39 SDS39 Returned south of Lyons to Staines. Bred by J.Paulger,Staines.

- 'Mercury' NURP37CEN335 Returned from a drop in Denmark. Bred by J.Catchpole

- NURP38BPC6 Returned to Bridgwater with information. Bred by S.J.Bryant, Bridgwater. N.B. the above seven birds were used by British Intelligence Forces for obtaining information on V1 and V2 rocket sites.

- 'Mary' NURP40SLE249 bred by C.Brewer, Exeter. In five years of service she received twenty-two stitches to her body. 'For outstanding endurance on war service despite wounds. (See additional information at end of chapter.)

- 'Tommy' NURP41DHZ56, bred by W.Brockbank, Dalton in Furness. Picked up in Holland by partisans. After two weeks recovery he was liberated with a message concerning enemy anti-aircraft measures. Although wounded he returned successfully with information on flying -bomb sites.

- 'Princess' 42WD593, bred by the Middle-East Pigeon Service. Dispatched at only five months of age with message for spares for radio transmitter broken by secret agent landing by parachute in Crete. She delivered the message and the spares were sent.

- 'G.I Joe' USA 43SC6390, bred by the United States Army. He saved hundreds of British lives by delivering message to Twelfth Air Support Command, of the British Infantry advance to a position formerly occupied by the enemy and scheduled to be heavily bombed. 'GI Joe' made his journey at over a mile per minute and reached there minutes before the bombers left on their mission.

- DD43Q879, bred by the Australian Voluntary Pigeon Service. Saved a patrol of United States Marines attacked by the Japanese. Though their radio had been smashed and two other pigeons carrying messages had been shot down, it delivered its message and the patrol returned to base safely.

- DD43T139 bred by the Australian Voluntary Pigeon Service. Flew 40miles in fifty minutes, in spite of heavy tropical rain, with a message from a landing craft in distress. The message was delivered and the landing craft and valuable cargo was rescued.

- ■ 'Duke of Normandy' NURP41SBC219, bred by G.Noterman of London. Landed with paratroops behind the German lines on D-Day. Liberated six days after landing, returning 27 hours later in severe rain and gales.

- ■ NURP43CC2418, bred by T.Markham, Kendal. Dropped with an Airborne force in Normandy. Released in bad weather after six days of confinement in a small container. She successfully homed.

This chapter has mainly confined commentary to the British successful use of pigeons but it must be remembered that many other countries used pigeons as a means of war-time communication. By the very nature of the British Isles, being just off the coast of mainland Europe, and for some time fighting almost alone, the use of pigeons became so very important for the maintenance of lines of communication to aid the war effort. The Osman family played a most significant role in this situation in both World Wars and continued to influence the sport of pigeon racing for many years after the conflicts.

Show of Service Pigeons (Army Division)

On the 2nd December 1944 a show was held for all fanciers who had supplied birds for Special Section operations. Despite being restricted to one bird only except for two classes for birds which had served in the operations, a remarkable 1017 birds were entered. The secrecy of the usage of the birds was at last lifted so that the public could be made aware of the role of pigeons, and the owners could have some information on how their birds had been used. The show was a great success and was attended by thousands. It marked the end of the service of pigeons in the Special Section which was closed down in January 1945.

Memorial

Tucked away in a garden of remembrance in Worthing, Sussex is a stone memorial engraved as follows: *'In Memory of Warrior Birds who gave their lives on Active Service 1939-45 and for the use and pleasure of living birds'.*

Great performances – terrible conditions

The most remarkable thing about the use of pigeons as messengers is that the top performances were achieved in some of the worst possible weather conditions and at times of the year not normally associated with pigeon flying. In pigeon racing, the normal racing season is from April to September when the weather is at its best. Race birds are conveyed to race sites in good quality transporters and looked after by experienced and dedicated fanciers. In wartime, the birds were handled mainly by non-fanciers as they were taken into battle and confined in small containers sometimes for long periods. They were often rocked and buffeted and made to endure extreme and unpleasant surroundings. and they were shot, shot at, wounded and otherwise injured. Yet they performed brilliantly and flew in weather conditions in which normal fanciers would hesitate at even allowing their birds from the loft.

One can have nothing but great admiration for the valiant birds which reached home despite being wounded, shot at, liberated in near dark conditions even moonlight and occasionally in the worst of flying and weather conditions. Much of the answer seems to be that the British fanciers supplied their best pigeons to the service of their country, and that the various pigeon services were manned by top quality pigeon fanciers who were able to get the very best out of their charges. They were the men of the day, selected by professionals within the pigeon sport, as being fanciers able and willing to produce top pigeon performances at the times of their country's need.

I commenced the chapter with a description of the performance of 'White Vision' so perhaps will end with a newspaper report of the time on 'Mary' the Dickin Medal winner and known affectionately as 'Mary of Exeter'.

'Mary Never Failed us'

A pigeon is going to a ball; She is 'Mary'
Veteran of five years' war service, who has just been awarded the Animals V.C.
At a charity ball in Park Lane, twenty-two stitches in her scarred body
Will be on view to the guests. Mary was lost for four days in 1942. She returned
To her loft with her breast ripped open by a hawk.
Five month later she came back after being posted 'missing' for three weeks. Half
A wing was shot away. She returned to active service and was found shot down in
a field, almost dead. Her wounds were stitched up;
a collar was put around her almost severed neck, and
Mary, holder of the Dickin Medal, is still in service raising
money for sick animals'.

Mary was owned and trained by Mr Charles Brewer, a shoemaker of Exeter.

To further illustrate the sheer determination of 'Mary of Exeter' the following information may be of interest. She was attacked by a hawk in 1942 when carrying a message for the 8th Corps, receiving a wound which required seven stitches. Five months later when again on service and carrying a message she was shot under the wing, losing most of her flights. Despite this she struggled home where her owner Mr Brewer removed three pellets and stitched her up again.

In the bombing blitz on the City of Exeter a 1100lb bomb dropped close to the house and Mr Brewer and his pigeons were evacuated. The following night another bomb exploded near the house in which they were temporarily accommodated and nineteen of the pigeons were killed. Mary was in one of the baskets blown to pieces by the explosion, yet was waiting at the loft for her owner the next morning. She was extremely shocked.

She again returned to service and when on another mission went missing for ten days. Amazingly she was picked up on a field nearly dead. She had a wound stretching from the top of her head to the base of her neck, the result of yet another hawk or falcon attack. Her owner lovingly stitched her up but her injury was so bad that she could not raise her head so Mr Brewer, a master shoemaker by trade, made a four-inch (10cm) collar for her. She had to be hand-fed and watered for many days, yet despite all adversities Mary once again returned to active service.

*   *   *   *   *   *

I thought that the extra information on 'Mary of Exeter' would enable readers to judge for themselves just how much the humble pigeon did to aid its country. Behind every description accompanying each of the Dickin Medal winners is a set of circumstances similar to that of Mary and of 'White Vision' and the few words can never adequately describe the suffering of the birds as they delivered their vital information messages. Vitally important information was delivered from behind enemy lines, information and intelligence which may well have shortened the war and also resulting in the saving of numerous lives - on both sides of the conflict.

Many good men and women owed their lives to the valiant pigeon messengers, described as the most gallant little bird the world knows. Who, when reading of their performances in wartime would argue with that statement.

PART 5

The Pigeon Year
A Month by Month Guide

Chapter 26

The Show Loft

JANUARY

It is tempting to stress that January is one of the most important periods in the show loft but for the pigeon fancier this applies to any period in the loft in the average year. It is true of course that decisions made in January will affect the success or otherwise of the show programme to follow later in the year, but each and every week in the year is tied in with matters affected by work and decision making.

For the purposes of this chapter however, it is the start of the calendar year but very much the start of the pigeon year. The serious fancier will already have been thinking about his potential pairings and the numbers of birds required for the breeding programme, both by way of key pairs and also those to act as feeders. I have no doubt that the best way to plan this is by listing the birds on paper so that the possibilities can be explored to ensure that the best possible birds are bred. A sound knowledge of parentage and family of the birds to be paired is necessary - also information on past breeding results. So, if a bird throws either large or small birds, or birds with faults, it is best to avoid using them or to try them with something completely different.

By committing everything to lists in writing it is an excellent way of getting to know the birds better and to clear the mind as to whether all the birds listed are necessary for the future of the loft's success. I tend to have numerous sheets of paper from November onwards on which I explore the probabilities of pairings and whether there is something else I need to bring in to supplement my stock. Remember, the smaller the number of birds at commencement of breeding the better, for there is nothing like having plenty of room and space. Also, spare birds can be a nuisance as they seek a mate, witnessing that all their loft mates are suited! If space allows a few spare birds to be carried, this is no bad thing. The spare birds can provide a little reserve should any of the main pairings go wrong in any way, and also a few unmated birds will be ideal for the early summer shows. They maintain their fitness and overall condition far better than birds going through the rearing process.

One can assume that all the birds are safely through their moult but those which are still going through it, having been later bred for example, can be assisted with extra light. Many birds will cease their primary flight moult unless provided with some sort of artificial stimulation. If extra lighting can be applied to a compartment or section this will enable the late-moulters to complete their feather change. Extra lighting is good for early breeding in any case, providing an artificial 'spring' with longer hours of light.

For those who enter the January shows this is one of the best times of the year to be able to find a team of good, fit entries. Generally the birds are at their best and respond well to good treatment and good show preparation. It is also an excellent time to obtain stock for most fanciers are carrying a few birds too many and are more willing to part with some as their breeding season approaches. A careful study of the birds on show can often reveal a bird of the type and quality to be brought in to improve chances of success at breeding.

Preparing the birds for the January shows is quite enjoyable. Some may well have used the Christmas period and quiet period, to 'break-down' condition or to reduce weight in their show birds. When this is done, it is normally fairly easy to bring the body weight back to requirements by supplementing the food with top quality grains and supplements. Birds cannot remain in top condition indefinitely so subtle changes to diet will allow the weight and subsequent condition to be varied to suit the show programme.

January is the time of hard work, for work done at this time can pay dividends later on. It is a good time to basket or crate all the birds in compartments or sections containing nest boxes so that the whole area can be thoroughly cleaned. If a good sunny and airy day can be selected for this so much the better. The area should be thoroughly scraped and cleaned with dust removed by sweeping or use of a suitable vacuum. The walls can be washed down using hot water containing disinfectant and soda or bleach to act as a germ-killer. The use of a blowtorch is recommended not only to assist in the drying process as a side benefit, but also to kill any worm eggs which might be on the floor area.

Then, the nest boxes. Each box should be thoroughly cleaned but they should be sprayed using a good virucide solution, but also sprayed against insect life especially the dreaded red mite. The latter will not be seen but may be hiding in cracks and other places, simply waiting for the right conditions to emerge and ravage the breeding birds and their young. The astute use of the blowtorch is also recommended but with the obvious advice to be very careful.

Once I am satisfied as to their fitness and cleanliness, I line the floor areas of each nest box with layers of newspaper using several thicknesses. It provides a good clean and replaceable base for each box but also a degree of insulation and warmth. Some birds like privacy and they are supplied with small cardboard box retreats within the nest box where they can achieve their quiet, undisturbed times. These also provide extra insulation and can be removed at any time for burning or other disposal.

When showing is over for the season, all planning can be directed towards the breeding. It goes without saying that birds which are in show condition are not necessarily in breeding condition. This is especially so in breeds which are required to have suitable 'body' when judged. Fat pigeons cannot breed properly so the first thought must be to reduce weight or to otherwise produce breeding condition in the birds - especially in the hens which will be expected to lay in good time.

I have never favoured starving birds as a means of weight reduction. It is far better to take an extra week or more to produce breeding condition, than to pair birds in the hope that they will achieve this through the mating and driving processes. Therefore a subtle change of diet is better than outright removal of foods. Such changes should be gradual and good fanciers will do this by gradually changing both the content and amount fed. The higher protein foods required for showing condition will be adjusted so that more carbohydrate is used with barley and clipped oats being my preferred grains as part of the new diet.

The oats will provide good energy and 'bounce' without weight and the barley is weight reducing with the added advantage of being a monitor or the bird's hunger. If birds leave barley - they are receiving too much - and I tend to wait until all is consumed before feeding again. Garlic added to the water or grains is a good idea and it is also a good time to administer purging salts and/or pigeon tea to sharpen appetite and constitutions.

The period between showing and pairing is also an excellent time for routine medication. The birds can be wormed using either flock treatment remedy, or by the tablet method for each pigeon. I also believe in flock treating for canker for birds carrying the problem will pass it on to their youngsters with subsequent losses.

The treatment of older birds to prepare them for breeding requires some thought also. Some of the old-timers need every assistance they can get by way of trimming surplus feather from the vent and reproduction areas. I would prefer not to have to do it, but in some cases am prepared for it to enable good reproduction. It is also sometimes better to pair the older birds later in the season when conditions are warmer and when they respond to spring-like weather and condition. The same applies to show breeds which are slow to get going. Unless there is a need to try to breed some early young birds, they are often better left until the warmer weather comes.

Talking about the weather, it is a good time to ensure that the lofts are both windproof and waterproof. Nothing strips condition like the cold winds blowing in and a damp or wet loft is a bad loft. Shutters can be used and any other means to keep the elements out and a settled environment in.

FEBRUARY

The days are short and the hours of darkness long. The use of artificial lighting is a considerable help with early breeding. The hours of light can be lengthened but must be accompanied by an automatic dimming system. An immediate cutout is exactly what is not required as it might happen when birds are off the nest at the drinker - or for some other reason.

The shutters or other means of windproofing and waterproofing should still be in place. In the event of a clear sunny day, it is a wonderful thing to be able to open up doors and windows for a while to allow as much natural sunlight and fresh air in as possible. Plenty of clear glass is the answer in window form or in adjustable louvres.

For many, the first of the young birds will be appearing and there is little better in the year in any pigeon loft to see the first discarded eggshells on the floor. The birds and their youngsters should be left alone as much as possible and there is no need to examine them until they are ready for ringing. By this time the young birds will be visible peaking out from under their parents and in any case the old birds will be a little easier at leaving them briefly to take a drink or to eat some food.

In the event of extreme frosts thought might be given to the provision of some heating. A tubular heater situated under nest boxes but not touching anything are all that is necessary to take most of the bite out of the cold. And if these can be controlled by a thermostat, so much the better. This is not an expensive operation and will repay the outlay quite quickly in ease of mind and in the production of good early youngsters. Our Belgian 'cousins' produce and sell an excellent form of 'heat-pad' for use on loft floors. It acts as a mild heater and as a warm area for newly weaned youngsters.

It is a good idea to provide additional insulation in the nestboxes. Plenty of newspaper on the floor area of each box is an inexpensive precaution and any draughts can be prevented from reaching the box inmates by some simple shielding and I favour the use of cardboard boxes in the nest box to provide this and some privacy.

With youngsters appearing only the best of food should be given to the birds to ensure that they not only maintain their condition but also give the best possible start to the squeakers. The use of garlic and other supplements can be administered and also a food supplement which includes cod liver oil and calcium. Calcium is most important at this time of the year and much will be provided by the provision of top quality grits especially oyster shell and of powdered minerals. All this should be administered fresh as damp will soon affect them.

The lofts should be kept as quiet as possible during this time of the year when birds are going to nest, sitting and producing young birds. That is not to say that they should be left alone, for a good fancier will simply sit and watch the birds as much as possible. The benefits are to be seen for both birds and fancier with the former getting used to the presence of the fancier, and the fancier being able to observe exactly what is going on.

The short days in the loft also result in long evenings indoors. What better time to get up to date with records, and other matters affecting the lofts and the birds? Pedigrees, correspondence and other records can be updated in the so-called quiet times.

Another matter to be sorted at this time of the year is to ensure that all show baskets and containers are properly emptied and cleaned. The weather may not allow them to be scrubbed and dried but just to empty them is a step in the right direction. I would also advise that all such baskets and containers are stored in a secure place so that vermin is unable to get access to them. Talking about vermin of course, always be watchful for signs of vermin. There can be little worse than in having mice or rats in or near the loft. The more likely will be mice so steps should be taken to keep them out using small mesh wire and to avoid leaving any food lying about.

MARCH

At last the evenings will be lengthening and the resulting extra light will provide the birds with a boost. In many lofts the young birds will be large and ready to leave their nests. Wherever possible, when they are two weeks of age, another bowl should be placed in the box so that the pair can start courtship for the second round. It is better to provide a choice of nests as when they have to lay in the same bowl as the large youngsters, all sorts of problems can occur.

Whenever possible, wean young birds in groups. as they provide each other with warmth, comfort and support. It is best to have an empty section for them away from any older birds. This prevents bullying and setbacks to the growing youngsters. Birds with obvious faults should be dealt with as should any which are in any way ill nourished or showing signs of weakness. It is always tempting when the youngsters are few in numbers to give the benefit of the doubt but in my experience such doubts are rarely wrong.

As much time as possible should be spent with the growing young birds as it encourages them to trust human contact and the tamer they are the better for their showing careers to follow. Where possible 'play' with them to provide that faith which will lead to their pleasure at human company.

Observation is very important. Any birds looking as though they might be leaving the nest of eggs of young birds should be looked at for red mite or for other problems. The presence of mice will most certainly upset the birds. When they look to leave their nest, there is generally a good reason for it. Exact dates of laying and hatching should be recorded so even if the adults leave the nest it may be possible to place the eggs/young birds under other pairs. Eggs should be checked after a week to check whether they are fertile or not. It is pointless allowing birds to sit out bad eggs, as much time will be lost.

Baths are important for the old birds and no opportunity should be lost when the days are fine and dry. The young birds will watch the old birds enjoying the bath and will quickly get the idea. Often they show their desire for water by trying to use the drinker when newly filled.

Winds can still be a problem in March so shuttering should still be available to keep the wind out and of course the driving rain or snow. Food supplements are most necessary and garlic and other products in the water can only help the feeding parents during this stressful time for them.

APRIL

Most lofts will be the possessors of some young birds by now. Indeed most will be on the second round and this is a good time to start to think about re-pairing some of the top producers or to try something different. Lofts with feeders are especially able to do this with the ability of taking off a round of eggs at an earlier stage freeing the adults for further duty or for a new pairing. It is also the best time to pair the older stock birds together in the longer days with warmer weather conditions. Boxes can be kept clear for them but it is still necessary to watch them very carefully to avoid fighting or other birds trying to take over the previously unused box. The best way to introduce an old stock bird is to use them as a replacement part of a pairing.

For instance, if the bird is an old cock, he can be kept separate until required. His intended hen could have already been paired to a younger cock for a round or two and when appropriate, the younger cock can be removed and the old cock allowed into that section. The hen will soon call him into her nest and as she is already in the right nesting condition, they should take to each other well and produce a supply of youngsters. The reverse applies of course for an older hen.

As much time as possible should be spent with the young birds. If they are flying breeds or are to be allowed their liberty from the loft, the earlier this is done the better. Or if there is a flight fitted, they should be encouraged to spend time out in the natural weather conditions. I always advise that newly weaned young birds are treated against canker, as many will be carrying the disease. Sadly if problems are noticed it is often too late to render effective treatment so a precautionary treatment is best. I also recommend that young birds be vaccinated against paramyxovirus soon after they leave their nests.

Pen training is a good thing to do and the time spent will be well repaid when the shows start. In any show lofts, the availability of erected show pens is a great advantage. A penning room is also a wonderful aide and whenever friends within the sport make visits, it is a good thing to pen a few youngsters for them to look at and judge.

I like to clean my nestboxes as often as possible and the use of newspapers on the box floor is a great asset for this. The top layers can be removed and burnt or otherwise properly disposed of leaving the box fresh and better smelling. A constant watch should be kept for 'wet-feeders'; birds which seem to pump a lot of water. Generally there is a clinical reason for this and in the first instance one should resort to the time-honoured remedies of charcoal and bicarbonate of soda to settle a malfunctioning crop. If this does not work, then veterinarian advice should be sought. If a pair experience problems with feeding, it might be a good idea to separate them for a couple of weeks in order to provide them with rest.

Keep a constant watch for insect life in the nest boxes and on the birds. Red mite will appear as soon as the weather gets a little warmer. It is hard to see and to detect but the advice is to treat for it whenever there seems to be a cause to do so. For instance whenever a pair leave their eggs or start spending a lot of time off their young birds, this must be the first suspicion. Red mite can be seen at night by torchlight or can be spotted on fledglings running around between the quills and developing feather. Deal with the problem instantly.

Plenty of good food, clean water and plenty of grit and minerals is the advice for April as in any other month. A supplement including cod liver oil and calcium is most useful to promote good growth and to keep the feeding birds in good condition.

With numbers in the lofts beginning to rise, it is a good time to think about ventilation to ensure that it is adequate for the numbers housed. Clean conditions will help in this and of course there is little like a good bath to give the birds a boost. There is less need for artificial lighting as the year develops and also a lessening of the precautions to keep out the cold winds.

The first of the show schedules will be appearing so thought will have to be given to whether a team can be entered. The shows are generally staged in May but the need for forward planning is necessary throughout April.

MAY

For many fanciers the breeding season will be drawing to a close. For those who have breeds which are good breeders and feeders, the chances are that a good team will have been built up of hopefuls for the approaching show season. In my early years in the sport I always reckoned to have completed my programme by the first week in May so that the birds could be prepared for the early summer shows - mainly those held in conjunction with agricultural shows. Now however I am not in the same hurry and tend to allow the breeding to extend on into June and even July to accommodate pairs which have been a little slow to reproduce, or where birds are being provided with different mates to evaluate potential value of the pairing.

Many breeds of fancy pigeon however will be requiring further time as so many take longer to complete their breeding. Those breeds needing feeders will also have needed a bit of good fortune to arrange pairings and the laying of the eggs to coincide as near as possible. This is what makes the breeding operation so fascinating and interesting with the only certainty being the uncertainty of it all.

With the days growing longer and warmer, I advise again to be watchful for the scourge of red mite. It is a dreadful thing to have in the loft and can easily ruin a breeding programme. I would also advise fanciers to take precautions against all other livestock by spraying the loft out or by dipping the birds. This is most important for birds likely to be entered in the shows.

Talking of the shows, the month is an excellent one in which to give attention to the baskets and show containers. At the very least mine are given a good scrubbing and cleaning using a high powered hose-spray and plenty of elbow grease. This is best done on a warm, sunny day so that they can dry off in the sun. I use wicker baskets and regularly varnish them. Every basket carries a label inside on which is written the last year they were varnished. Every two years is quite sufficient but well worth every bit of effort.

With the moult beginning it is important to provide a weekly bath for the birds. This is beneficial for the physiological well being of the birds as they really do respond to having a dip and the young birds get quite excited by it. The moulted feathers should be swept up and removed on a daily basis and it goes without saying that the lofts should be kept clean and fresh. Allow as much access to the sunshine as possible. Where there is a flight or aviary this is easily attained but for birds which are confined to the lofts, then as much sunlight as possible should be allowed in to the loft by the use of open doors or by clear glass windows.

As much time as possible should be spent with the birds observing them and watching their development. Handling and playing with the young birds is a good idea to keep them tame and under control so that they have no anxieties about human contact. A routine involving pen training will be a most useful exercise as it will prepare young birds for their first experience of being shown,

Many fanciers avoid showing at the summer events claiming that it can be harmful to the birds. I have now found this having shown in the summer events throughout my showing career.. I tend to take the positive view that the shows act as a wonderful shop window for the sport in enabling non-fanciers to examine the various

242

breeds of pigeon, and perhaps develop an interest in them. My only proviso would be to try to make a two-day show the maximum period for any pigeon especially when conditions are hot. There then needs to be a two-week period of rest before they are shown again.

Whether showing is contemplated or not, good management should ensure that at all times the birds look in show condition. Good food fed on a regular basis is the minimum and I like to see food supplement feeding continued using the small seed mixture or one with cod liver oil and calcium. A regular use of garlic in the water also assists a healthy moult and regular use of pigeon tea will be beneficial.

May is the time when thought is given to the reduction in numbers on the basis that the fewer birds in the loft, the better the overall environment will be. If there is overcrowding the birds will never be able to properly settle and my sentiment has always been that an empty perch is often worth more than than the pigeon which might have been occupying it. In thinking of reducing numbers however, do not be too hasty in disposing of birds from the breeding pairs. All too often birds are disposed of and then there is a realisation that they have bred a superb quality young pigeon.

Showing can be a most enjoyable pigeon occupation at this time of the year providing that the main aim is to enjoy the social aspect with the winning of prizes being acceptable but not the principal aim.

JUNE

The shows continue into June and present an opportunity for social enjoyment and for the pleasure of seeing some youngsters exhibited for the first time. It is always useful to be able to enter some young birds and to compare them with what others have bred. Of course it is no certain guide to the rest of the year but I have always maintained that a good pigeon is a good pigeon at whatever time of the year bred.

Breeding will be drawing to a close for most. The birds begin to show signs of weariness at the process and while they are content to remain with their mates in their boxes, the urge to reproduce is mainly spent. Fanciers contemplating entering the summer shows may well keep the pairs together sitting out pot eggs as a means of holding the moult as long as possible. The birds seem to enjoy this time of the year in a state of relaxation after their labours of rearing and keep themselves in wonderful condition until the middle of July and even beyond. However, once separated they go into a very heavy moult so it is all a matter of timing.

Even where it is intended to keep the birds sitting out eggs, it is a good idea to clean the boxes, getting rid of all the debris of the breeding season. The use of newspaper or other base is good for this and when the boxes are cleaned, more paper keeps them looking clean and fresh for the remainder of the season. It is a good idea to have a couple of hand-sprayers available for use at all times. I have one charged with a Jeyes Fluid solution as the moths hate the smell of this and I also have one containing an insecticide for a routine spraying of the perches and nest boxes. I believe that I have mentioned before that I also have a larger hand-pumped sprayer which contains some virucide which I use on the floors and perches prior to cleaning. This loosens the droppings which quickly become dry and hard in the heat, and makes scraping much easier.

Think all the time about reducing numbers by disposing of the not-so-good and keeping only those which look promising. It is not good to be too hasty, in fact it is all a matter of judgement but the lower the number kept, the easier it is to manage and clean the loft. By this time the fancier will have a good idea about the success or otherwise of the year's pairings and this will act as a guide on the future of some of the older birds. I always advise care in the disposal of breeders for all too often they are disposed of just before the true value of a youngster becomes obvious. I have never been afraid to hand on to a young bird even with faults, if I believe that it might possess potential as a breeder. It helps to have a stock section to facilitate this but it is one of the pleasures of being a pigeon fancier in being able to back one's judgement and to be proven right (or wrong!).

Newly-weaned birds should be treated against canker. If fanciers manage to remember to do this they will reduce mortality rates enormously for I believe that in most cases of young birds suddenly taking ill and dying, can be down to canker in its internal form. The problem is that if the illness is noticed, it is often too late to treat especially in the more frail breeds.

The lofts should be kept clean and fresh smelling. Baths should be provided on a weekly basis especially before and after shows. Immediately after a show the birds really relish a bath and it does much to relieve their stress of being exhibited.

The month is really one of clean lofts and plenty of sunshine, clean air and good food and water. This will produce an environment which will suit the birds and help prepare them for a settled moult.

JULY

The moult begins to be very noticeable even with the adults. Birds which have been sitting out eggs will be looking good enough to show. The shows continue and there needs to be thought as to how to find a few entries for them. Birds in the show pen, especially in hot conditions, fall into a heavy moult and we have all seen birds almost lying in a bed of their own feathers at the July shows. Of course, just as the older birds start to moult, some of the young pigeons will be looking good and every fancier knows that wonderful feeling of suddenly recognising a young bird in its new plumage it having been in moult until then.

Some later breeding will still be going on in the breeds which are slow to start in the year and which require a lot of time to produce the required young bird show team. Keeping the birds interested in their nests, eggs and young birds is a matter for good management with each breed having its peculiarities. Even in the easier breeds such as the show racers, some later youngsters will be in the nest as the result of re-pairings for instance.

Within the lofts one should guard against moths and Jeyes Fluid is still as good as anything for this purpose. In the summer heat insect life flourishes so take care to keep the birds free of it and the feathers need to be removed on a daily basis and dust should also be swept away or removed by vacuum cleaner.

Plenty of time with the birds is a good aim in this month as in any other. Little problems can be spotted so much earlier if time is spent with them: things such as the start of respiratory problems in the form of greasy wattles or one-eye cold. The show enthusiast can do worse than to try to emulate the efforts of racing enthusiasts who are very active during July, not only in racing their birds at the distance events but also in preparing the young birds for training. The use of tea, garlic and other supplements will ensure good health and this is the peak time of effort in the average racing loft. Garlic is very usefully employed during the moult and when administered say for instance in the drinking water, there should be a noticeable increase in the shedding of feathers indicating a good healthy state of the moult.

Green foods are more available in the summer months with the birds enjoying a few lettuce leaves. I also favour a few tit bits of seed to help the birds through the moult and such seed should include linseed and other small seeds rich in oils. My birds enjoy a few peanuts and will take them from my hands. This is a good way of inducing good trust and understanding.

The long summer days need a careful bit of management and clean lofts and clean birds are the result of such measures of offering plenty of baths and by cleaning the lofts regularly. Keep the birds happy and quiet to produce a quiet and settled environment for the stress of the moult.

AUGUST

This is the month when hardly any shows can be held owing to the moult. Most of the adults will now be shedding feathers in profusion whereas some of the young birds will be looking quite spruce as they emerge from their body moult. The feathers present a problem and need to be removed on a daily basis. A small piece of board (12 inches by 12 inches - or 30cm by 30cm) resting against the wall in the corners will collect the majority of the feathers in a convenient fashion.

The management in this quiet month is one of quiet effort in keeping the lofts clean and by allowing as much natural sunlight as possible to get to the birds. It is a good month to thoroughly clean the lofts - section by section when the breeding is finally over. Some nest boxes will still be in use for the birds which have had a slow start to reproduction. When the weather gets hot it is not an ideal environment for breeding and rearing and a careful watch will have to be kept in case the parents or feeders look like tiring of their task. Hand feeding might then become necessary.

For the cleaning of the lofts when the breeding is finally over, the easiest way is to remove all the birds from one section by either penning them or placing them in show containers. The section can then be cleaned from top to bottom with a scrubbing of the floor and the washing down of the walls ceiling and the perches. All dust and feather bloom should be removed so that the section starts from scratch again. The use of Jeyes Fluid on the floor will not only help kill the germs but will act as a deterrent to the moths. Good sunny days should be selected for such work so that the areas cleaned can quickly return to normal and the birds returned.

When cleaning the lofts in this way I consider it most important to wear a mask. Indeed if there is the slightest suggestion of being slightly allergic to the pigeon protein then a mask should be worn whenever in the pigeon lofts. As a word of warning also, with August being the traditional month for holiday taking. The biggest danger time is to have been away from the birds for a period of two weeks or so, then to return and to start cleaning the birds immediately. This can produce a violent reaction with influenza type symptoms and if this happens medical advice must be sought.

I also advise August as being a good time to take a look at the exterior of the lofts to decide whether any alterations need to be made and whether they need to be painted or otherwise treated with a good wood preservative.

Plenty of baths will assist the birds through their moult as will the provision of a good varied diet including oil-bearing seeds such as linseed and sunflower. Green food is quite plentiful and should be given to the birds whenever possible. Garlic bulbs in the water greatly help the moult and when the birds are given it in this manner or where it has been crushed first, the result is apparent to be seen with a good fall of down feathers as a sign that the moult is progressing well.

It is also a good month to ensure that all birds have been vaccinated against paramyxovirus. Even is the law does not require this, I believe that it should be done. Birds at show can so easily mix with a bird with it and before long the whole loft will be affected. For this reason I tend to vaccinate my young pigeons as they leave the nest. I also advise fanciers to check to ensure that all birds in the loft are registered in the correct name with transfers of ownership duly notified in accordance with prevailing rules.

Baskets and show containers should be thoroughly cleaned and treated for the advancing show season. I use wicker baskets mainly and these are scrubbed using a hot solution of detergent and bleach and then thoroughly hosed down using a powered hose. Good dry and sunny days should be used for this chore and when dry, they may require to be varnished. My wicker baskets are varnished every other year and each carries a label inside on which is inscribed the dates when varnished. Treated in this way good baskets will last a lifetime and look as good as the day they were made.

Assuming that fanciers are continually assessing their birds, the month is a good one to acquire additional stock. Most fanciers tend to be overstocked at this time of the year and therefore are more likely to part with either stock birds or a youngster or two. It is therefore a good time to get hold of some new blood or a useful pigeon or two to supplement the show team.

SEPTEMBER

This is the month when the worst of the moult is over. The piles of feathers for collection get progressively smaller and the time comes when the cover feathers have all been renewed and fanciers can count the primaries, secondaries and tail feathers as a means of gauging the progress of the moult. By the end of September therefore most of the birds will be looking fresh and lovely and ready for the commencement of showing.

Some of the earliest shows commence in September and while it is still difficult to find a team of old birds, the youngsters are mostly in superb condition. The early season shows can be wonderful social events but just as importantly they provide a first outing for the youngsters.

It is a good month to enjoy visits to other lofts or to receive visits from fellow fanciers. When going visiting it is a good idea to take a basket of birds for mutual inspection and for some basket training. When receiving other fanciers, it is useful to have a few young birds in the pens to be examined and judged as a useful form of pen training. The exchange of ideas at such times is a most enjoyable and productive form of judging progress and the success or otherwise of the recently completed breeding programme.

The astute fancier will use the month to get a few jobs done to be ahead of his tasks so that when the shows start in the last quarter of the year there will be more time for spending time with the birds. The tasks which can be seen to during the last of the 'quiet' months can include

- Spraying the lofts and birds against insect life - a task which will need to be repeated as the show season progresses
- Cleaning and treating all baskets/show containers
- Ensuring that all birds are vaccinated
- Checking that all rings are properly transferred
- If not already done, to thoroughly clean the lofts and the nest boxes.
- Treat all birds against canker and worms.

These steps will keep the fancier one step ahead which is far better than continually working to catch up with tasks. The month must also be used to select the birds which will be required for the showing programme and for the breeding to follow. The aim must be to reduce numbers as much as possible to allow for a more settled environment. With regard to late-breds or even just the later-bred birds, it is always a good idea to allow them to develop on their own away from the main team of birds. If this isn't possible they might be placed in with the stock birds. Most fanciers carry a few late-breds especially from the breeds which are difficult to get to produce, the short-faces and so on, and as these late birds take a while to develop, they should not be compared to their older brethren until later in the year.

It is also a good idea to try to facilitate the late-breds to complete their moult in the year of their birth. If there is the ability to keep them on their own in a section, they can be provided with artificial lighting to lengthen the hours of light to bring this about. It is always a thrill to have a later-bred bird suddenly blossom and appears as a bird of quality - making the effort well worth while.

All time spent with the birds is time well spent. It enables the birds to remain calm and to be trusting of human company, preparing them for the stressful situation of being shown.

OCTOBER

The first of the winter shows will now be scheduled and most of the show dates for the season will be known and advertised. It is therefore a good time to make a plan of showing intent and I have always found that the best way to do this is to put it all down in writing. A list of all birds is a good start, listing stock birds, birds available for showing and others - including later-bred pigeons. Apart from doing this for the show programme, it is a good management idea to do this in order to be able to make management plans for the loft. There is nothing like seeing a full list to direct the mind towards numbers, potential and necessity and the aim should be to take a stern look at the quality available.

The list of shows can then be weighed against the available team. The two together will determine the numbers of birds which can be entered in the various events so as to avoid overshowing and to use the strengths of the team to best advantage. Much of the success or otherwise of a normal show season can depend on the decisions made at this stage of planning. I would urge any serious show enthusiast to make a written plan.

The October shows are not the easiest to find complete teams for. Many of the older birds will be completing the growth of the primaries and be just under their best condition. No such problems exist at finding youngsters except in some of the breeds where birds are often a little later. It is a good time to have a new show notebook to be taken to the shows to record all birds entered together with details of success, number in the class, the judge's name and any other information which might be useful at some future time. Most judges have fads of type, colour or size and some knowledge of them may help to determine the entry to be made at subsequent shows.

Second opinions at shows are always useful when they come from fellow exhibitors and enthusiasts. The decision of the judge on the day is one thing, but the views of fellow fanciers can be even more useful. It is amazing how observations can confirm opinions or doubts about certain pigeons and we all know that some birds seem to win at whatever the class of competition.

I would always advise against taking drastic action following a lack of success at a show. All too often I have seen disappointed fanciers taking drastic culling action when disappointed at a show but as I always point out, the opinion of the judge is merely one factor and that in the long run the fancier is the best judge of his own birds. By all means, listen to views and opinions, but in the long run it is you the owner of the birds who pays for the corn and all other outlays, and who must stand or fall on decisions made.

If the work has not already been done, the final preparations for showing must be carried out with all birds vaccinated, treated against worms and canker and sprayed against insect life. I would always advise fanciers to spray each bird immediately after a show to ensure that any passengers in the form of insect life picked up at the show, can be dealt with instead of being allowed to spread throughout the loft. The birds should be sprayed or otherwise treated against insect life at various stages of the show season as it always reflects badly against a fancier's management when birds are discovered to be infested. The use of the 'Ivomec' treatment is an ideal one for show purposes but will need to be administered again during the season.

Pen training is a good use of time at this time of the year to prepare the birds for their show outings. Good hard work is hardly ever wasted and how much more satisfying is the success when it follows genuine work and effort.

NOVEMBER

This is the first of the two main showing months so everything which follows now involves time, work and effort, both physical and mental. It is the season at which all work and planning has been directed. Providing that the work has been diligently carried out throughout the year, the season should be fairly easy to manage but for those who have allowed management to lapse, will now be working extra hard to catch up - and they will be far less likely to succeed. Neither do they deserve the same success as the methodical manager of a loft and team of show pigeons.

Of course, as the importance of the shows increases, so too do the precautions necessary to keep things on course. The weather will have deteriorated and there will be need to keep the lofts dry by preventing the possibility of rain being driven in. All work at show preparation will be undone if the loft is in any way damp. Likewise, allowing winds into the loft will strip good condition off birds especially the cold breezes.

The aim should now be to have the lofts clean at all times with the scraper being applied where possible on two occasions a day. By this time the diet should have been worked out and kept consistent for the duration of the show season. A suitable supply should be stored so that no mid-season changes are needed. Within a diet some subtle changes of content can be made but a complete change can lead to upset and loss of condition. Fresh water every day with garlic being added to it on at least one occasion a week. It is a good sign to see a good fall of feather down after the birds have taken garlic.

Pen training is time usefully spent - in fact all time spent with the birds is good. Regularity is very important so that the birds receive their food on a regular time basis and have no need for anxiety about the next feed. Careful observation should highlight any birds which have been stressed out by attendance at a show so that individual attention can be provided to them. Such birds may well get used to being shown but may also require longer periods between shows. The observation and attention to detail will also spot birds which are putting on too much weight or birds needing some more body. The former can be treated by penning a bird and feeding it sparingly while the bird requiring more, should be fed more and possibly checked to ensure that there is no medical cause for the lack of body.

Stress needs to be addressed at all times both at the shows and afterwards. When one considers the upset to the system of the birds being removed from their loft and basketted, then checked in the pre-show preparation period, taken to a show possibly many miles and hours away, then handled again to be penned. They are then handled by at least one judge, kept confined in a show pen for the period of the show in difficult surroundings, before being re-basketted and driven home again. If every fancier could look at the problem in that manner there might be a better understanding of the stress levels.

I firmly believe that the post-show recovery period is most important as part of the preparation for the next outing. The quicker the birds are settled back into their lofts and routines the better and this is why, whatever time I get home from a show - be it four in the morning - the birds are returned to their loft and provided with a light feed and a drink under lights. Dimmers allow the light to diminish like a normal dusk and the birds then start the next day back in their own surroundings. For me, to witness the great pleasure a show bird shows when it gets home is one of my joys in pigeon keeping, just as enjoying the spectacle of a bird returning to a race is another of similar nature.

Baths must be supplied whenever weather conditions allow especially in the days prior to a bird going off to a show. When the birds are really show fit, they can be bathed right up to the day before a show although on average I would prefer two or three days between. In the event of sunny days, the birds respond to being given access to the sunshine as much as possible.

I would hope that most of the work for show preparation had been completed well before the November peak of showing. The baskets should be clean and fresh, the birds free from insect life and the settled environment should be producing birds in wonderful show condition. Therefore, most of the effort can be directed towards the birds and their personal preparation. However, between shows the baskets should be cleaned and provided with fresh sawdust or wood shavings and as stated before, birds should be treated against insect life. The work is never complete - merely made easier by a generalised approach spread over the whole year rather than having it crammed into the space of a few weeks.

DECEMBER

What has been said for November equally applies to December for the management is very much a case of observing the birds, spending time with them and in keeping the lofts and perches clean. Most of the jobs will have been completed in lofts with good management so there is plenty of time to sit with the birds.

Such time as is spent with them is most useful for not only does it help towards show condition but also in the planning of the pairings for the approaching breeding season. Every fancier will have a good idea on what he intends pairing to what as part of the ongoing planning. Already some birds will have revealed themselves as being unsatisfactory for future breeding or showing and this will help the desire to reduce numbers to bring them down to breeding numbers.

The aim throughout the month is still to enter the best team available and to produce it for the show pen in the very peak of condition. After all, this is what pigeon showing is all about.

The biggest difference between the two months is that by mid-December the show birds are beginning to show signs of tiredness of being constantly entered and handled. One can almost hear the birds groan when they see the approach of the show baskets/containers! The need to keep them interested and alert is one of judgements every fancier will have to address. The Christmas period intervenes and allows a certain breathing space both for birds and fanciers. Both will appreciate a rest. It is a good time for a reduction in rations so that they become a little leaner and ready to take the increased intake once another show approaches, so as to reproduce their top show condition.

This will be the thoughts which enter into management for show preparation and condition but towards the end of December, many fanciers will be turning thought towards early breeding, either using stock pairs or by removing a bird or two from the show team. Early breeding requires careful thought and is best accomplished by having the breeding operation well away from the show team wherever this is possible. If the show team can see or hear their fellow inmates being paired together it could easily cause them to fret and to lose show condition. This must be avoided as the December and January shows are the main ones of the season.

With thoughts of early breeding the calendar is brought back to the beginning of the year and to January and the new year of pigeon fancying. It is always a full-year activity with each section of the year running into the next, varying of course with nature and special demands of the breeds kept. Each pigeon requires management but a different detail for each of the wonderful breeds which are available to be kept, flown and shown.

Chapter 27

A Month by Month Guide

The Racing Loft

JANUARY

Calendar-wise, January is at the beginning of the year but in terms of many racing lofts the new year is well under way with fanciers pairing up in December in order to have early-bred young birds and as preparation for the widowhood system of racing. It is all a matter of choice in how and when to commence the breeding operation and will depend almost entirely on the method of racing to be employed.

It can therefore be assumed that in the 'close' season, i.e. in the months between the end of racing and the end of the year, that most racing men will have decided on the method they intend to employ for their racing campaign. This merely emphasises the fact that racing, like showing is a year-round occupation with a constant appraisal of situations past, present and intended. In the period after completion of racing, much thought will have been directed towards the strengths of the team. If the season was a very successful one then little needs to be done or added, whereas if a bad season ensued, and many birds were lost, the thought will have to be given to new blood and the ways of supplementing the team for breeding and for future racing.

Therefore the chances are that in the period in question, fanciers will have been checking possible sources of good stock by contacting suppliers, checking the sales lists in the fancy press or by attending auctions. These tasks have to be completed in good time so that the newly acquired birds can settle in to their new surroundings to be able to enter into the breeding programme.

With that basic introduction, attention can be turned to loft events in the month of January. Where breeding has not commenced, the majority will be pairing their birds in this month. Only the extreme distance fanciers who fly their birds on the natural system will wait until mid-February before pairing. Such fanciers are not interested in the sprint races but develop all effort towards the long distance events in July.

In terms of basic management in the anticipated foul weather of the month, some effort will have to be made to keep the wet out and to prevent the worst of the winds from blowing in directly. For many years I have found that there is little better than the use of adjustable glass louvres for this purpose. In times of good weather they can be opened and when conditions are bad, they can be closed or nearly closed.

I like to have the birds out on the wing whenever conditions allow and of course some fanciers provide an open loft for their birds. Having the ability to have the birds out is a great asset when pairing the birds as being out together assists in bonding and helps the breeding process considerably. When birds are paired, being allowed out together is good for them as a means of making them into the start of a family. It follows also that whenever the birds are out it is good if they are allowed to search for nesting material and some of the best nests are those made of materials the birds find themselves. If they can be allowed an open loft for an hour or two they will work hard and this helps to bring them into breeding condition much better. Observation of wood pigeons, crows and magpies when they are foraging for nesting material will confirm the wisdom of this.

The last of the Winter shows will be held in January and while this may have little impact on the racing enthusiast, they present an ideal opportunity to do the final shopping for specifics and any other products useful for the breeding and racing seasons. Not many fanciers have pigeon shops immediately available to them so it is good to take the opportunity of visiting the trade stands.

It should not need saying that all the nest boxes should have been prepared and properly prepared well before the breeding season is due to commence. It is a job firstly whenever the breeding finishes, and then again in good time before it re-starts. Steps must be taken to ensure that all clocks have been prepared or serviced in readiness for the racing season.

FEBRUARY

Many racing lofts will already have young birds to show for the early pairings whereas the long distance fliers will be preparing for their mating programme in about the middle of the month. They argue that they need the race birds at their best and either sitting or rearing, when the longest races are held and it also makes no sense to have to feed youngsters for a couple of months longer than necessary.

For many however the birds will be sitting tightly prior to the hatching. It is a good idea to provide the breeding birds with extra lighting in order to stimulating them into the breeding process. This would especially apply to those who pair their birds at very early dates and any system should be accompanied by an automatic dimming system because instant cut-out will cause disturbance and even loss of eggs or young birds.

Whilst the weather conditions are likely to be quite extreme and care needs to be taken to ensure that the rain and winds are kept out, it is a good thing to allow the birds out whenever conditions permit. When the weather is good to allow as much access to the air as possible as there is nothing better than sunshine to spur the birds on.

There is one matter which must be faced and that is what to do with the hens when the widowhood racing commences by the separation of the cocks from the hens. The safe custody of the hens is just as important as making provision for the cocks. The hens should be housed where they have little access to privacy when they might pair together, and if possible they need access to the outside world - say in an aviary or small flight. It should also be close to the cocks' compartment without being in sight or within hearing. In order to show the hens to the cocks before racing or before some training tosses, there is a fair amount of work involved and the easier it is, by proximity, the better it will be done.

The diet needs to be a good one with plenty of good quality grains with the addition of pellets and a food supplement. Good clean water, which is changed regularly, is important especially during periods of freezing weather. Apart from that and when allowing the birds out in good weather the quieter they are allowed to be the better.

Fanciers who employ the 'darkness' system will now have to think of methods to block out most of the light during the hours from about 1700hrs until 0900 hours or whatever variation is best suited to the hours and work of the fancier. The earlier the birds are placed on the system the better for them and within a few weeks they will be shedding their cover feathers in profusion.

MARCH

The first of the young birds will now be due for weaning and in lofts where the management is good, a section or compartment will have been prepared for them. Wherever possible young racers should be weaned in groups so that they can provide comfort, warmth and company for each other. Some fanciers will wean birds straight into a racing crate so that they get the idea of where the food and water is. A good bed of shavings will help the birds get used to their surroundings. If they are being housed in a compartment, shavings, sawdust or straw should be placed in a corner for the birds to use for their first few days and nights. They will soon get the desire to get up on to the perches.

Young birds should be provided with a mixture of grains they like and a high percentage of peas will be taken and will ensure that they receive a high level of protein. They will benefit from being able to get a look at the outside world at a very early age and the earlier in their lives they are able to be allowed out of their loft the better. The weather does not help this aim. Once they are enjoying their liberty it is important to provide them with some early training, both by basket training and by taken away a few kilometres and liberated. Picking a good day is important and the birds really will respond to this early training.

Another thing I recommend is that when young birds are weaned they are treated against canker which is often fed into the youngsters from their parents. Unfortunately if the symptoms are noticed it is often too late for treatment so preventative treatment is seen as the best way forward. Following this treatment, routine application of garlic will reduce the chances of canker getting a hold. Vaccination against paramyxovirus is also necessary and better done early in their lives.

If not already done, it is time to prepare the training crates and baskets in time for the start of the racing season. All club subscriptions should have been paid and every fancier should ensure that he possesses sufficient entry forms for the racing season. All rings should be transferred and distances obtained for every racepoint.

Training will now be commencing depending on the type of racing to be employed. Whatever, the weather will be changing for the better so that the birds can be allowed out more and more. Therefore some training is an extension of this. Training includes having the birds under control and this can be achieved by careful control of the food. When called the birds should instantly come when called and this effort will be repaid when racing commences and when speedy trapping is required.

As many baths as possible should be presented to the birds and the best idea is to have a bath available outside the loft. Birds able to spend time flying free to an open loft and to be able to bathe and collect nesting material are at their best for their physical and mental well being.

APRIL

Training will now have to be taken seriously, as racing will be commencing. I always avoid trying to train the birds when the winds are the cold ones, in the case of Britain, those from the East and North. This especially pertains to the treatment of yearlings which must be considered as youngsters. Just think of it like this. About nine out of ten stray pigeons which enter the lofts of fanciers at this time of the year, are yearlings. This should be a strong enough message to take extra care of yearlings, especially the later-bred birds from the previous year. What is the point of keeping and feeding them for the best part of a year, and then waste them by failing to avoid the cold weather conditions.

The same will apply to the early races as far too many teams are ruined by the impatience of fanciers who insist on entering every race. Whatever the weather conditions, they enter their teams including yearlings and then lament when they have half their team missing before the intermediate races start. Club averages are much to blame for this state of affairs and I have always steered clear of getting involved in the averages competitions. I would much rather start a few weeks after the rest to ensure that my birds are given the best possible chances.

All racing men will recognise that training will have to be as good and comprehensive as possible with birds responding to racing demands if they have been properly schooled and are as fit as possible. The training will depend on the type of racing which will be employed and each fancier will have a good idea on what to do and when.

In racing lofts which use the natural system of racing with breeding commencing so much later, the youngsters will be ready for weaning and the same advice about trying to do this in groups is good advice. The later youngsters will enjoy better conditions for their first days away from the nest and can be settled so much easier and provided with access to the outside world when weather conditions allow. The youngsters should be carefully watched and any finding it difficult to cope or failing to develop should be discarded. It is pointless keeping birds which provide doubt for the chances are that they will more often than not fail when put under pressure.

Basket training for the youngsters is a good way of schooling them. A period or two in the crate or baskets including a night's stay, and being fed and watered whilst in them will benefit them later on. It is also a good idea if they can be liberated within the garden or yard area from the basket as a further lesson in the way of things to come. In areas which are subject to having birds attacked by the hawks and falcons, special care will have to be taken to vary times of flying out and to try to teach the birds as much independence as possible. They will be able to cope so much better if they are aware of the likelihood of attack and will not panic so much if subjected to one.

Providing that the weather conditions are favourable, the April races can be most enjoyable and the pleasure of witnessing the return of race birds to their loft is good so early in the season. However, if the winds are cold, it is better either to keep all the birds in the loft or to race only the older and more experienced birds.

MAY

Racing will now be at its best and providing the early season disasters have been avoided, fanciers should be able to start to plan for the important races, generally the more prestigious at the intermediate distances. It is an exciting time when the weather conditions are often getting better and more conducive to serious pigeon racing. However big or small the size of the race team it is necessary to make a plan so as to decide which birds will be schooled for which races. A plan on paper will be best and it is a good idea to have a chart of all available birds and to be able to record every training outing and every race. This will provide pictorial evidence of whether the birds are being overworked or not.

Each and every week the birds should be the subjects of observation to note how they come through their training and racing. Some birds respond to plenty of work while others seem to require a longer convalescence period after a strenuous race. The one thing which must be avoided is to use a bird if there is the slightest doubt about its fitness. Any sign of a knock or injury should be noted and the birds given the benefit of a period of rest. The manner in which they fly around when out on the wing is a very good indicator as birds which are bruised will want to remain reasonably static until well again. I always give the pigeon the benefit of the doubt over such matters and provide rest rather than risk it again prematurely. Even so, they will only receive a short race or a training to toss to assess their recovery.

Those who race on the natural system will also have to be careful about sending hens while in egg, or too soon after laying eggs. It is cruel to send such pigeons to races and again the advice must be to rest them rather than to risk them.

The training of the young birds can continue using baskets and crates and if conditions and time permit, perhaps a training toss a mile or two away will teach them a great deal and allow them to build up a great deal of confidence. They should not be stressed, merely given some prudent experience.

As to the old birds, there is a great deal of stress involved in racing them week in and week out. It is possible to get to the stage when they express apprehension whenever they see the fancier approaching with a training crate or basket. This is not good and it should be avoided, especially the sending of birds each and every week to the races. Even with a very small team it should be possible to stagger the entries so that the birds enjoy the luxury of a weekend at home. It is better to send a couple of very fit and willing birds than a larger team of birds which are jaded by constantly being shipped away from home. I am quite aware that some birds respond better to hard work than others but I maintain that it can be overdone to the detriment of the birds.

JUNE

The longest days, the best of weather and the best of the racing are what June means to many racing enthusiasts. In club racing the intermediate distance races will be staged during the month with some stretching into the longer distance events. However for those who choose to enter for the national and classic events, some of the finest races are to be enjoyed.

By this time the birds will have settled down and most will be properly prepared for almost anything. It is a good time to have some crop swabs taken and some droppings examined professionally to ensure that the birds are fit enough to undertake the tasks required of them. Birds which are being raced are mixing with birds from other lofts and areas and if there is disease about, it can soon spread through basket contact and by the use of communal drinking vessels.

If birds are carrying an illness they cannot perform and no amount of training will make them into fit pigeons. It is far better to know of any problems so that suitable treatment can be provided and a week's rest at such time is generally all that will be required although the advice of a veterinarian expert should be heeded.

Records should be made of almost everything which happens. The training and racing chart will be an excellent guide but it is also good to record details of every race and of every pigeon. A card system can be very beneficial in determining future entries especially when racing birds on the natural system. It is a good thing to note when birds put in a good performance, their state at that time e.g. when sitting, or when rearing, or when driving to nest and so on. Even when birds are on widowhood, they will point out when they are at their fittest by their method of flying around the loft and the same applies to birds on the celibacy system. Notes of everything can be one of the greatest aides in any racing loft and its management.

Young bird teams which have been on the 'darkness' system will now be brought to more natural hours of daylight to ensure that they are able to complete their primary flight moult before the end of the year. Mid to late June is the time normally accepted for this and those which have been on the system since early in the year will be looking almost like adults with their new plumage.

Care is needed with the treatment of strays which come into the loft. I always isolate them but treat them with every care and kindness. Wherever possible they can be helped on their way home and it takes but a little effort to do this. It is better to isolate them because they may have something wrong with them and going astray is but an indication of this. I invariably spray them against insect life at the very minimum and arrange for help should a bird have injury of any sort.

The astute fancier will also be making decisions about the future racing of the loft. Yearlings for instance often benefit from being provided with some racing but then 'retired' for the year, to be used again as two-year-olds. These enables a fancier to start a new year with a more experienced team as in too many cases just about all yearlings can be lost leaving a gap in the racing team. The situation is always one of planning ahead and making plans for tomorrow and next year than in putting everything into the current round of races. Patience is a wonderful thing for a pigeon fancier but unfortunately many fanciers fail to recognise this and lose out by being neglectful of the needs of future years,

JULY

The racing season 'peaks' in this month and all the work of the past year is put to the ultimate tests of the distance and mid-distance events. Not many fanciers are able to house sufficient pigeons to be able to compete at all types of racing. The shorter sprint races require a far different type of bird than those which are expected to perform at the extreme distances. Those who enjoy the sprints will in the main also be able to enjoy the intermediate distance events including the classics and national races. The same applies to the fanciers who want their birds to fly the greater distances, for their birds are also able to cope with the intermediate events but will be too slow for the shorter races when competing against the sprinters.

The long distance races however require great experience on the part of both fancier and birds and often need the backing of a team of pigeons built for endurance with a long history and pedigree of extreme distance racing. It is the ambition of most to win at the extreme distances but the specialists with the proven teams and families are those best suited for it.

The widowhood cocks will often be losing some of their enthusiasm for racing and fanciers will have to consider ways of stimulating them again. They might re-pair them again and then put them back on to widowhood but this takes a period of two or three weeks. For the final race a simple pairing will change their attitude with the cocks being sent to a top race while sitting on eggs. There are many possibilities for bring their best out.

The month is an extremely busy one with the top racing events being held with all the work and travels involved. It is also the time to start training the young birds properly and this task alone will be extremely time-consuming. The youngsters take a great deal of time and effort to get them trained and experienced and I guess that every year they provide fanciers with frights when they fail to return in good time. Hawk attacks are more and more to blame for this state of affairs.

Plenty of ventilation is required in the summer heat and of course baths should be made available to the birds at least weekly. Good food and plenty of clean water is the minimum requirement but good grits, clay blocks and mineral supplements will help the birds through their season. A good garlic supplement is a most useful aide for the racing birds both young and old.

The lofts must be kept as clean as possible so that they smell sweetly and free from odour. It is easier to condition birds which are kept in good clean surroundings. The young birds should be at their very best especially those which have been on the 'darkness' system. The main advantage of this system is that they race with most of their flights in place and have the best possible feather condition at the end of the season when the most important young bird races are held.

In very hot conditions the birds have to endure considerable hardship to reach home in good time so the provision of electrolytes in the drinking water coupled perhaps with honey will assist them in making a quick recovery. The faster a pigeon is able to return to its normal demeanour is quite important and it is one of the things that a good fancier will be observing and working to assist. The sheer pleasure at being home is generally enough for the bird to forget its hard flight but having sustenance in the water is an aide to it.

Where a loft is able to house a team of stock pigeons, these will now have completed their breeding though it is to their advantage to allow them to sit out a set of pot eggs before separating them in the month. They will then go into a heavy moult, as will the racers as they complete their racing by the end of the month. The better the moult the better and efforts will have to be made to ensure that the birds have excellent foods and supplements to assist them through the moulting process.

AUGUST

In some ways the month is a most exciting one when the youngsters take over the responsibility of racing. After the successes or otherwise of the old bird team it is something to look forward to see how the new crop will perform. It is a time of hard work for the youngsters will only do well if they have been well schooled and provided with plenty of experience and fitness.

They will go through a considerable amount of stress by being entered in the races although much of this can be avoided by suitable home preparation in basket training and by the provision of some shorter tosses to build confidence. The stress involved can only be imagined but the unfortunate thing is that the majority of fanciers do not even see it as a problem. These pigeons are not machines and need careful and considerate handling.

I am never too keen to take part in the first young bird race or two because of the sheer panic which ensues when they are liberated in large numbers from the transporters. It is a new experience for them and I believe that many lose their direction at such a time and can then get led astray by other pigeons. The clashing of liberations is a dangerous matter for young birds especially in the opening races until the birds have gained sufficient experience and confidence to be able to cope.

As with old birds a careful fancier should employ a plan. The chart of training tosses and races is a most useful aide but there also needs to be a strategy to cope with the young bird season. The questions which need to be addressed are those of whether all the young birds should be sent to a race or whether the team is split so that a half stay at home each week and rest. This ensures that even the worst racing disaster will affect only half of the team. Likewise, many fanciers who plan for their loft's future, will carefully guard their young birds and decide at a fairly early stage whether they will stop some of them racing and put them by for their yearling stage. I do believe however that every young bird should experience the racing for two or three outings before such 'temporary retirement'.

Meanwhile with all the effort being directed towards the production of a successful young bird team, the basics within the loft must be watched and carefully controlled. The lofts must be kept clean and there must be good food and clean water. With the heat of the summer special attention must be paid to the provision of water for there is little more stress inducing for the birds to be thirsty and anxious where their next drink will come from. However the young birds should be under control and should respond to the call of the fancier. This will assist trapping on race days especially as when they arrive home from their first races they are often very nervous.

The months of July and August are two of the busiest in the racing left when the peak of old bird racing coincides the start of young bird training and racing. The management must be at its best and this includes ensuring that the birds are at their peak of fitness and free from infection. Professional testing of samples should ensure this state of affairs.

SEPTEMBER

September sees the ending of racing for yet another year. By September each racing enthusiast will have a very good idea of how his youngsters are performing and will therefore have the means to plan for the remaining races of the month. The birds must be free from any disease and access to expert pigeon veterinarian advice is a great asset.

The young birds which have not been on the 'darkness' system will start to look rough as they proceed with their body moult and fanciers should avoid sending their youngsters to the longer races if they have bare areas in head and body area. No fancier would think of sending adults in such condition, yet for some reason think that it is quite in order to race young birds like it. It is far better to keep them at home if they have entered into the body moult.

The piles of feathers in the race loft will be growing and need removal on a daily basis at the same time as dust and droppings are removed. Good management is very important to ensure that the best is produced from the young birds in the remaining, most important races. By this time the old birds will be enjoying their deserved rest and many will be moulting heavily. Even when they are encouraged to sit out pot eggs, or in some cases to rear a round of late-breds, they still moult heavily. Garlic provided on the food or in the water will help produce a good and sustained drop of down and cover feathers.

They will not be too anxious to exercise but will enjoy being provided with access to the outside world where they can relax and perhaps bathe in the open air. I favour keeping the sexes together at this time of the year for if separated they fret and sulk for a while. They are far more likely to remain contented if paired and it is some ways a reward for their racing efforts.

It is an excellent month to take stock of the old bird team and to dispose of birds which have obviously failed. This is not to say that unless they have won awards that they have failed, for often they are building experience and may one day produce the top performances. The distance pigeons take far longer to develop than the sprinting families. Harsh decisions however will have to be made for it is not good to carry a surplus into the 'close' season of birds which have proved an inability to compete. The situation must be faced and the sooner it is done the better. The success or otherwise of the future race team may well depend upon the decisions made at this time.

However the main effort must be to maintain the young bird team to ensure that it performs to its best ability. Every fancier will have methods to stimulate performance such as racing them paired or on widowhood, racing them separately but inducing some jealousy into them and so on. The methods are continually changing and this is what makes it all so fascinating.

OCTOBER

The racing is over. However this is no time to sit back and relax for the future of the racing loft may well depend on the work to be done in this month. With all the birds in a heavy moult it is not the best of time to make decisions based upon appearance, but of course it is merely on past performance and potential that they should be made.

The good fancier will never be completely happy with the season even when super success has been enjoyed. The enlightened fancier will be thinking on how best to improve the team to make it even better for succeeding years. This is why the month is so important to decide on what to keep and what to dispose of. The young birds which are left following the programme of racing, will be the main base and future providing that they have done well. They will be the yearlings of the next year and will join their older brethren on the established race team. They will form the main part of many sprint teams but for those who use distance racing as their aim, their yearlings will need more time to develop into top distance racers.

The other judgement which will have to be made is whether the fancier feels that he performed well enough to provide the birds with the best possible chance. Was there too much involvement in other fields to reduce the time input into the birds? Was there an energy gap at the crucial time of the season or some other cause of deficiency in management? Did the system used suit the team or is there need to consider something different for another season. The fancier must question himself just as much as his pigeons.

Neither should the effort cease with the racing. In every loft there will be birds which have provided doubt. There may be birds which got injured or which fell by the wayside through other means. It is no bad thing therefore to continue to train these birds in order to be able to evaluate their potential. Where later-bred birds are being retained it is just as important to provide them with some training experience. A little work in training in the good and settled weather conditions can be most useful in determining which are duffers and which can be expected to perform later on.

The management of the racing loft is quite basic in this month. The lofts should be kept clean and should have all moulted feathers removed on a daily basis. A good diet should be provided to assist the moulting process with some addition seed such as linseed to provide extra nutrients. As much as possible the birds should be given a quiet environment as close to natural and relaxing conditions as they can get.

Young birds which have been on the 'darkness' system will start a fast moult of their primary flights two to three weeks after the racing season finishes. The use of extra lighting may have to be considered to ensure that they complete their primary moult by the end of the year. The situation will have to be carefully watched and judged.

After the management comes the construction of the loft. Did it meet the requirements and demands of the race programme or could it be adapted to make it better for the next season. Does it require weather treatment before the onset of winter and are the fittings suitable for the methods to be used in the future. Now is the time to get alterations planned and actioned.

NOVEMBER

If there is one month which can be called the 'close' season it is November. Fanciers can enjoy their relaxation in the month although those with ideas for the future will be working towards them. It is one of the best months to procure new stock as so many sales of birds are held at this time of the year and it is an ideal time to be on the look out for valuable breeding stock.

It is the time of year for socialising at shows, dinners, sales and other pigeon functions. For those who enjoy some showing it is a good way of maintaining interest throughout the year and the reader might find something of interest in Chapter 18. It is a good time not only to socialise but also to listen to what others have to say about their methods. Visits to other successful fanciers will always provide stimulus for future endeavours.

The month is a good one for updating all records in readiness for the approaching breeding season. The yearbooks will be about to be published so there will be plenty of additional reading material on pigeons and racing methods. It is useful to get up to date on methods used by the successful and to judge whether their ideas would suit the management of one's own loft and team. Every fancier should keep a file or folder of matters of interest which can act as a reference in those quiet November evenings. Those who seem to succeed at racing are those who mix and involve themselves with the successful fanciers of the day. There is always a good reason why they are so successful and many will be quite open about methods and pleased to share parts of their success.

The fancier should never stand still but always seeking improvement. Remaining isolated is no recipe for future success but talking and listening to others can be a step towards success for the future. The idea is to look beyond your own dropboard to see what goes on in other areas and in other loft establishments.

The birds enjoy bathing when finishing up their moult. Indeed many of the birds will now be looking resplendent in their new feather cover and will be full of energy and vitality. It is no time to be complacent and to take a rest from management duties for the success of any season can depend on the methods deployed at this time of the year. Time spent with the birds is always useful as a means of creating trust and by providing the birds with a home to which they will always seek to return.

It is not too late to continue training the later-bred youngsters or the birds which made mistakes or which became injured or damaged in some way. On good days a toss of a few miles will keep them on their toes and provide them with experience, and provide the fancier with an insight into their potential.

As I said earlier, the good fancier will never be seen sitting back and relaxing, but will be using this time of the year to plan for the future either by acquiring new stock or by creating a racing plan. There is nothing like having a goal to aim at and if this requires loft alterations these should be done well before it is intended to start pairing the birds. November can be a quiet month but for the ambitious, it can be one of the busiest.

DECEMBER

All the planning should now be coming to fruition. Any loft alterations should be complete so that the facilities are ready for the breeding season. Many fanciers will be commencing the pairing in December so as to have their youngsters early and so that the racing plan can be put into place.

The birds still require good management. They will be looking at their best but some may be still clearing up on the last primary flights. Birds which were held on the 'darkness' system may have a flight or two to grow and may benefit from some extra lighting to lengthen the hours of daylight. Late-breds may also benefit from this as they will be better birds if they can clear their moult rather than to have a dual-moult in the spring. The value of extra lighting should never be under estimated. The extra lighting should have been started in September/October but this is worth doing in December only to ensure that the final flights are thrown and then re-grown.

For those who intend to pair their birds early, the month is one when the birds will be wormed, checked for canker and possibly for coccidiosis. Professional assistance in this matter will be useful for there is little point in treating for problems which do not exist. One treatment however which will always be necessary is the treatment of the birds and lofts against insect life. If this hasn't been done for a while, it is a good time of the year to spray the lofts and to dip the birds or to treat them individually with the use of Ivomec or similar.

December at the end of the year is for many the beginning of their new year as their plans start to develop into positive action. What was said for the month of January is the result of the work and planning which has been going on in the so-called 'close' season. However for top racing men there is no such thing as a 'close' season and this is why they are so successful as they work at their birds every day of the year.

Pigeon fancying is all about that, whether in racing, showing or competition flying, the working season is a year-long one with no breaks and no holidays but with a whole lot of positive enjoyment.

Index

Glossary of terms

A.O.C.	any other colour
A.O.V.	any other variety
Apple bodied	neat body form, plumpish, not thin
Argent	applied to Modenas having a white centre to a coloured feather
Back skull	rear part of head
Badge	pigeons carrying pied markings and white flights
Bald or bald-headed	white plumage on head of coloured pigeon
Band	pigeon ring
Barred	bands of alternative colours running across the back
Barred tail	coloured or light band across tail
Beard	white feathers below beak of coloured pigeons
Bib	patch of coloured feathers below beak of white pigeons
Blocky	bird with broad, substantial build
Bloom	gloss or sheen on plumage
Bolting eye	prominent, bulging eye
Booted	feathering on legs and toes
Box-beak	close fitting beak, stout-beaked
Breast	front, crop area
Breed	variety, race, family
Broken coloured	birds having more than colour
Broken-eyed	colour of eyes lacking uniform of colour
Bull-eye	eye with dark coloured iris (appearance of black)
Canker	protozoal disease in three forms, internal, navel and pharyngeal (throat).
Carriage	general bearing and stance of pigeon
Cere	bare skin around the eye
Chain	fore-part of frill as in Jacobins
Chequering	pattern of feather colouring on wing covers
Chuck	white patch below under mandible
Clean-legged	no feathering on shanks or feet
Close-feathered	feathers lying flat against body, not loose-feathered
Close-season	the time in the loft between racing or showing

Cobby	English version of 'blocky', heavily and solidly built
Cock	male pigeon
Condition	the quality of the pigeon in body and appearance
Condition (verb)	to train, prepare, and wash birds in readiness for shows
Corn	collective name for grains
Corn (U.S.)	maize, sweetcorn
Cream	yellowish white colour, a dilute of ash red
Crescent	white or dark crescent shape marking on crop
Crest	feather tuft at back of skull either as shell crest where it runs across the head, or pin-crest if it ends in a point
Crop	pouchlike enlargement of gullet in which food is stored or softened before it passes into the gizzard
Damson cere	dark coloured eye cere
Deep-bodied	noticeable depth of keel and of body from back to the lower breastbone
Dominant	characteristics which predominate in breeding
Down	fluffy part of feathers, also profuse soft feathering around thighs and abdomen
Down-faced	full sloping beak
Expression	the facial look of a pigeon
Family	strain or breed
Feeders	pigeons used as foster parents
Flecking	additional colour in a primary flight e.g. black in light coloured flight
Flight coverts	short feathers at base of primary flights with part cover
Flights or flight feathers	primary feathers in wings
Foul feathers	feathers of a colour not belonging to the breed
Fret mark	damage to feather in growth
Frill	fluffed feathers on throat as in Turbits, Oriental Frills
Gay pied	excessive amount of white
Gazzi	Modenas with white bodies but coloured elsewhere

Globe	air-filled throat area - as in pouters and blowers
Hackle	the neck area of the pigeon, lustrous feathering
Hen	female pigeon
Heterozygous	cock impure for colour, carrying two colours
Hock	the joint between shank and thigh
Homing	ability or faculty to be able to return home
Homozygous	Cock pure for colour, both chromosomes same colour
Hood	inverted feathers on neck- as in the Jacobin
Hoppers	containers for food
Inbreeding	the mating of closely related birds e.g. father to daughter
Incubation	when the hen sits the eggs
Keel	lower edge of breastbone
Kit	a number of pigeons trained to fly together e.g. rollers
Lacing	edging of a feather, darker than the main part
Late-breds	birds bred late in season
Leggy	pigeons having legs which seem to be too long
Line-breeding	breeding within a family line but not so close as in inbreeding
Magnani	Modenas with dappled or spangled mixing of several colours
Mandibles	upper and lower portions of the beak
Mane	rear part of the Jacobin's frill
Mealy	colour of pigeon, powdery silver with red bars
Mottled	small patches of white on a ground or self-colour
Moult	the process where the old feathers are shed and new replacements grown
Muffed	growth of feathers on shanks and toes
N.P.A.	National Pigeon Association
O.C.	Old or adult cock
O.H.	Old or adult hen
Opal mosaic	British name for opal chequers, recessive diminution of colour, chequering with opal edging

Outcross	the use of an unrelated pigeon for breeding purposes
Pair	Two pigeons mated together
Pairing	the process of pairing birds together
Pearl eye	very light or white eye
Pied	where a solid colour bird is splashed with another colour - normally associated with white
Pigeon milk	the soft substance secreted by crop and fed to newly hatched young birds
Pin Crest	see - crest
Pipping	eggs starting to hatch, the shell being punctured
Pot eggs	false eggs
Powder	A lightening of a colour especially in blue and mealy
Primaries	Primary flights
Progeny	the young birds produced from a pairing
Racy	slight build, slender, tight feathered bird - often used in respect of show racers resembling the real racer
Reach	tallness, length of neck
Retrices	tail feathers
Ring	numbered identification band
Roach back	hump backed
Rose	centre of the rosette on Jacobin's frill and some other markings or feather formations on other breeds
Round	A span in the breeding cycle from the laying of eggs until the young birds leave the nest
Saddle	the back of a pigeon to base of tail
Schietti	Modenas coloured all over including white self-coloured
Scraper	implement for scraping/cleaning
Secondaries	the long quill feathers of the wing between the primaries and the body
Self-colour	solid or uniformly covered colour
Sheath	the covering of a new feather
Shell crest	see crest
Short-faced	birds having very short beak and front face
Shoulder	front of upper part of wing
Shoulder-butt	as above but the leading edge of the wing

Silver	delicate shade of blue, a dilute of blue
Slippered	lightly feathered toes
Smooth-legged	legs with no feathering below the 'knee' joint
Snip	patch of white or coloured feathering above beak
Solid colour	one colour throughout
Spindle-beak	thin or pointed beak
Splashed	uneven markings of colour and white
Split-eyed	where the iris colour runs from bright colour to dark
Squeaker	a young pigeon before it gains its adult voice
Stance	the way a pigeon stands
Stock birds	pigeons kept solely for breeding purposes
Stockings	short feathers covering the lower leg and toes
Stop	angular appearance between beak and rising forehead
Strain	a family of breed of pigeon
Stud	collection of breeding birds
Team	collective name for a team of two or four, or of a complete show entry of a fancier
Thighs	upper part of leg
Throat	as in gullet
Ticked	spots of colour, often a white tick behind eye
Toy	small pigeon
Trap	method of entry to a loft but with no exit
Trimming	superficial shaping of feathers
Tucked-up	wings held nicely up, not drooping
Type	the carriage and body of a pigeon, its conformity to standard or ideal
Utility	bred for commercial production, not for showing etc
Ventilation	method of keeping air clean in lofts
Wattle	fleshy nostril cover
Weaning	when the young birds leave the nest to fend for themselves
Wing coverts	cover feathers covering base of secondaries
Yearling	the year after the year of birth
Yellow	dilute of red
Y.C.	young cock(s)
Y.H.	young hen(s)

Bibliography

The Pigeon	by Wendell M Levi
Book of Pigeons	by R.Fulton
Pigeons in the Great War	Lt.Col.A.H.Osman
Pigeons in World War 2	Major W.H.Osman
Racing Pigeons	Joe Rotondo
Encyclopedia of Pigeon Breeds	Wendell M Levi
Pigeon Fancying	R.Bissett
General Management of Pigeons	by 'Violette'
The Book of the Pigeon	by Carl A Naether
The Secret of Speed	by E.J.Sains
Pigeon Racing	Major A.Neilson Hutton
The Homing Pigeon	by Edgar Chamberlain
Pigeon Racing	Dr W.E.Barker
Guide to the Pigeons of the World	A.McNeillie
Fancy Pigeons	by W.Watmough
Pigeons of Today	by W.Watmough
Fancy Pigeon Standards	National Pigeon Association
The Show Racer	by Douglas McClary
Pigeon Showing	by Douglas McClary